Value Stream

Generally Accepted Practice in Enterprise Software Development

Mark Kennaley

Software Development Experts

mark@software-development-experts.com

Twitter - @sdlc3

Visit Software Development Experts at www.software-development-experts.com

Library of Congress Cataloging- in-Publication Data available

ISBN 978-0-9865194-1-3

Text printed on recycled paper

First Printing December 2014

For the investors in software

Foreword:

Most of us are faced with serious software related challenges. Our current software track record is weak and we struggle with quantifying how weak. Mastery of software is getting harder. Business cycles, development cycles and delivery cycles are accelerating. There is a greater premium on the trustworthiness of software. There aren't enough good software people to go around and the growth in demand is outpacing the growth in supply. If your business or career depends on software this book will help you address these challenges and help you steer toward a more prosperous future.

We all need a strong foundation for understanding the economics of software. In this book, Mark Kennaley walks the reader through many strategic elements of improving software economics that attracts the reader to learn more about how to best cope with the software challenges. There are no prescriptions, but Mark lays out a nice framework of knowledge for applying many patterns of success, and avoiding patterns of failure, in your own context.

One recurring theme throughout this book is treating software with more empirical discipline. Software measurements and forecasts in most enterprises sound a lot like the sleight-of-hand statistics quoted by politicians. Politicians have a well-deserved reputation for under-delivering on their committed forecasts. The software market suffers from the same disease. Software productivity and quality improvement forecasts are plagued by hyperbole and spin.

Software delivery is much more a discipline of economics, having a high degree of uncertainty, than it is of engineering where laws of physics and properties of materials provide a foundation of predictable outcomes. We need better standards for measuring in the face of this uncertainty.

By listening, observing, synthesizing and participating first hand in many success and some failures, Mark has walked the walk. Value Stream is loaded with from-the-trenches knowhow and it provides practical guidance in the disciplined use of modern practices for software delivery enterprises. Mark has packaged a tough topic in an attractive read with a provocative style and a well-balanced mix of innovation, theory, data and experience.

Walker Royce, Chief Software Economist - IBM

Preface:

You may be wondering why the front cover of this book has a gargoyle on it. In fact, this is not just any gargoyle, but probably the most famous gargoyle of all known as *Le Stryge*, which sits high atop *Notre Dame du Paris*, commissioned to ward off enemies of the faith. Knowing full well that invoking religion through an image of a church, synagogue or mosque within this work might be highly controversial and might lead to stoning or crucifixion, I chose other imagery to make an important point.   Deliberations about how to approach the development of software these days has become similar in many regards to debates on faith and orthodoxy and closely mirrors the ideology of those engaged in the debate.   This is the elephant in the room that many will agree has been present for some time in our industry.   For those within IT, perhaps you have felt a strange feeling from time to time, which feels like a form of intense peer pressure to conform to some "one true way". It must have been what McCarthyism felt like back in the 1950's, although perhaps in reverse?

Le Stryge was the creation of *Eugène Viollet-le-Duc* during the gothic restoration of the cathedral. It just so happens that the works of this famous architectural theorist serves as an ironic back story for the crossroads that the software development industry faces.   The irony is related to the debate and intellectual competition with another architectural theorist from the period, *John Ruskin*, an Evangelical Christian, known for his social activism and strong support for the *Arts and Craft Movement*. Ruskin was most concerned about the "feeling and emotion" of architecture, and strongly believed that it was the craftsmen alone who were the true artists that created the beauty and goodness of a structure. In stark contrast, *Viollet-le-Duc* (an agnostic) was very practical and forward thinking. He was considered the first modern architectural theorist who believed in the designers understanding of the logic of rational construction, and was open minded to exploring application of the progressive new steel and glass building materials in his conceptualizations.

If you listen closely to the current state of debate regarding software delivery approaches and technologies, you can easily draw parallels with the documented ideological struggle from this historical period. In effect, software is the new cathedral, and the battle over its future is a continuing struggle between the viewpoints of *artists versus engineers*, liberals versus conservatives, socialists versus capitalists. Nothing really has changed in human nature since the gothic period, only that the medium of economic pursuit has changed and the arena of ideological competition has evolved. More importantly, as it was with the investors of architecture and structures from that period, so too are the investors in software being disenfranchised by the self-indulgent pursuit of intellectual stimulation and profiteering by opportune methodologists and consultants.

To put this quite bluntly, the business is tired of all of the dogma, rhetoric, kool-aid drinking, populism, manifestos, navel gazing, pontification, profiteering, partisanship and piety. Peddlers who have made bold *silver bullet* claims without the results to back them up, and we will discuss many such instances of this throughout this book, have run with impunity for far too long. Regardless of which methodology we are talking about, the evidence of efficacy is either sparse, non-existent or less than credible. What remains in the industry are superficial anecdotes, folklore and de-contextualization. Instead of genuine discovery regarding why certain software delivery practices work and in what circumstances, what is transpiring is all manner of money making scams, certification pyramid schemes, and "Alliances" of one clique against some other "evil empire". Somewhere along the way, the business and those who pay for software were forgotten. Lest we forget, the stakeholders to software development don't care about such petty arguments and definitely don't like getting ripped off. In fact they have very real concerns about maintaining their very existence in an increasingly hypercompetitive world. Without the ability to keep up with the demand for software innovation, there will be no workplace to improve for individuals wanting a more humane, fun and joyful *world of work*. Activism and lobbying has its place, even for those whose causes are obviously riddled with bias. Focusing first and foremost on creating "happy" software developers is all well and good, but such a pursuit must not be obfuscated or misrepresented. After all, freedom to assemble and the right to free speech is something we enjoy in democracies, but there cannot be a conflict of interest when one is also getting paid by an employer. It takes a village to raise some software, and having an axe to grind against management, analysts or architects is counter-productive. Advocacy for a sustainable pace should be driven by debate about motivational theory and return on investment, not the rhetoric of Socialism. It is noble to want a better society, but accentuating a stance of *an honest day's pay for an honest day's work* is the productive and stable way to get there. When present, anarchists must be shown the door, as software development is too important to society. Software development is first and foremost an economic activity that just so happens to lead to intellectual stimulation that can improve the lives of the humans that take it up as their vocation and profession.

Hopefully putting this work "out there" will stimulate credible debate which will propel the software industry forward. In the true spirit of openness and transparency, the ideas in this book will be tested through peer review and unbiased discussion (see the LinkedIn Group of the same name to participate). More importantly, the integration and contextualization of software development is being enacted in working software through the use of expert systems and the *Advisor* platform. Enough pontification about big ideas and next big things. Books and slide-ware offers no direct value in driving better business outcomes. Instead, tangible, credible software systems are what is needed to make ideas concrete and real at the scope of large scale, distributed and contextually diverse enterprises. Driving industry-wide empiricism reflects a philosophy most closely aligned with the world of business - pragmatism. A practical focus on the software Value Stream means optimizing the delivery of value by maximizing flow, minimizing scrap and rework, maximizing learning through triple-loop feedback, and attending to the critical cultural issues that enable change and improvement to occur. Instead of pushing the flavor du jour on organizations, the ideas within this book clearly articulate a strategy for embracing the diversity of modern enterprises, and instilling the concept of *The Learning Organization*. Focused experimentation and pattern reuse replaces faith and reliance on emergence, or the continual reset button due to methodology fads. Finally, a clear articulation of what it takes to achieve better outcomes through better human decision reasoning is presented in an actionable form in what I term *Decision-centric Capability Improvement*.

For the software industry to get out of the rut we have been in for a long time, we must constructively and integratively build upon a knowledge. We must stop ignoring so much of the sea of knowledge because of *bias* and must start placing experience in context. We must "reach across the aisle" in non-partisan fashion to end the methodology gridlock that plagues the land and materially improve software delivery results for our stakeholders. The most recent wave of software development productivity improvement - *The Agile Movement* - has had its chance with ample time (at least 14 years depending on how far back you go) to prove itself. Yet we still see the same number of software debacles and extremely costly train wrecks. We still have organizations embarking on their 5th "Agile transformation". Why is that? Could it simply be that <u>those other people</u> that must change <u>their</u> ways are merely being resistive? Or is there something lurking that is much more systemic and innately human related to this problem. Perhaps it is related to continual "conversion" attempts coupled with countless roadmaps to enlightenment and salvation? One thing however is clear. Something is obviously not working with the status quo, and the continual practice of pushing something on someone seems to be the culprit.

What we need to move beyond this stagnation is *Generally Accepted Practice*. We need to mute the noise in our industry so we can get on with addressing the growing gap between demand and the tapped out supply chain. We must return our focus to investors, and recover the $200 billion per year being left on the table and being wasted through software delivery failures.

Many thanks to the team at Software Development Experts including Carson Holmes, Chris Corey, Philippe Kruchten, Scott Ambler, Meilir Page-Jones, and Stephen Mellor for travelling this journey with me. A special thanks to all those who influenced, reviewed or provided commentary on this work including: Walker Royce, Diego Lo Giudice, Mike Gualtieri, Kurt Bittner, Glenn Alleman, Pat Howard, Jesse Jacoby, Joe Lowther, Doug Stewart, Julian Holmes, Lee Ackerman, Dave West, Capers Jones, Rolf Reitzig, Arun Zachariah, Chris Armstrong, Steve Adolph, Randy Lexvold, Tom Weinberger, Mark Lines, Adam Murray, Ricardo Garcia, Hadar Ziv, Cecile Peraire, Geri Winters, Al Shalloway, Pete Franklin, Bill Curtis and Grady Booch. My hope is that together we can jolt the industry out of its collective trance.

Mark Kennaley - December, 2014

Table of Contents

Table of Contents

Table of Contents

Chapter 1: Sifting through the Rhetoric

"Plato is dear to me, but dearer still is truth." *Aristotle*

Have you ever had the feeling that your Information Technology (IT) organization has become more akin to religious clans or medieval tribes than a business unit accountable for contributing to the bottom line? Do you sense that many of your IT people engage in intellectual warfare related to their favorite methods or practices rather than focusing on the delivery of value to your customers? I would hazard to guess that the answer to these questions is anywhere from a skeptical "yes" to "absolutely". How many times have you seen the *next big thing* walk through the door related to an approach, method, or process for delivering IT value? How many bodies-of-knowledge (BOKs) does your organization support through communities-of-practice or centers-of-excellence for the various roles within the value stream of your organization? I would also hazard to guess that the answer to these questions is "frequently" and "many". You should know that you are not alone, and this phenomenon is real. Historically, wave after wave of silo'd experience in the form of software development methods, community reinforced and protected bodies-of-knowledge, or "best practice du jour" have plagued the delivery of software. Given the above observations, can you imagine how much this must cost? The impact of this key business issue is a major reason for the almost $200 billion in waste that occurs each year out of an overall IT industry-wide annual spend of $2.1 trillion dollars as of 2014. This represents an opportunity cost of somewhere in the neighborhood of $1.6 trillion dollars per year [1,2].

The issue for large enterprises to consider as they attempt to solve their portion of this industry-wide business problem is to understand what the root causes are related to this phenomenon. To attack this business risk requires us to first explore sociology, human psychology and the differing philosophical viewpoints that exist in any organizational context of increased diversity. To start, we will elaborate upon the scope of the business problem, and explore the tell-tales that can lead us to credible solutions that have eluded the software industry to date.

1.1 – The Business is Getting Screwed

In my travels, I have seen endless debates and turf-wars about which single IT *scripture* is the right one, along with the ensuing pressure for non-believers to convert. Similarly, I have personally seen the reset button hit on process or capability improvement initiatives on a number of occasions, unfortunately for suspect reasons. When this happens, all prior progress from Method X is deemed of no value, and Method Y is stood up with reinvention in the areas potentially not covered by the *ideology* of the new approach. In other words, either flush the current methodology entirely, or slap a new coat of paint on something that is effectively the same, but give it a new label or brand. Not surprisingly, this is not a recent occurrence; it has been going on for over 50 years. This phenomenon occurs within each of the different IT functions (i.e. Enterprise Architecture - EA, IT Service Management - ITSM, Project & Portfolio Management - PPM, & Software Development - SDLC).

Figure 1.1 illustrates what I call the "method soup" of what finds its way into modern IT Departments for consideration. Each ellipse represents a community-specific articulation of processes and practices which all too often has become inward looking, bloated, overlapping and often inconsistent with potentially competing neighbors. I will argue that this is one of the biggest sources of waste in Enterprise IT due to the fact that it directly and negatively affects the productivity of the biggest factor of success in software delivery - the people involved.

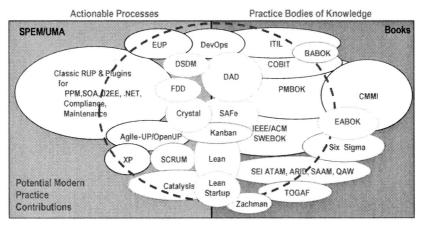

Figure 1.1 – Enterprise IT Method Landscape

Drilling deeper into this assertion related to overall industry impact, each time a new *methodology fad* is embraced by an organization, a rather large change management initiative is triggered. Within IT this means a typical 3-5 yr campaign and beyond. Such an initiative typically involves the following direct costs for a 1000 person IT organization:

- Consulting costs and training/mentoring associated with traversing the Dreyfus Model [3] from Novice to Competent and sometimes higher (to Master) - say $1-2M;

- Knowledge Management risk mitigation costs to avoid vendor lock-in due to reliance of tacit knowledge in the heads of coaches or consultants. If performed, the capture of standard work or "our way of working" results in enormous costs spent related to process-ware – add another $1M;

- Such changes in approach can trigger new process management tooling – anywhere from "free" to $1M is typical;

- Changes with approaches typically have implications related to socially acceptable software delivery infrastructure – hitting the reset button on this can cost upwards of $5M for such an organization.

As you can see, these costs are not insignificant if they recur periodically. However, one cost that is hidden and which arguably far outweighs those identified above is the lost productivity due to passive aggressive behavior [4]; or in other words, lost efficiency and effectiveness due to people digging in and arguing about methodology.

To look at the magnitude of this cost, consider various historical studies on strategic change initiatives. Such studies show that around 70% of transformational investments fail to achieve the expected outcomes [5] We know that worldwide IT spending for 2014 is estimated to be $2.1 Trillion, according to Gartner [6]. Out of this, the investments made in software development and integration services is estimated at $930Billion. Typical IT Budget allocations suggest that at least 10% of this can be associated with process improvement/strategic IT change initiatives [7], so we can expect that 70% of $93B, a total equaling $65B worldwide is doomed to failure. Additionally, some portion of the total worldwide IT spend for 2014 is implicit spending on process improvement, which could be thought of as "just-in-time" process improvement at the beginning of and during a project. For assessing this cost, we know that roughly 14% of software engineering efforts are outright failures [8]. While many chastise the Standish Group *Chaos Report* [9] due to the questionable research methods and their flawed definitions used for Success and Challenged, none of the critiques question the validity of the Failure category; and the trend for this category is flat and not materially improving. In the reasons cited for failure from the Standish surveys, it is arguable that people issues are the real root cause, as opposed to the more symptomatic list presented. In other words every project with a newly formulated team of people has to Form, Storm, Norm and Perform [10], and many failures could be viewed as directly attributable to a poor progression through this team lifecycle. For teams failing to evolve through this team lifecycle efficiently, if you treat this microcosm as a form of "change initiative", you can link poor project performance to involving a major contribution associated with change. For the roughly 50% of all IT spend is on IT projects - ($930B), we can estimate this root cause as costing $91.1B worldwide this year (70% of $130B). Put another way, somewhere near 70% of software development project failures might be attributed to *us-vs-them* passive aggressive behavior totaling some $91B worldwide. This does not include the "Challenged" category in the surveys which would suggest less than optimal delivery performance on average 33% of the time. Conservatively, you could argue that there is another $30.7B or so being lost worldwide for 10% budget overruns.

Re-asserting the point made in the above analysis, the hidden or indirect costs associated with software development methods being *"more akin to fads and fashion than engineering discipline"* [11] represents a very large number indeed – as stated somewhere around $186B this year alone along with an associated opportunity cost of somewhere between $1.6 and $2.5 Trillion industry wide.

The typical cycle in enterprises of large scale is something akin to an 18 month cycle with three distinct phases: the *honeymoon* period, the *stay-the-course* period, and the *wrap-it-up* period. In fact, it is not unlike Kurt Lewin's 3-phases of change theory (Unfreeze, Transition, Freeze) [12]. Figure 1.2 illustrates the common capability improvement cycle observed within most enterprises:

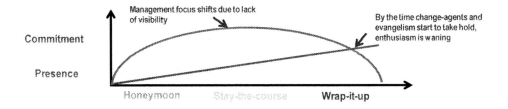

Figure 1.2 – Frequency of Enterprise Methodology Reset

From the above, we can see that process improvement efforts typically start out in a "honeymoon" period, where the organization and its leadership are enamored with the potential for change. With the natural lag in gaining traction inherent with influencing large organizations, patience starts to shift away from the transformation and on to other more tactical and emerging issues, with the assumption that everything is fine. This is the "stay-the-course" period of time. Finally, as attention has shifted, business conditions have changed, results are slow to take hold and impatience grows, executives have moved on. The organization enters the "wrap-it-up" period. The pace of change is outstripped by the perceptions of results, and only when a new entrant decides to revisit the elusive challenge of addressing the business critical issue of software improvement does the cycle repeat. Unfortunately, the continuity between visionaries is disjoint, and so the cycles are akin to starting over from scratch.

Given that you agree with the above analysis and view it as credible, perhaps you have also observed the increasing frequency of *rhetoric* within the industry related to software development methodology. It is sometimes not so easy however to separate the sharing of knowledge with *spin*, and attempts to influence large audiences for economic gain. Some of the tell-tales that rhetoric is being leveraged include the unbalanced use of ethos (appeals to the audiences values or customs, leveraging such things as culture, age and other demographics, national customs) or pathos (appeals to the audience's emotions, leveraging such things as social justice, populism or underdog positioning), rather than logos (the content itself, and its credibility and substantiation as it seems to prove). Typically in social media, or even talk around the corporate water cooler, you might observe overly argumentative debates occurring if rhetoric is being employed, as most good *rhetors* learn to counter arguments regardless of how credible their position [13].

You may be wondering why the public art of shaping opinion, usually reserved for politics, the law or religion is finding its way increasingly into the world of IT and software development methodology. Such a communication style has typically been confined to product marketing when discussed in the business context. Historically, going as far back as Plato, rhetoric has been a controversial approach to communication. Early philosophers argued that *"while rhetoric could be used to improve civic life, it could be used equally easily to deceive or manipulate with negative effects, as the masses were incapable of analyzing anything on their own and would therefore be swayed by the most persuasive speeches, rather than that by which a credible argument is made by someone experienced in the field."* [14]. Today, as in ancient times, rhetoric is often viewed pejoratively as a means of obscuring the truth and attempts to strategically manipulate the masses, with modern day examples including lobbyists and corporate public relations.

To understand the origins of the increasing incidence of the invocation of rhetoric in the software industry requires exploration of philosophy, organizational psychology, sociology and the nature of "methodology politics". Usage of rhetoric is only a tell-tale that something else is really going on within the industry. While it is typical to think that software development methodologists are only concerned with devising tasks and workproducts, the reality is that all methods and managment systems necessarily involve and influence people. Therefore it is understandable that researchers are now increasingly turning to the "soft sciences" to understand how to improve the state of affairs in our industry.

1.2 – The Sociology and Politics of Software Development

One of the social undercurrents related to the increasing use of rhetoric in software development methodology discord seems to hinge on myopic, typically intolerant beliefs related to *creativity*. In other words, who owns "innovation" or is in the best position to "innovate". It would seem that everyone wants to own this high ground. At times, vitriolic debates have flared up related to software product development and what the essence of software is and is not [15]. On the surface, you typically see the battle lines drawn between Software Factories akin to a manufacturing metaphor [16] versus Artisanry aligned with a craftsmanship metaphor [17]. Ultimately this is reflective of a dipole that has existed in society for quite some time and one that has been leveraged many times in the past by those wishing to influence market dynamics. This power struggle is between The Arts versus Engineering. Look no further than the imagery leveraged in the 1984 Apple Computer campaign [18], which invoked imagery akin to George Orwell and his novel 1984 [19], or the reincarnation in 2005 with *PC versus MAC* and the geek versus the cool dude [20]. The contrast is quite polarizing to the constituencies involved, and this has a funny way of finding itself penetrating business enterprises. In other words, the very nature of society does not stop at the doorstep of an IT shop. One world-view believes the "pure thought stuff" needed for enterprises to achieve *Disruptive Innovation* [21] is exclusively through artistic creative genius inspiring beauty, and that the pocket protector wielding engineers and their rigor or discipline are only part of the problem. On the other hand, those very engineers hold the view that creating *what has never existed before which yields utility to society* should never be entrusted to those hippy artists down the hall. So who is right? Clearly this is an important question, as innovation is a paramount business imperative in today's competitive environment.

It should be no mystery that various factions are fighting over control of the economic engine of software. Software touches every corner of society, and the world's appetite for software is increasing exponentially. Whether it be engineers, craftsmen, computer scientists, technologists, industrial designers or business people, software seems to involve all and yet we constantly hear rhetoric claiming it for a single title exclusively. Figure 1.3 below captures a sociological domain model for software development.

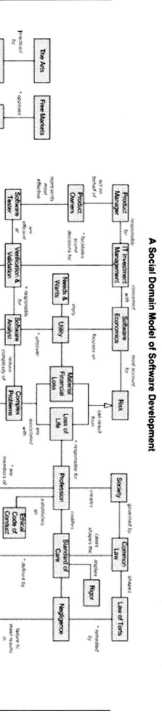

Figure 1.3 – Sociological Domain Model of Software Development

With the backdrop of infighting over control of software development, there has been historically very little detail in the analysis of social dynamics in software projects. The above model attempts to start to frame the debate moving forward using a more robust and credible sociological tautology. From this model, it is difficult to argue that these abstractions are not somehow present in relation to software development.   The key observation to make from this domain representation is that software development is not divorced from other aspects of society; in fact, it is just the opposite. The Law as a major instrument of order in our society is prominent, and closely related to the discipline and fiduciary of Engineering.   Craftsmanship is also prominent in this model, and has affinity to such concepts as industrial design and pride in workmanship. Yet one may notice that there is separation between abstractions. This separation of context has the natural effect of creating the conditions necessary for intolerance and division to thrive when it comes to differing viewpoints. This has been referred to as "making faces across the gulf" [22] in research circles studying the state of the relationship among differing ideologies attached to ontology, epistemology and tautology and therefore how we study the world around us. Clearly, social dynamics is a very complex subject.   Humans have a strange way of oversimplifying what they don't easily understand. What does occur is superficial treatment and anecdotal observations of complex phenomenon, typically in myopic fashion only exploring a small piece of the sociology quilt for often suspect reasons, again laced with rhetoric. The challenge to date has been to explore sufficient scope to understand the various influences that are present in any software project; this scope is *all of society*.

Your enterprise will surely have all walks of life represented, each with their own vantage point or perspective on things due to where they are situated in this social landscape. This will carry forward as to people's perspective on software development methodology. Various communications will resonate louder than others depending on where they sit within the domain model in Figure 1.3. Whether someone has a social axe to grind, or whether their context just mandates certain business realities, diversity of opinion can be assured.   Anyone suggesting that uniformity of thought is the goal is sadly mistaken. Everyone in the enterprise has their perspective for good reason. The challenge is to embrace this diversity and instil empathy and tolerance in the debates regarding efficiency and effectiveness. This assumes that this is what enterprises should be talking about, rather than broader social causes that seem to creep into the conversation from time to time. It is important to understand where people are coming from in the daily Enterprise IT discord so that convergence can be accelerated on optimizing investment outcomes and the approaches that will enable them. Ultimately though, the agents within the enterprise ecosystem are people and therefore have various levels of agenda in relation to their interests and careers. When people have an agenda, one needs to accept the reality of the discipline of politics in any enterprise of scale. Politics is typically defined as "competition between competing interest groups or individuals for power and leadership" [23].

Due to the fact that software development is not immune to societal forces, structures, networks or institutions, it is natural that various political parties have emerged as a result of the constant jockeying for position and the associated attainment of power. Almost yearly "methodology elections" are held within IT organizations when it comes to bodies-of-knowledge (BOKs), with the plethora of parties tribes and factions represented as illustrated in Figure 1.1. Such a potpourri looks more like "Italian Politics" than political consensus. From these, the over-arching power struggle of recent years and easily the most polarizing and disruptive to enterprise investors is arguably between the caucuses of management and developers, and reflected in their party platforms (the Project Management Body of Knowledge - PMBOK [24] versus the *Agile Manifesto*) [25]. Most of the time, it feels like your are either within a "Blue State" or a "Red State" as you walk the IT shop floor. On the left we have the political tool of *populism* which juxtaposes "the people" against "the elites", and urges social and political system changes. Notable populist movements in history includes *The French Revolution*. One doesn't have to reach very far to see the parallels with the *Agile Movement*, embracing slogans like "changing the world of work" [26]. On the right is what some could argue is the reciprocal political strategy of elitism, where those who are elected to the Project Management Office are therefore entitled to govern in such a way as to control rather than lead and enable. Similar to a dictatorship, some overzealous "governors" in the software development world feel that ownership of everything that happens in the ecosystem is theirs, and success will be theirs' and theirs' alone. A slogan that would exemplify this is "I am delivering <u>my</u> project, on-time and under-budget". Figure 1.4 presents a tongue-in-cheek perspective on how ridiculous it can be within IT organizations that are supposed to be first and foremost delivering software, rather than engaging in political gridlock.

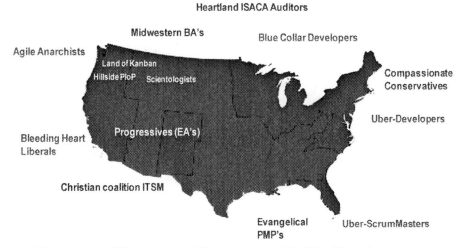

Figure 1.4 – The Software Development Political Landscape

For an enterprise, these political forces matter, and breaking out of "politics as usual" is increasingly important. Due to the fact that software development is a critical element within the value-chain of most modern businesses, forces that affect labour cost, competency and availability warrant close attention.

In recent years, the momentum and traction of the phenomenon surrounding Agile has received increasing management attention [27]. Arguably the stronger political party these days, the Agile constituency has been under some scrutiny. In fact, some brave souls on social media even have gone so far to as to ask the question "Is Agile Communist/Socialist?" [28], while others blatantly invoke such ideology [29]. These feelings likely have resulted from an allergic reaction to the potential for over-reach for power within enterprises. At a minimum, one could make the case that unionism forces are in play [30], with the Agile Movement exhibiting many traits of the Guilds [31]. Guilds were groups of self-employed skilled craftsmen with ownership and control over the materials and tools they needed to produce their goods. Looking back in history, the Guilds were closely associated with Craftsmanship [32] which has become more prevalent within software development in recent years, apparently not by accident. Craftsmanship originated with writings and social commentaries of John Ruskin and *The Arts and Crafts Movement* [33]. The mid 19th century writings of John Ruskin laid the foundations for many of the craftsman style values. His writings predicted and commented on social issues such as environmentalism, sustainability, craftsmanship, and fulfilling labour. Ruskin thought the machine was at the root of many social ills and that a healthy society depended on skilled and creative workers. Ruskin attacked orthodox, 19th-century political economy principally on the grounds that it failed to acknowledge complexities of human desires and motivations (broadly, "social affections"). In *The Stones of Venice* [34], Ruskin attacked division of labor (industrialized workforce specialization) and industrial capitalism. He warned about the moral and spiritual health of society, where he argued that Venice had slowly deteriorated because its cultural achievements had been compromised, and its society corrupted by the decline of true Christian faith. Ruskin also argued that the worker must be allowed to think and to express his own personality and ideas, ideally using his own hands, not machinery, the goal being the Artisan's joy through free, creative work. Ruskin believed that the economic theories of Adam Smith expressed in *The Wealth of Nations* [35] had led, through the division of labor, to the alienation of the worker not merely from the process of work itself, but from his fellow workmen and other classes, causing increasing resentment. He argued that one remedy would be to pay work at a fixed rate of wages, because human need is consistent and a given quantity of work justly demands a certain return. The best workmen would remain in employment because of the quality of their work (a focus on quality growing out of his writings on art and architecture). The best workmen could not, in a fixed-wage economy, be undercut by an inferior worker or product. These views reflected the notion of Craft Unionism [36].

When the software development political landscape is viewed in this light, one then can filter out much of the noise of rhetoric that is not directed at achieving outcomes intended within the software investments. It allows us to have some context behind the passion within recent notable software debates like #NoEstimates [37]. Such grounding allows us to explore whether bona fide methodology innovation is being advocated, or rather an alternative populist agenda. In the case of #NoEstimates, proponents leverage dogmatic arguments that appear to be disingenuous when pressed for clarification or substantiation. Look no further to requests for clarity in whether the movement is anti-management, intentionally obfuscating their position so as to penetrate the established management tier within enterprises. Perhaps #NoEstimates is something akin to a Trojan Horse virus?

1.3 – Philosophy and Software Development Methodology

With such a broad social and political spectrum represented in some way within the scope of software and software development, it is inevitable that differing ways of thinking about software development will exist. One often hears the words *mind-set* or *world-view* [38] being used when scanning the chatter on social media or in various books on software development. Each of these terms describe the *frame/frame of reference* that is the basis of the views expressed. From Wikipedia, a frame is described as follows:

> *In the social sciences, framing is a set of concepts and theoretical perspectives on how individuals, groups, and societies organize, perceive, and communicate about reality. Framing is the social construction of a social phenomenon often by mass media sources, political or social movements, political leaders, or other actors and organizations. It is an inevitable process of selective influence over the individual's perception of the meanings attributed to words or phrases.*

Two common yet opposing viewpoints that consistently surface in software development debates are also dramatically different philosophies on understanding the world around us and the epistemology of knowledge: the philosophies of reason - *Empiricism, Positivitism, Rationalism and Pragmatism*; and the philosophy of faith [39]. You will likely observe management and academia based in the former, where evidence of efficacy assertions is sought. As in *prove it*. You will likely see the latter tied to various forms of marketing spin or social activism under the auspices of "thought leadership", yet with little credibility in terms of conceptualization or broad experiential data. As in *trust me*. To understand where methodologists are coming from with their agendas, and thereby understand the bias that they exhibit, requires a quick study of each of these philosophical underpinnings.

1.3.1 The Philosophies of Reason - Empiricism, Positivism, Rationalism and Pragmatism

The English term "empirical" derives from an ancient Greek lineage and translates to the Latin word *experientia*, from which we derive the word "experience" and the related "experiment". The term was used by the Empiric school of ancient Greek medical practitioners, who preferred to rely on the observation of phenomena. This was a rejection of the prevailing prominence of the *Three doctrines of the Dogmatic School*, which was an ancient school of medicine that relied heavily on reason rather than experimentation [40]. Dogma represents "*a principle or set of principles laid down by an authority as incontrovertibly true. It serves as part of the primary basis of an ideology or belief system, and it cannot be changed or discarded without affecting the system's paradigm, or the ideology itself.*" Modern *Empiricism* originated in the 18th century during the period of "Enlightenment" with the likes of Sir Francis Bacon [41]. The philosophical offshoot *Positivism* was built around the principle of verification in which adherents argued that the only meaningful statements of truth were those which were empirically verifiable. In contrast, *Rationalism* as a philosophy of reason holds that some knowledge can be arrived at through intuition and reasoning alone and that we have innate ideas. Rationalists have such a high confidence in reason that proof and physical evidence are unnecessary to ascertain truth – in other words, "there are significant ways in which our concepts and knowledge are gained independently of sensory experience."

In 1903 Charles Peirce from Harvard University founded the philosophy of *Pragmatism* [42] suggesting a link between sensory perception and intellectual conception as a two way street. He agreed with the idea that rational concepts can be meaningful and go beyond the data given by empirical observation. In later years he even emphasized the concept-driven side of the then ongoing debate between strict empiricism and strict rationalism, in part to counterbalance the excesses to which some of his cohorts had taken pragmatism under the "data-driven" strict-empiricist view. Among Peirce's major contributions was to place inductive reasoning and deductive reasoning in a complementary rather than competitive mode. Peirce also added the concept of adductive reasoning. The combined three forms of reasoning serve as a primary conceptual foundation for the empirically based scientific method of today.

In the world of software development, these philosophies generally relate to "prove it", "provide me with credible reasoning", or "be reasonable and do both over time where it makes sense contextually". In the noise of current software development debate, some methodologists may claim that these philosophies represent a world view that is symptomatic of a "low trust" culture or other such rhetoric.

1.3.2 The Philosophy of Faith

In this frame, faith is seen as those views that one holds despite evidence and reason to the contrary. Accordingly, faith is seen as pernicious with respect to rationality, as it interferes with the ability to think, and inversely rationality is seen as the enemy of faith by interfering with beliefs. Within the world of software development methodology, one could easily argue that Agile represents a social movement that ironically leverages belief and faith heavily even though empiricism is espoused. Some have gone so far as to compare it to religion, often resulting in very passionate backlash and the vitriol labeling of the apostate as being a heretic [43]. However, it is hard to not agree with many of the parallels that can be made. Going beyond labeling those who rely exclusively on faith simply as zealots, one needs to understand that a faith-oriented ideology enables very powerful community preservation. Similar to major religions, which invoke such concepts as sacraments, rituals/ceremonies, and altruism, software development phenomenon like the Agile movement has been so successful due to its ability to invoke Prosyletic, Adversative, Cognitive and Motivational ideas in relation to its propagation [44]. In this regard it can be compared to the strength and perseverance of religion and the philosophy of faith. With such apparent parallels, it is hard to imagine that the community and culture of Agile didn't just happen void of such forethought of what it takes to sustain and grow such a social network. Note that the philosophies of reason are both critical and comprehensive, yet religion is not by definition so critical. In much the same light, movements such as what Agile has become are not subject to the careful scrutiny of reason and logic. Leveraging faith implies an attitude of trust or assent and therefore requires an act of will on the part of the believer. You either believe in Agile or you don't, and it is not the movement which must prove or disprove efficacy. The power of leveraging this ideology is that by valuing faith over evidence from experience or reason inoculates the movement against the most basic tools that people use to evaluate their ideas - thinking. Similarly, movements leverage highly emotive communication and norms so that the community reinforcement can spread more quickly, and because of the implied sociological as well as personal economic rewards.

In software development methodology debates, this philosophy can generally be summed up as "trust me". Much has been made of the high-trust culture and embracing whole-team between the business and IT where investment is not to be scrutinized (see #NoEstimates). A reasonable business-position that could be taken by stakeholders when confronted with leap-of-faith decisions related to methodology advice might be to request that those asking for trust related to their advice and guidance back it up with a money-back guarantee.

1.3.3 Philosophy and Theory

A scientific theory is a model that describes and codifies the observations we make. A theory will describe a large range of phenomena and will enable predictions that can be tested. Theories explain the why of things (i.e., causal explanation) and put boundaries and context on the subject being examined. Good theories are generative and will inspire new research, and will serve an integrative function thereby providing a coherent picture that expands the existing body of knowledge. While the philosophies of reason embrace the use of theories, philosophies of faith find theorizing potentially threatening. In the case of the Empiricism and Positivism perspective, the *Inductive Grounded Theory* [45] approach attempts to arrive at a theory of knowledge under consideration through exploration of data, deduction and the emergence of a theory. The Rationalist perspective will conceptualize a theory, followed by the deduction of hypothesis and design of experiments, and in some sub-disciplines, attempt to verify through empirical observation and measurement of data. This ontology is an approach called *Hypothetico-deductive Theory* [46]. The Pragmatist school of thought is to embrace both approaches to arrive at a theory - both inductive and conceptualization, which represents a hybrid approach to theorizing. To arrive at a theory of how software development endeavors function using this approach involves intelligent conceptualization and the accompanying empiricism to enable and inform calibration or re-calibration of our conceived ideas. This serves as a form of "theory feedback loop" to flesh out our paradigms.

Theories are important to business because they can be valuable to understand *what makes succeeding projects succeed and failing projects fail* The Pragmatic approach is valuable because it provides a bridge between industry and academia, enabling the integration of research with practice in the field in the quest for seeking an answer to the above question. It is likely however that attempts to explore the essence of software ecosystems will be rebutted by those espousing faith-based philosophies as Reductionist and akin to applying archaic Newtonian thinking on something inherently abstract, complex and artful. Such rhetoric can be countered by pragmatic enterprises by reminding those who do not have to exercise due diligence that while Holism studies the relationships of the whole, this requires an understanding of the properties of the parts to contribute to our understanding of the whole. When these two perspectives are combined, an enterprise is practicing "Holistic Reductionism". This approach to theorizing and observation is also popularly referred to as *Systems Thinking*, which perhaps is more palatable. That is to say, we need to study the parts that comprise any system, and also study and understand the whole so as to explore the emergent behaviours and dynamics of the system itself.

Sifting through the rhetoric means decoupling issues of social activism and power plays from operational strategy. What any business enterprise must decide is what mindset and therefore methodological school of thought would their investors prefer they follow. In general, this boils down to the schools of *Management Science* and *Reasoning* versus *Faith-based* decisions. Through this lens enterprises can assess which theories or lack thereof will be relevant and valuable in their pursuit of operational excellence. Hopefully it is clear that the pragmatic school of thought most resonates with the realities of today's business climate, and such an approach avoids the *pedantics, rigid orthodoxy* or other forms of baggage that often accompanies the quest for capability improvement.

1.4 – Software Development and the Law

We live in a collective society made up of laws. Regardless of what one might think about the current state of the Law, this is the system that we have that maintains stability both civically and economically. All modern enterprises exist within this framework, and therefore are not exempt from the rule of law. While some methodologists have taken up the crusade to challenge the order of things and use software investments as a vehicle for their cause [47], we also know what happens when *anarchy* is allowed to reign. Within the field of software development, notable examples of train wrecks includes the recent Healthcare.gov fiasco with cost overruns amounting to $500M and the associated political capital and goodwill that was lost to President Obama [48]; Toyota's Prius' 1.9 million car recall due to software glitches[49] ; the Patriot Missile System glitch in Saudi Arabia that cost the lives of 28 servicemen [50]; Heathrow's Terminal 5 baggage handling system which lost 42000 bags in the first 10 days and forced 500 cancelled flights [51]; or the Denver Airport baggage system costing $560M [52]; the EDS Child Support System epic failure costing UK taxpayers $1Billion; the Mars Climate Orbiters' miscalculated landing, costing $125Million [53]; the Ariane 5 rocket destruction due to overflow conditions, costing the $8Billion program dearly and the loss of a $500M satellite payload [54]; the Defence Integrated Military Human Resources System - DIMHRS being summed up upon cancellation as an acronym Robert Gates couldn't pronounce after spending $1B [55] - you get the idea, the list goes on. To ignore that the Law is somehow not the governing environment when things go wrong is naive. Enterprise software development is no place for social activism, yet this is what surfaces from time to time in the world of software development methodology. You will often hear rhetoric that espouses the virtues of a "high-trust culture" when legal realities like contracts are discussed. Needless to say, apparently the lessons of Enron and Arthur Anderson have been lost in the sands of time for such advocates. When oversight fails when it is most needed, the result is very large order losses.

It is instructive to discuss the topic of the legal system that enterprises operate within and the realities they face every day. Particularly relevant to North America and the Commonwealth countries is the Common Law system that emerged in society over many centuries. One area of law is the *Law of Torts* [56], the word Tort coming from the Latin word *Tortus* meaning "a wrong". One area of Tort is that of *Negligence* which would be the relevant area of what was discussed in the previously mentioned spectacular failures. Within the law of Negligence is the concept of *Duty of Care* or *Standard of Care*. This is the standard of performance that "a reasonable person" would discharge. Such a general duty is upon all within Enterprises, whereby individuals are held to a standard that asks would it be "reasonably foreseeable" that things could go wrong. Duty of care generally represents a social contract and the implicit responsibilities held by individuals towards others within society. In business, when large investments are involved, the duty of care addresses the attentiveness and prudence of managers in performing their decision-making and supervisory functions, assumed to be carried out in good faith. Management can be said to have what is referred to as a *Fiduciary Duty* to the investors of IT, ultimately the shareholders in the Enterprise. A fiduciary duty requires a stricter standard of behaviour, with the fiduciary conducting themselves with undivided loyalty absent of any conflict-of-interest. For example, when we see management behaving in "empire building" activities, it could be argued that they are breaching their fiduciary duty to the stakeholders of the Enterprise because they are making decisions for their own benefit. Similarly, when developers insert risky, pet technologies into projects solely for selfish purposes to enhance their personal learning and marketability, it could be said that they are breaching their general duty of care.

Indeed, due diligence must be exercised within any publicly traded company to a standard that a "reasonable man" would discharge. Such due diligence has been codified in various ways, including the Sarbanes Oxley regulation, Section 302 and 404 [57]. This requires that Enterprise Risk Management and Governance functions within IT adhere to a Fiduciary level standard-of-care for modern software development practice entrusted by the CEO and CFO. However, a major problem is that the evidentiary standards within this field are lacking, and the body of "case law" is sparse, let alone not formally or centrally registered for *a priori* usage on software projects. Indeed, what is needed is the establishment of such a "common law" registry for the world of software development.

1.5 – The Making of a Profession

The Common Law of present day had its origins in medieval Anglo-Saxon law, with it descending from ancient continental Germanic legal thought and custom and strongly influenced by the Roman Empire. This early law of the "barbarian" nations was essentially oral, where laws were periodically recited publicly and relied on word-of-mouth and memory for their maintenance. With the advent of a new "technology", this reliance of what obviously was an error prone approach akin to "folklore" and strongly subject to interpretation and conveyance was ended. The maturation of the laws that reflected societies' needs were codified through the advent of writing [58]. This resulted in the ability for society to reference past experiences and rulings when faced with pressing decisions, and enabled incrementalism of the application of laws and the non-disruptive evolutionary "steerage" of society. It would be fair to say that the software development industry is at a similar cross-roads. Either the field of making software is going to be based on something akin to religion and "barbaric custom", or it is going to evolve through the use of technology and implement similar structures like the major social institutions that implement the laws of the land. Due to the fact that society and software are becoming so intertwined and software is becoming so important and pervasive, it would seem reasonable that more formality and tighter integration in knowledge capture and application would add significant value to the world of business. In a similar line of reasoning to the Common Law, practice in software development should be instructive rather than prescriptive. Only in the cases where policy is necessary due to large order risk should the notion of "Statute Law" and "standards" be applied. Unfortunately, the standards and certification game is alive and well in the software development industry, having entrenched itself without having the benefit of the historical "case law" to rely on.

Codification of the "laws of software development" largely implies the need for a mechanism to establish and record *precedents* within an integrated registry. Similar to the Common Law Courts, such a "court registry" for software development precedents requires some degree of governance and oversight in the form of *rules of procedure* such that the adjudication process is effective in rendering decisions about a matter needing attention in a timely manner. Today, no such mechanism exists but is sorely needed. Conflicts of interest are rampant within an industry focused on gaining competitive edge rather than serving broader society and the businesses that drive economic prosperity. Only a few organizations can refute this assertion of impartiality, with the most common scenario of the capture and certification of software development expertise and knowledge bases coming by way of for-profit standards bodies, and "communities". Examples of organizations that do seem like candidates for owning such a responsibility include the IEEE (Institute for Electrical and Electronic Engineers) [59], the ISO (International Standards Organization) [60] and the ISACA (Information Systems Audit and Control Association) [61]. It just so happens that these bodies are tied to professional bodies - Engineering in the case of IEEE, and Accounting in the case of ISACA.

The debate naturally arises as to whether a profession should oversee the "rules of procedure" of codifying **Generally Accepted Practice** in software development that is based on "case law", or whether it should be left to some other form of organization. It is clear that a battle over this turf is underway, with the idea of Guilds or Trade Unions being at one end of the spectrum, and professions at the other. When faced with a choice, most business enterprises would agree that software gone wrong has the ability to materially harm shareholders, or could result in wrongful death. It is fair to say that art or crafts can't practically do such damage, but software surely can. That would suggest that what is required is a **Profession** and associated code of conduct and governing body [62]. Professions are defined as having a professional association, a cognitive base (storage of adjudicated knowledge), institutionalized training, licensing, work autonomy, colleague control and a code of ethics. A very high standard is set related to professional practice and intellectual excellence. Currently this is non-existent within the industry. As software becomes more and more important to enterprises, they must be able to rely on an impartial body to move beyond the broad stroke assertions of efficacy, the rhetoric, spin, partisan politics and dogma that is representative of what the software development industry has devolved into, most noticeably in the "software development method wars".

Ultimately, the creation of a professional body for software development would span existing communities and standards bodies. Its charter would be to integrate disparate knowledge across the various disciplines and specializations and would be inclusive of the various perspectives that exist within the methodology landscape. No longer would rhetoric, implied or explicit like "we don't need PM's or BA's anymore" be credible. Instead, the registry of experience would adjudicate the useful precedents of practice based on empirical observations that would achieve higher evidentiary standard of care required by the Common Law environment that our society relies upon.

Chapter 2: The Emergence of Generally Accepted Practice

"What do you think was the most important physics idea to emerge this year? Answer- We won't know for a few years." - Stephen Hawking

When one rejects the myopathy and division associated with the current state of rhetoric related to software development methodology, very little has fundamentally changed over the past 50 years in terms of the practices and techniques we employ on software development endeavors. The subtle changes that do occur are evolutionary in nature and some fundamentals are emerging. Through many years of effectively trial and error within the world of business, *Generally Accepted Practice for Software Development (GAP-SW)* has emerged. It is time to embrace the notion that there are generally accepted tactics that can be said to be efficient and effective. Support for this efficacy can be made in a credible manner such that the longstanding philosophical divisions and dogmatic ideologies can give way to professional practice. Rather than continue the pattern of the past, the software development field is sufficiently mature to attempt to codify Generally Accepted Practice and thereby bring together software professionals in such a way to divert their passions towards the delivery of software value and away from petty, pedantic arguments. The world has woken up to the new reality of an insatiable appetite that society now has for software, and the gap in the ability to supply this capability is being far outstripped by demand. It is time for the collective industry to grow up and enter the big leagues for the benefit of accelerating the progress of mankind and serving the investors that pay for software.

2.1 – "Agile is Dead, Long Live Agility"

Subsequent to the articulation of the Agile Manifesto, where the authors felt compelled to issue such a political declaration, "Agile" has become a bit of a *cottage industry*. All manner of profiteering has accompanied the social agendas, anti-management/architect/analyst axe grinding, left-wing ideology and even the undercurrents of craft unionism as described in Chapter 1. Contrary to the original pragmatism espoused by these pioneers, it has been twisted, contorted, and diluted beyond recognition. While the Agile movement served to jolt the industry forward out of a purely mechanical and almost de-humanizing slant almost 15 years ago, it is pretty telling when those of the 17 idolized individuals recapitulates and asserts *Agile is Dead, Long Live Agility* [1]. In a show of credibility and personal courage, "Pragmatic" Dave Thomas opens up about the Agile Pandora's Box, stating rather forcefully:

> *"The word "agile" has been subverted to the point where it is effectively meaningless, and what passes for an agile community seems to be largely an arena for consultants and vendors to hawk services and products."*

Another slightly older example of calls for renewal from one of the original authors is Alistair Cockburn's *"Oath of Non-Allegiance"* [2], whereby he attempts to stuff the genie back into the lamp:

> *"I'm tired of people from one school of thought dissing ideas from some other school of thought. I hunger for people who don't care where the ideas come from, just what they mean and what they produce. So I came up with this "Oath of Non-Allegiance:* **I promise not to exclude from consideration any idea based on its source, but to consider ideas across schools and heritages in order to find the ones that best suit the current situation.** *".*

There have been tell-tales that the Agile brand has been waning for some time. The early signs of this were mentions of *big-A Agile* versus *little-a agile*. Then came along the attempts to re-write the Manifesto due to perceived shortcomings of a declaration that at the time was just that, a point in time declaration. Some have even gone so far as to articulate an *Anti-Agile Manifesto* [3], grounded on common sense. Later very public disputes, most notably between the Agile and Kanban communities, started to take on a surprisingly vitriol tone. Finally, some research analysts are beginning to question whether the data exists to support claims of efficacy, suggesting that Agile methodologists have run with impunity for far too long [4].

Nowadays, it is hard to distinguish rebranding from any form of advancement. Plays on words increasingly attempt differentiation in the marketplace, with whomever serving up the flashiest snake oil taking a temporary windfall out of the enterprise space. Too often in this scenario, selection of the latest shiny object is akin to not having to think. Other disturbing examples highlight an increase in bias, including *The Scotsman Fallacy* [5], in which unfounded assertions are made that no true Agilista would develop software without application of a specific popularized practice. A case in point is the recent hand-raising related to the questioning the efficacy and appropriate context for TDD - Test Driven Development [6], one of the core darling practices of the Agile Movement, specifically found within the eXtreme Programming method (XP) [7]. The first to question the efficacy of what was once accepted by rote was James Coplien in his essay *Why Most Unit Testing is Waste* [8]. This was notable because he is also one of the original Agile Manifesto authors. TDD efficacy was again questioned recently, many years later, by David Heinemeier Hannson (@DHH), the creator of the Ruby on Rails development framework through his blog admonition that he did not want to use the practice anymore [9]. This led to quite a backlash from proponents of the practice, and also those who had some emotional attachment to their sacred baby. The debate increased in intensity when two of the Agile Manifesto authors (Kent Beck and Martin Fowler) decided to engage @DHH in debate within a public Google Hangout forum [10], subtly attempting to dissuade this dissenting opinion under the auspices of learning. Nothing of any significance was achieved in this exchange, other than perhaps retrenchment of positions and the fact that dissent does exist, contrary to popular "Scotsman" lore.

To explore these TDD dissenting voices a little requires a contextual example that will highlight the potential inefficiency of the TDD practice and rebut the claims of universality that are often made. Take the case of the control software for the Large Hadron Collider at CERN called Detection Control Systems [11]. These systems monitor and control variables such as voltage, temperature and humidity within the particle detectors for 4 main experiments - The Compact Muon Solenoid (CMS), Large Hadron Collider Beauty (LHCb), A Toroidal LHC Apparatus (ATLAS), and A Large Ion Collider Experiment (ALICE). The software operates many pieces of hardware that measure and control over a million parameters concerning these environment variables. The complexity of single nodes is relatively low: on average a node contains about 8 states in CMS and ALICE and 6 states in LHCb and ATLAS. The complexity of the system lies in the number of nodes and the communication between them: the DCS of CMS consists of over 32000 nodes and in LHCb's and ATLAS's DCSes there are even more: over 79500 nodes. Their systems yield state spaces of about 10^{25000} and 10^{57600} states.

Clearly, preventing unwarranted entry into any of these states is important because doing so can lead to the destruction of the very expensive experiments. Validation of guard conditions required to allow transition implies the need to perform precondition checks on each and every state. If this is to be achieved through TDD and the use of Unit Tests, we are faced with having to maintain a parallel set of tests in addition to the code that implements these pre-conditions - obviously a huge number. When such an extreme example is raised as a nonstarter TDD situation on social media (which it was on Twitter by me) there is no rebuttal. The reason is that better practices exist that reduce the overhead of such a large state space and yield the same preventative poka yoke effect. Such contextual options are discussed in the next section. Instead of creating separate and apart tests, simply code the pre-conditions inline in the program. Unfortunately, this does not confirm to orthodoxy. When it comes to test cases, these should be reserved to important acceptance test cases at full nested state machine scope, and guided by the reduction of the state space achieved through linear algebraic approaches that determine state reachability. Such a need for pragmatism is abundantly clear when faced with such an extreme context, and illustrates the principle that myopically following a practice by rote and using brute force to solving software delivery ecosystem problems might bring comfort or the feeling of a safety net to developers, but ultimately it is foolish.

Very recently a number of industry leaders convened to chart a new direction for the software development industry. The result was an articulation of how to move forward, agnostic of existing divisive brands and past the limited research and credible management science that many methods are lacking. The charter is intended to be a living and evolving statement of how to integrate methodology experience into a coherent whole. The intent is for continued conversation, effectively launching a counter-meme to the damaging effects of Agile dogma. More importantly, it grounds the industry in the reality that people pay for software, and have a fiduciary duty to maximize the return on their investment. Similarly, those that have the responsibility to meet almost ridiculous deadlines driven by ruthless competitive pressures like *Digital Disruption* [12] and other forms of *Disruptive Innovation* [13], require a "new deal" with management whereby they are granted reasonably and responsible autonomy to perform their jobs. **The New Deal** movement (the-new-deal.org), grounded on the philosophy of pragmatism, will attempt to realize these ideals for the betterment of the industry.

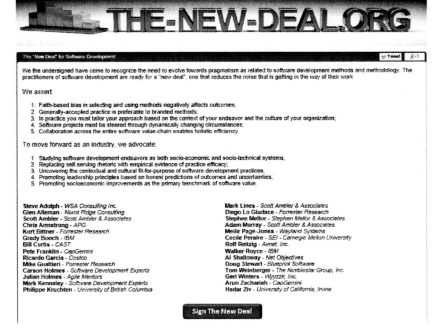

Figure 2.1 – The New Deal

2.2 – Identifying Equivalency & Variation

With all the rhetoric going on in the industry, it is often difficult to perform apple-to-apple comparisons of practices. Misinformation, lack of due-diligence in making one's case, or limited research engagement has made identifying bona-fide differentiation very difficult. With much distrust, one finds oneself more often attempting to discredit ones opponent, more akin to showing how much smarter one is on social media than actually having an adult conversation. Part of this is due to the lack of any form of registry, rules of evidence or all the other things that serve society to help integrate the "common law" of software development. The literature is divided between popular folk-lore and high-brow academia papers.

Continuing with the increasingly controversial flash point surrounding the Unit Testing debate and claims of universality, consider the example of an extremely sarcastic interview that was staged by the proponents of TDD against the inventor of Design-by-Contract (DBC) [14]. Rather than drive to the specific nuances between the approaches, the interviewers approach the conversation by attacking the foreign practice. In reality, each of these practices serve as detailed design practices, and they do not stand alone in this space as other less popular variants exist, including Desmond DeSouza's Operational Contracts [15]. If one looks hard enough and mines various practices across the spectrum of methodology, this is not a unique phenomenon. Many practices are equivalent to others, with only names and branding being the essential difference.

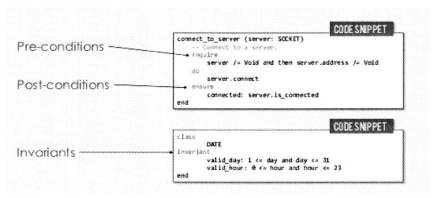

Figure 2.2 – Design-by-Contract

The table below compares and contrasts these four similar practices, each focused on the purpose of preventing the injection of defects at a design level:

	Test-Driven Design (TDD)	Design-by-Contract (DBC)	Operational Contracts (OCs)
Discipline	Code	Code	Design
Artifact	Unit Tests	Pre/Post Conditions	Pre/Post Conditions
Persistence	External	Integral	External
Mechanism	Mocks	Ensure/Assert	Guard Conditions

Table 2.1 – Defect Prevention Practices

As will become evident in the discussion of a universal kernel to follow, such debates must be arbitrated through rules that establish the context and purpose of the practices in question such that variance can be intelligently explored. For now, it is suffice to say that commonality does exist in the sea of software development practices, and identification of common ground, practice variants and equivalence is a bounded problem and is possible.

2.3 – A recap of SDLC 3.0

Five years ago, a work was published which sought to drive an integrative agenda within the software development world, both socially and methodology wise. It represented a call to action, one that was inclusive and tolerant to differing ideas. The book promoted the retirement of the "waterfall" approach on the basis that it can be proven to be destabilizing [16] and extremely unproductive, both efficiency-wise and effectiveness-wise. The basis for this will be discussed in *Section 7.1 – The Optimization of Flow* . I would go so far as to additionally say that in light of such credible explanations, anyone attempting to advocate Waterfall efficacy is flirting with **negligent practice**. Only for reasons of obfuscating actual learning progress and delaying a day of reckoning with investors so as to milk a project for profit would someone leverage this approach. How strange it is that so many continue to embrace its usage, which by the way represents a clear misinterpretation of the original 1970 paper by Winston Royce [17].

SDLC 3.0: Beyond a Tacit Understanding of Agile [18] was grounded in an ideology of credible study via scientific principles, leveraging both known and emerging models of the way things on software projects work. It also represented a vision that set the course for future directions and work. In fact, it represents the vision for the technology that will be described in this book, the concrete realization of the ideals presented in SDLC 3.0.

The first key concept presented was to apply the principles of software configuration management and parallel development to the high degree of branching that has occurred within software methodology. As illustrated in Figure 2.3, other than retiring the Waterfall branch, the book advocates performing a merge or "re-baseline" on the Iterative Methods branch and numerous sub-branches to prevent the division and drift that has occurred not only in the methodology concepts and terminology, but also the communities and followers attached to them. Finally, also advocated was the continual integration of future emergent innovations that are discovered and codified by methodologists from time to time due to corporate and contextual experience.

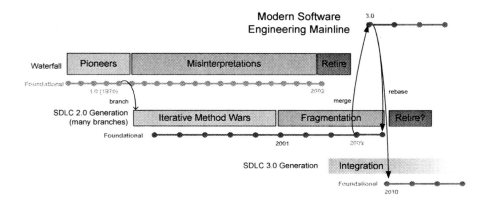

Figure 2.3 – Software Engineering Method Branching [18]

To achieve such a goal, SDLC 3.0 performed the meticulous task of charting and mining where all this methodology stuff came from in the first place.   Instead of just taking the origins of ideas or effective practices as a given, the attempt was waged to sift through all the noise out there and to track the *context* for their emergence and usage.   This research is extremely important for this more recent work, as context is everything when trying to determine what approach tactics are likely to be effective at delivering software.   All too often, credit is claimed by those who are best at marketing their wares, or who simply tweaked some words or labels or even took some liberties on when things were "invented" to stake a claim as the "father of X", thereby losing this essential context.

Such archaeology had been attempted before SDLC 3.0, but never for this purpose. Figure 2.4 illustrates a map of where methods emerged in relation to the culture/ideological lineage, and the corporate experience that enabled codification.   It is updated to reflect the recent industry experience that will be described as the *SDLC 3.1* baseline, with contributions to be discussed in the section that follows.

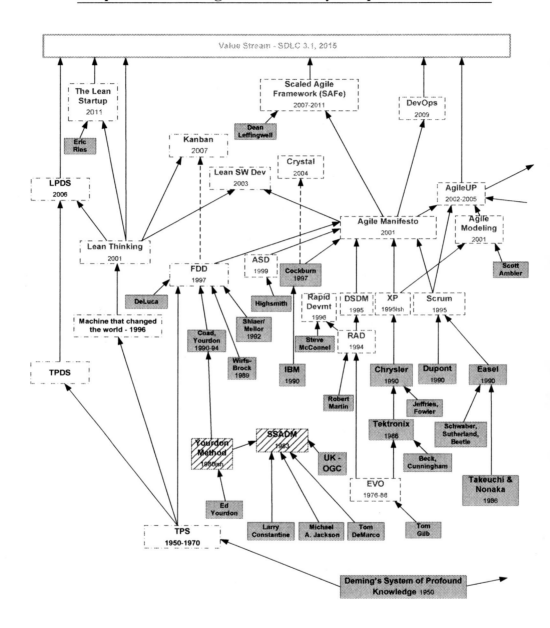

Figure 2.4 – History of Modern Software Development Methods [18]

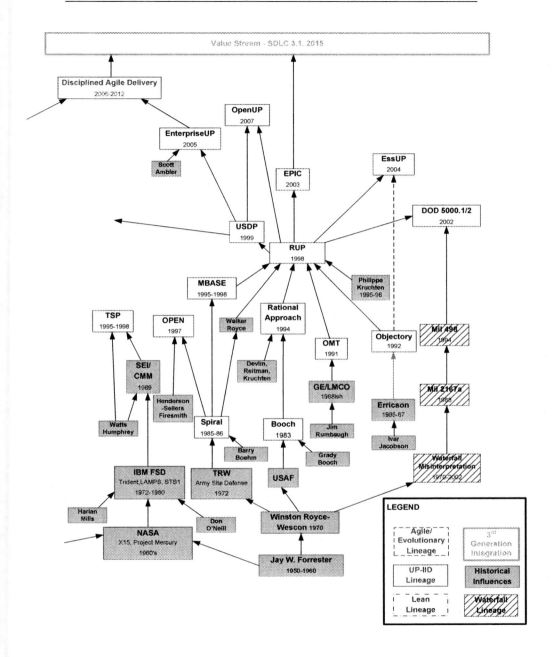

Figure 2.4 – History of Modern Software Development Methods [18]

Finally, SDLC 3.0 performed the heavy lifting of identifying recurring patterns across the spectrum of methodology perspectives. From this emerged "common ground" or a nucleus of ideas in the form of patterns or "practices" which have consistently proven to be effective. This commonality is essential to enable the communities to rally around such an integration effort, as there is no shortage of opinions when it comes to methodology brands. Figure 2.5 illustrates the decomposition of the major lineages of methods into their unique contributions in terms of practices or "approach tactics", and the common ideas or practices that are shared among modern methods.

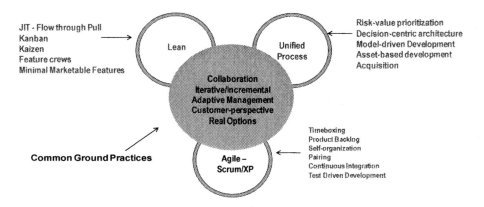

Figure 2.5 – Common Ground [18]

From looking at the common ground practices, agnostic of branding or differentiating labels, the connection was made and described that all software development endeavours represent systems with necessary feedback. Knowing full well that the potential to be perceived as threatening to those who seek to profit from their "flavour du jour", the discovered model for how software development projects work was backed by some engineering discipline. The book for the first time described an approach for studying feedback systems familiar to me and readily available to those who want to go beyond rhetoric and slogans to improve the state of the practice.

Figure 2.6 illustrates this model at a high level and represented the beginnings of identifying a universal kernel model, one that would explain why succeeding projects succeed and failing projects fail.

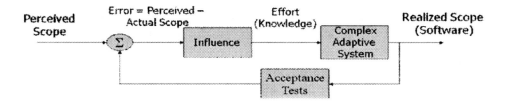

Figure 2.6 – Systems Thinking and Software Development [18]

The latter chapters of the book built upon this model of software development to begin explaining common issues being tackled within the various communities including issues of scale, technical debt, and empiricism. From this, the grand unifier was presented for enterprises, the notion of integrating the entire end-to-end value stream leveraging practices. Typical "value networks" that result from the selection of competing practice choices across the various activities of the value stream were presented covering such key value-added enterprise functions as   Alignment, Acquisition, Portfolio Management and Service Transition. Finally, the book took a stand against the rhetoric of "Individuals and Interactions over Processes and Tools", specifically in the sense that technology is a key enabler to how those human interactions may be empowered. Instead of buying into the rhetoric of tools always thwarting the necessary human collaborations that are at the core of the software development ecosystem, the book chose to attack the complexity of modern enterprise software development infrastructure rather than assume overly simplistic solutions to be universally applied, independent of context. Such a stance was likely unpopular compared to socially acceptable approaches in the Agile community, but necessary for progress in our industry.

This book amplifies these latter chapters, and takes a radically different strategy than any other book on software development methodology. Instead of just capturing ideas and pontificating on their merit, sometimes with less than credible empirical evidence, this book will describe how these rather revolutionary ideas have been put into concrete practice through working software. Strangely enough, this is very rare in our industry. Perhaps because it is a very difficult problem we are facing, and I can attest to the complexity of the ultimate solution. Notable exceptions that have put their money where their mouth is and have manifested their ideas in software that can actually yield the true value of the work include Kent Beck with *jUnit* [19], Martin Fowler with *CruiseControl* [20], Robert Martin with *Fitnesse*, and Ward Cunningham with the *Wiki* [21]. Continuing this pragmatism, this book will describe the concrete realization of what ultimately is working software to solve the capability improvement goals that are so badly needed yet historically illusive. Hopefully not too many methodologists will label this pejoratively using the word "tool".

2.4 – Recent Industry Experience – SDLC 3.1

The capture and codification of corporate experience has continued since the SDLC 3.0 baseline was articulated. In the past five years, innovations have emerged that have furthered the state of the practice and addressed prior shortcomings. Unfortunately, these new entrants into the methodology landscape still, to varying degrees, stand on their own island as unique and isolated methods. Each has attached new communities, certifications, consulting emphasis and to varying degrees knowledge persistence and management in the form of whitepapers, books, process management facilities and conferences. To continue with the methodology integration philosophy to establish "Generally Accepted Practice", integration of this recent experience is necessary along with prior methods. To do this, identification of the unique and independent practice parts is necessary, separate and apart from the whole method container. The following represents an assessment of the unique practice contributions from each emergent body of knowledge or method.

2.4.1 – Scaled Agile Framework

The *Scaled Agile Framework (SAFe)* emerged from experience by Dean Leffingwell during consulting engagements, most notably with John Deere [22]. The content of SAFe is delivered via a static content repository that delivers the framework over the internet for free public usage. Figure 2.7 illustrates an older example of the interface to this knowledge base:

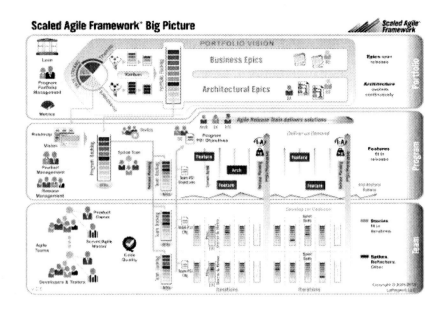

Figure 2.7 – Scaled Agile Framework v2.5 [23]

The core context for this framework is lightweight investment identification, allocation and formation of programs that comprise multiple Scrum product management lifecycles. The Scrum lifecycle is essentially wrapped by the Alignment-stage tactics advocated by the framework, which are modified to address more coarse-grained release cycles of *potentially shippable increments* (PSI's) of working, tested software. The framework has enjoyed market success as representing a fresh attempt at addressing the shortcomings of the minimalist and overly simplistic Scrum-of-Scrums approach to scaling Agile. However, it is not without controversy, with much backlash emerging from within the Agile community who believe that scaling up is not the answer, but rather that the organization should be the ones to change and restructure around small autonomous teams [24]. Aside from some of the more radical activist overtones within the chorus of this backlash, others have pointed to the issue of contextualization related to SAFe usage [25]. Specifically, any attempt to force all IT investment into an aggregated *Program Management* structure represents batching, and represents a contradiction to the purported emphasis on Lean Thinking, specifically principles of flow.

One key practice that is new and unique within the framework is the *Agile Release Train*, and approach to deal with coordination of complex program releases at a reasonable frequency of delivery. This practice extends Scrum backlog management and advocates newer *Product Management Team* ideas. Figure 2.8 illustrates the core idea:

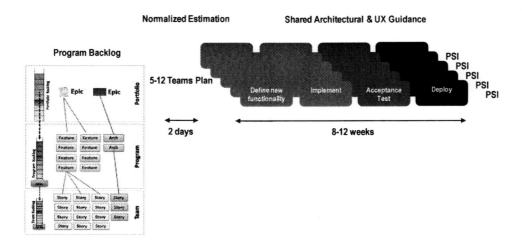

Figure 2.8 – Agile Release Train

Core to this scaling strategy is an expanded "agile" approach to requirements. The beginnings of the strategy originated within the work published in the book *Agile Software Requirements*. This work advocates extension of requirement types beyond User Stories at the system development level to Epic and Features at the Investment Portfolio and Program Management levels. Both business and architectural Epics are advocated to accommodate demand management categories of business alignment and innovation, and technology strategy respectively. Leffingwell, having long been known for Requirements Engineering tactics stemming from Requisite Inc and Rational Software, continues the work in this space. With the core emphasis being based on capturing, aligning and elaborating software product intent, the connections to scaling Scrum deficiencies with larger programs becomes apparent. Figure 2.9 illustrates the requirements taxonomy implicitly manifested within the framework.

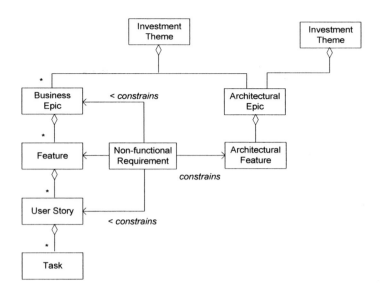

Figure 2.9 – Agile Software Requirements Taxonomy

The extended requirements taxonomy positions the unique contributions of SAFe to be within the Alignment stage of the IT value-stream. It could be said that this framework represents an alternative to TOGAF [26] with the objective being to establish flow related to IT investment planning, with an implicit reliance on emergence related to Enterprise Architecture. This is clearly a difference from the types of reasoning and reliance on visual modeling within the Business, Application and Integration domains as advocated with the heavier TOGAF Enterprise Architecture ADM (Architecture Development Method). Reliance on Epics, which are notoriously ambiguous and high level, assumes that identification of as-is to to-be transformation strategy can emerge over time without up-front investment justification and any up-front reasoning about cost-benefit analysis. Such over-simplification assumes that stakeholder concurrence of investment themes as sunk costs has already occurred, that essential complexity can be addressed through emergent Product Backlog grooming activities, and that real-time conversation can result in the knowledge required to refactor large scale legacy assets or reason about the necessary BPR within COTS Acquisition constrained developments. Figure 2.10 distills the SAFe framework alignment portion into a workflow model:

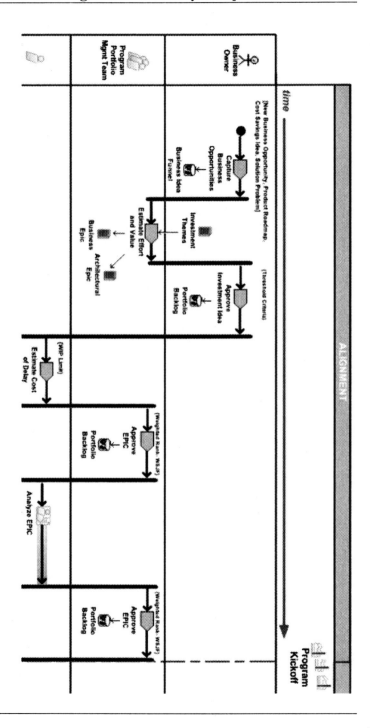

Figure 2.10 – Workflow of the Scaled Agile Framework (SAFe)

2.4.2 – Disciplined Agile Delivery

Disciplined Agile Delivery (DAD) [27] captures the cumulative efforts of Scott Ambler during and after his tenure at IBM Rational. It represents an example of the trend towards hybrid approaches in line with the advocacy of SDLC 3.0. Its origins stem from the work related to Agile-Unified Process [28], and incorporates much of Ambler's *Agile Modeling* [29] practices. Core to this framework is the extension of the Scrum lifecycle to incorporate something akin to the Unified Process (UP) lifecycle. Advocacy is given for inclusion of an Inception phase to seed the product backlog, although the term *Work-item List* is given preference.

While somewhat controversial, DAD advocates an implicit rather than explicit period of time akin to the Elaboration phase with UP to reflect the fact that true "architecture" is not always necessary on all projects. Instead, favoring lightweight milestones over the more formal phase gate milestones of UP is preferred. Modeling in a way consistent with Agile culture and collaborative ideals is described extensively within this approach (Figure 2.11) including practices like *Model Storming* which embraces the emergent social behaviors attached to *swarming* phenomenon; and inclusion of modeling in the *Iteration Planning* effort.

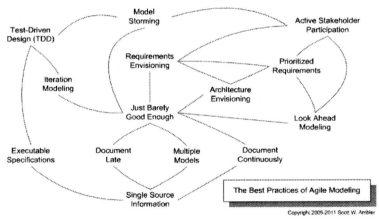

Figure 2.11 – The Practices of Agile Modeling [29]

Figure 2.12 below illustrates the high-level lifecycle model of DAD.

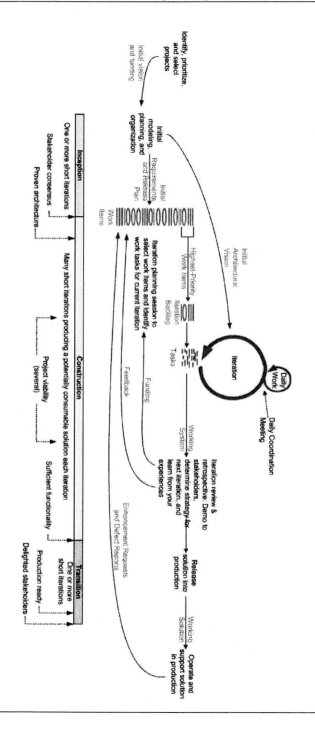

Figure 2.12 – Disciplined Agile Delivery Basic Lifecycle [27]

The standard DAD lifecycle can be seen to visually represent an extension of the core Scrum time-boxing approach to encompass and explicitly call out a full product delivery lifecycle through phase-themed iterations. It also makes attempts to generalize Scrum terminology to be more consumable to a broader constituency within the IT industry. Since the original publishing of DAD, it has morphed to include other visual articulations of lifecycle, most notably a Lean one-piece-flow lifecycle model [30].

Through work at IBM Rational, the ideas of contextualization and situationally appropriate practices started to gain popularity through Amblers efforts. The *Agile Scaling Model* [31], building on top of the work of Boehm and Turner in *Balancing Agility and Discipline* [32], identified practices required for scale. The context factors identified for making fit-for-purpose decisions, while only ranged in nature in the original articulation, serve as a more or less good going-forward set for exploration of efficacy.

Recently, DAD has started to advocate contextual reasoning of practice choices across the UP-like phases. Similar to the idea of phase objectives, DAD leverages goals to structure a set of attributes which in turn enable presentation of practice options. Alongside the feature called "Enterprise Aware", the new "Goals Driven" feature has accompanied the evolution of the framework towards being a "Process Decision Framework". While these phase-wise goals and associated subcategory "process issue" attributes cover contextual choices faced by teams, their scope is limited to delivery and currently do not cover the breadth of the full IT value stream. Additionally, the selection of the goals are based on the unique perspective and experience of DAD's creators and caretakers, and do not correlate to an underlying kernel that is system's based, one that clearly identifies the system context within which the practice plays a role, and one that can explain how the ecosystem works. As will be seen, these robust and advanced aspects are reserved for the Universal Kernel to be described in detail in Chapter 5. Nonetheless, it is to be applauded for stimulating the contextualization discussion, and it represents a view that can be overlaid and mapped onto the Universal Kernel to enable integration of this valuable experience. Such a view of the kernel also results in a different choice architecture in what will later be described within expert system technology.

2.4.3 – The Lean Startup

Delivered in book form, this body of knowledge was captured and codified by Eric Ries based notably on experience from IMVU [33]. Influence over this work stems from seasoned Silicon Valley venture capitalist Steve Blank, and observations from colleagues and mentors like Scott Cook from Intuit. Core to this approach is the necessity to prove hypotheses related to market demand when the customer is unknown. The practices contained within this work can be said to be a derivative of Henry Mintzberg's *Emergent Strategy* [34], long established in Product Management literature. Figure 2.13 illustrates the controversial Emergent Strategy practice as articulated in business circles:

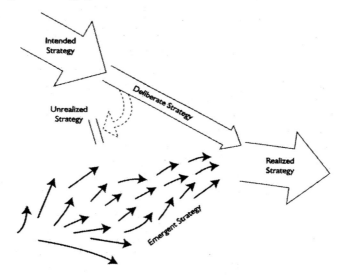

Figure 2.13 – Emergent Strategy [34]

In any startup, key to success is understanding the viability of a market opportunity. Even if an innovation has been discovered, it only represents a guess as to the market potential of the idea. As such, the practices contained within the codified experience of *The Lean Startup* can best be described as "Speculative Development". The key differentiator here is that the customer is not known for certainty but is rather conceived of in the fictitious sense. The core practices in this approach, while not being exclusive to the world of startups (as in the emerging examples of The Lean Startup being applied within enterprises), are focused on rapid feedback from experiments. It is the high frequency of the feedback loop that allows for emergence of clarity to ensue. The practice of *Minimally Viable Product* acts as a constraint on the development team to ensure that delay is not inserted into each development cycle which would reduce the effectiveness of the required learning. As such, it acts to limit WIP (Work-in-progress) in the truest Lean Thinking sense. Figure 2.14 illustrates what constitutes a Minimally Viable Product (MVP) which constrains hypothesis testing cycles:

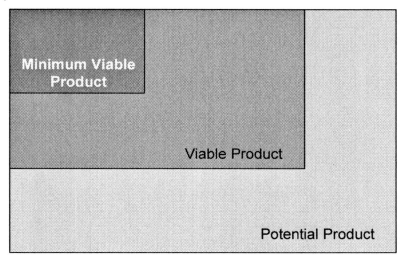

Figure 2.14 – Minimum Viable Product

Each cycle within the articulated cycle of *Build-Measure-Learn* is structured to achieve flow, specifically the idea of "continuous innovation", similar to continuous delivery. The core measures related to innovation are focused on learning about the fictitious customer and the un-validated market opportunity. Accounting for progress in this highly speculative context is focused on learning and reduction of uncertainty, not delivery of value. Governance is represented in the practice idea of *Pivot or Persevere*. This is most often the objective of the discovery and alignment period of time, and can be said to be an approach that fits within the "fuzzy front end" of product development. It competes with other alignment approaches like TOGAF, which are leveraged in large scale enterprises which are much more established, and for which the customers of the enterprise architecture are more well known.

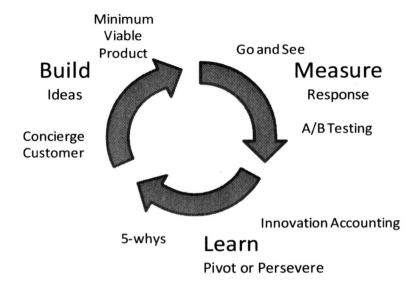

Figure 2.15 Build-Measure-Learn [33]

Recently, Enterprises are leveraging this approach internally to drive innovation within their Research and Development organizations [35]. The approach is ideally suited for such efforts due to its tight feedback loop, something that is required if emergence of market-resonating products is to be discovered. Similarly, such an approach acknowledges the high degree of uncertainty that exists when the customer is largely unknown and product development is entirely speculative. Unfortunately, as historically been the case due to overzealous consultants trying to make a buck, some are attempting to make this approach universal within enterprises, independent of context and culture [36]. Segments of the portfolio related to sustainment of existing corporate assets, COTS acquisitions of well-known business processes, or large scale transformation programs would find limited value of the approach and related practices beyond that of the Discovery Stage of the IT Value Stream.

2.4.4 – The Kanban Method

Kanban [37] emerged from experience by David J. Anderson while at Microsoft and later Corbis. Originally applied to Sustainment Engineering, claims of universality for all phases of development are made. Much of this approach borrows from the Lean Thinking origins of the Toyota Production System (TPS) where Taiichi Ohno invented the signaling approach for implementing JIT [38]. Regardless of the fact that application of Little's Law [39] should be reserved for steady-state dynamics, teams leverage the approach in attempts to identify Critical-WIP for all their work.

The story within the story is that The Kanban Method (with a capital K) represents an **emergent approach to organizational change management**. Specifically called out as evolutionary, Kanban represents an application of Eliyahu Goldratt's Theory of Constraints (ToC) [40]. The approach advocates the opposite of Scrum's radical redesign approach to capability improvement, instead favoring keeping an organizations existing division-of-labor profile and role names.

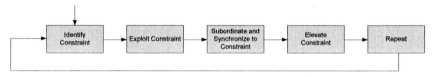

Figure 2.16 – Five Focusing Steps from ToC [40]

Kanban boards realize a principle of Visualizing the System, with an almost myopic focus on establishing Work-in-progress (WIP) limits. The innovation as described by its creator involves *exploiting* existing constraints as much as possible before the more costly *elevation* of constraining activities. Elevating constraints through the establishment of other process topologies and introducing parallelism is argued to be more expensive. Instead, through the *kanban* mechanism to implement a pull system, attempts at optimization are focused on establishing flow - a practice referred to in the method as *flow-through-pull*. Metaphorically, you can think of a kanban signal similar to conventional current in electric circuits. The flow of holes left by the flow of work units (the electrons) are the kanban signal to pull work down the value stream. Figure 2.17 by Karl Scotland illustrates the concept of a Kanban Board for managing work very effectively which makes use of this *valence* concept:

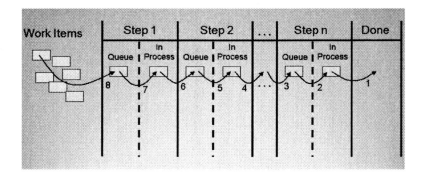

Figure 2.17 – Kanban Board [41]

While a Kanban board represents a visual representation of the states that a work-item goes through, adding color is a common convention to represent differing *Classes-of-service*. As an attribute of each demand element going through the system, common values are expedited, representing requests that are disruptive to steady-state flow; fixed delivery date, representing items that must be prioritized to achieve the desired service; standard for typical work; and intangible for ancillary work like remediation of technical debt.

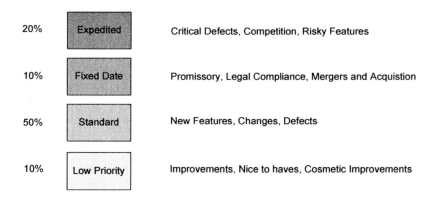

Figure 2.18 – Classes of Service and Heijunka

2.4.5 – The DevOps Movement

DevOps [42] is a movement and community that advocates better collaboration between what is typically a segregated Development organization, an independent Quality Assurance organization, and IT Operations as a separate organization. The core emphasis is to integrate these potential silo's through increased generalization in skillset, proactive development of automated deployment procedures and assets, and highly automated environment provisioning. It's amazing how cute slogans and clever marketing labels continually emerge within the IT industry. For something that is quite a simple idea based on common sense, it is telling why some anagram or concatenation sweeteners are required for the ideas and meme to spread. As discussed in the first chapter, one needs to study political science to understand why this is so effective. The DevOps Movement can be traced back to 2009 and the confluence of several industry forces and ideas coalescing at once including 1) conferences that highlighted notable examples of multiple deployments per day as described at the Velocity Conferences [43]; 2) Agile Community presentations and talks including *Agile Infrastructure* or *Agile Administration* and books such as *Continuous Delivery* [44]; :3) the entrance of Startup conferences [45] and the work of Steve Blank and Eric Ries; 4) the advancements in PaaS, most notably Amazon Web Services Platform [46] and stack based development tools like Wavemaker [47] or IBM Bluemix [48]; 5) Cloud computing and virtualization.

The principles of DevOps can be summarized as follows::

Defect prevention, not merely discover
Feedback loops that integrate actual customer experience
Removal of segregation of duties
Infrastructure and deployment assets as first class citizens
Extending continuous integration to continuous delivery
Heavy reliance on automation
Continuous Learning through repetition

Table 2.2 – The Principles of DevOps

The key new practice that has emerged within this movement is that of Continuous Delivery. Other than that, the need for fast feedback is understandable through management science and already exist within other movements or communities. The science of flow has also been around for quite some time as a way to build more effective value-stream integration. Figure 2.19 illustrates the Continuous Delivery workflow and the high degree of automation required for achieving this degree of flow:

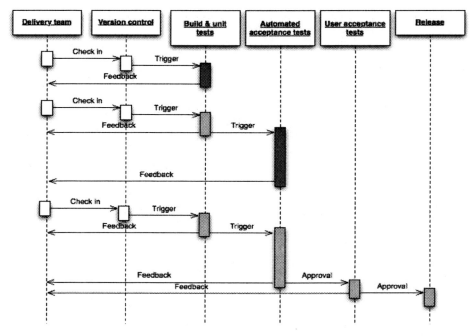

Figure 2.19 – Continuous Delivery [44]

What is also unique is the continued emphasis towards skillset generalization started by the Agile movement. The blurring of organizational boundaries within the DevOps way of thinking is an attack on the ideas of segregation of duties or the so-called low-trust compliance requirements of "two pairs of eyes" common in high-compliance contexts. Regardless of the benefits that frequent automated deployments provides, it is important to understand that the strategy is contextual and that shades of grey necessarily will temper the ideal of one-piece-flow all the way through the value-stream. Depending upon those who are in the position to judge the fidelity of controls in high compliance environments, human judgment may be forcefully inserted to govern deployments when subjected to ISACA SAS-70 level standards. Likewise, blackout dates and moratoriums may be imposed that create a back up in the deployment pipeline and therefore could contribute to less than ideal stability. A notable example of this would be in retail surrounding the period up to and after Black Friday in the United States. Such constraints are now finding their way into the calculus of the DevOps movement, with rolling deployments using such practices as *Canary Deployments* being struck as a compromise.

2.5 – Addressing the Complexity – Expert Systems

With all of the methods and bodies of knowledge that have been chronicled in SDLC 3.0, and recently revised in SDLC 3.1, how can humans on the ground efficiently make choices on which method is best for their software endeavor. Moreover, if you subscribe to the notion that methods are only "snapshots" or baselines of experience, and that a method constitutes a set of practices that together led to the success of a software project in context, then what if only parts of those methods are relevant to the different variants that are seen in any typical enterprise? How can we consume only parts of those methods that are relevant, and do so in an intelligent manner?

To explore this problem, we need to understand the complexity that is faced in real-time in every project that is instantiated. For an enterprise at scale, this problem manifests itself on the order of 200-300 times per year based on typical portfolio sizes. This says nothing to the fact that conditions within projects change over the course of the schedule and require non-biased choices to be made based on the needs at that moment in time. Complexity comes from many sources, but the essential complexity that needs to be addressed is due to the fact that there exists a very large number of permutations and combinations of possible "methods" that can be leveraged for a software project. That is to say, there are many practices that together make up the ecosystem for the project, and with many possible equivalent choices that are available to pick from to achieve roughly the same function. In our estimation, and based on some of the innovative work we will discuss in Chapter 5 related to the Universal Kernel that underpins all software endeavors, there are around 115 attributes associated with the components that comprise such a delivery system. Doing the math below in Figure 2.20:

# of Practice Choices to configure Value Stream = 115

Average # Options per Choice = 5

Number of Possible "Methods" = $5^{115} = 2.4 \times 10^{81}$

Figure 2.20 – Possible Method Permutations and Combinations

Clearly, this is larger than the 3 or 4 that are popular today within the IT industry. One may ask - is addressing this complexity necessary? In my view, to arrive at optimum deliveries that reflect the needs that all software projects have, yes. In fact, what is needed to understand industry wide is the data as to which ways-of-working are effective and why, and this requires emerging the patterns of sets of practices that lead to better outcomes. The nature of the business problem discussed in Chapter 1 is extremely complex. A simple solution is foolhardy. Having said that, this is the basis by which *Expert Systems* are needed to make such a strategy based on optimum usage of practices derived from empirical observation and a priori experience necessary.

To drive towards Generally Accepted Practice, whether at the scale of the enterprise or for the entire industry requires collecting the choices that humans make for software endeavors related to their way-of-working. These choices occur in a specific context - meaning certain external forces shape the appropriateness of these necessary choices. For example, the decision to follow a risk-value based prioritized lifecycle versus purely a value-driven lifecycle with as-needed risk mitigation events depends highly upon the criticality of the software being developed, and the risk tolerance of the investors. To achieve this, an **expert system** was developed to make this approach to achieving optimum deliveries on software investments a reality. This expert system, the first of its kind in the newly emerging trend related to Cognitive Computing [49] is called *The Software Development Practice Advisor*, or *Advisor* for short [50].

As a brief overview of the technology, *Advisor* helps humans on software development projects select an optimal set of practices. It integrates all known practices to avoid bias, and allows reuse of codified patterns of practices (current industry methods), quickly facilitating an understanding of what each method represents by way of their realization of the components and attributes that are common to all software delivery ecosystems. In other words, it provides templates to act as a starting point for all projects, along with the workflow models that such methods advocate. The system allows the aggregation of selection data across projects and enterprises such that the emergent Generally Accepted Practice can be backed by credible empirical data. Credible data means correlation between the choices made in context and the ensuing results, something achieved by performing periodic retrospectives. In the case of *Advisor*, these retrospectives are "smart" and their capture is additive with the reach of the system.

Building this system was no small task, as it required 1) capture, contextualization and reconciliation of all common and meaningful software development practices - something that has been underway and pioneering in the work of SDLC 3.0; 2) initial assessment as to the factors that would likely enable identification of contextually good versus poor choices; 3) codification of a starter set of rules representing common advice espoused by coaches and consultants; 4) articulation of practice knowledge including heuristics, history and synonyms; and most importantly, 5) a Universal Kernel based on systems theory [51] that represented the inventive step for facilitating the mixing and matching (i.e. mash-up) of software practices into a coherent whole and able to be represented in a simple value-stream network. Figure 2.21 illustrates the entire breadth of functionality enabled by these new system capabilities:

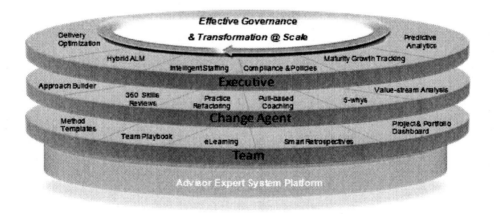

Figure 2.21 – The Advisor Transformation Platform

Through the aggregation of data, the starting hypotheses regarding the power laws (i.e. should a scale for "size" of project be logarithmic, exponential, or something entirely different to be able to filter out risky choices) for each factor will be deduced, part of the notion of applied grounded theory in concert with Hypothetico-deductive reasoning as a starting position [52]. The system infers these power laws over time as more and more data is collected through the method of Maximum-likelihood-best-fit approach [53], whereby the data collected by *Advisor* will statistically determine the most likely probability density functions. Further, Bayesian [54] re-calibration of the emergent model parameters is performed as time proceeds so as to facilitate better risk identifications. The platform represents an application of Artificial Intelligence, specifically Reinforcement Learning [55] whereby the system learns about optimum software delivery patterns as time goes by. Decision-trees reflect the Markov Decision Process [56] which occurs during startup of every software development project, and is leveraged to explore method optimization within different contexts. The goal is to move towards an Artificial Neural Network (ANN) [57] constrained in the Restricted Boltzman Machine sense, to facilitate Deep Learning. Not only do results contribute to recalibrate the Forward-chaining inference rule engine [58], but also through Negative chaining and the human interaction related to refactoring of practice choices and attempts to optimize results. The rules currently most closely resemble Fuzzy Propositional Logic [59] which are approximate and heuristic-based due to the lack of industry causality related to practice usage. Eventually, data mining will enable Fuzzy Predicate Logic for rules related to the parameterization of the *Advisor* Expert System Universal Kernel (described in Chapter 5). This model hypothesis for software development represents the Domain or Universe of Discourse [60] , which for Expert Systems is necessary to constrain the problem space and establish a shared Ontology for project ecosystems.

Chapter 3: Contextualizing Ways of Working

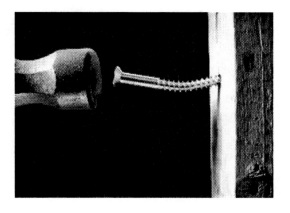

" I suppose it is tempting, if the only tool you have is a hammer, to treat everything as if it were a nail" - Abraham Maslow

There is a concept in common-law legal statutes that originate as far back as 1893 in the United Kingdom related to consumer rights, contracts and commercial transactions. One derivative example, in British Columbia, Canada, is the *Sale of Goods Act - [RSBC 1996] CHAPTER 410*. It has within it the following sections that provide relief for customers who feel their purchase was a "lemon". *Sections 18A - Fit-for-Purpose, and Section 18B - Merchantable Quality*, as stated below are directly relevant:

Implied conditions as to quality or fitness

18   Subject to this and any other Act, there is no implied warranty or condition as to the quality or fitness for any particular purpose of goods supplied under a contract of sale or lease, except as follows:

(a) if the buyer or lessee, expressly or by implication, makes known to the seller or lessor the particular purpose for which the goods are required, so as to show that the buyer or lessee relies on the seller's or lessor's skill or judgment, and the goods are of a description that it is in the course of the seller's or lessor's business to supply, whether the seller or lessor is the manufacturer or not, there is an implied condition that the goods are reasonably fit for that purpose; except that in the case of a contract for the sale or lease of a specified article under its patent or other trade name, there is no implied condition as to its fitness for any particular purpose;

(b) if goods are bought by description from a seller or lessor who deals in goods of that description, whether the seller or lessor is the manufacturer or not, there is an implied condition that the goods are of merchantable quality; but if the buyer or lessee has examined the goods there is no implied condition as regards defects that the examination ought to have revealed;

These two provisions reflect a societal view that not all objects are made of equal quality, and not all provide the same utility for the job at hand. One could argue that the same concepts can apply to the "sale" of software development methodology. Specifically and to the point, the software industry seems to continually imply the condition of fit for purpose, regardless of any situational awareness. Just because some *wares* are "for sale" up on the method rack doesn't make them appropriate for the job at hand. Needless to say, there is a lot of *method-ware* out there to choose from, with peddlers and cobblers of every make and persuasion trying to sell you theirs. The challenge with software development is that vendors will attempt to sell you what they know and can profit from, but unfortunately the Sale of Goods Act or equivalent in your jurisdiction doesn't seem to apply for pure thought-stuff, as in the case of a way-of-working. The vendor always has the out to say that it was incompetent execution of the approach that led to less than optimal results. So without relief possible in this type of corporate purchase, I would say **buyer beware**.

3.1 – The History of Situational Method Engineering

Situational method engineering as a term has existed within the IT industry since the early to mid-1990's in research and academic circles [1]. Its goals are to design and define methods that are "fit-for-purpose" for the particular situation faced by the software project. Some attention and R&D investment in the corporate world also has surrounded the term that far back, most notably Anton Harmsen's Doctoral Thesis from University of Twente in the Netherlands engaged in joint research with Ernst & Young [2] as reflected in Figure 3.1 below. From these early pioneers, many different meta-models, ontology's, fragmentation and chunking approaches have been discussed, mostly within academia, and usually centered around object-oriented expression and a CASE (Computer Assisted Software Engineering) implementation.

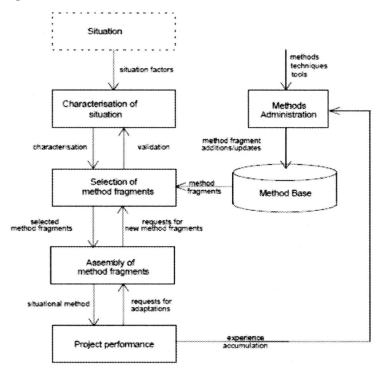

Figure 3.1 – Situational Method Engineering Concept [2]

Commercial and publicly widespread application of the Situational Method Engineering concept has been extremely limited, with the notable absence of computerization. One notable instance that gained some degree notoriety includes the "Development Case" approach within the Rational Unified Process (RUP) [3]. Figure 3.2 illustrates the essence of this approach:

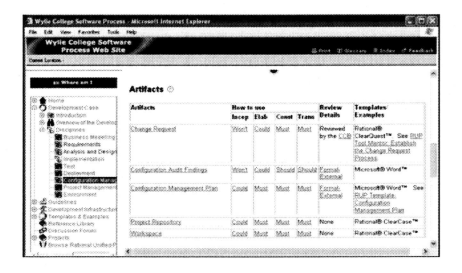

Figure 3.2 – RUP Development Case

This declarative approach which included a defined RUP artifact included within the process framework, entailed specifying which Roles, activities and artifacts would be produced during a software development. In the case of the latter, the degree of formality was also to be declared along with the relevant template. Over time, this gave way to a different delivery mechanism in what started as the "RUP Builder" based on Rational Rose and later Rational Method Composer [4]. The intent of each of these early commercial Situational Method Engineering approaches was to tailor down the framework within an object-oriented meta-model.

Other, more robust yet less formal and semantic attempts to articulate the various degrees of freedom that exist with project types and classification included the *Crystal* framework from Alistair

Cockburn [5]. This was one of the first articulations of project discriminating factors based on his work, most notably at IBM. In Crystal, the method is tailored based on three dimensions, size, criticality and legality/compliance as illustrated in Figure 3.3:

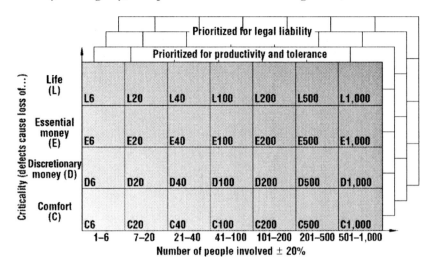

Figure 3.3 – Context Factors for tailoring Crystal [5]

The resulting approach established a three-dimensional matrix comprising roughly 56 method instance cells. The main point of the grid presentation was to highlight that a very small discretionary project should use a different methodology than a loss-of-life project. The third dimension illustrated that a project with time-to-market pressures should be set up differently from one working against traceability pressures. The framework columns were color-coded with "Clear" representing the smallest and lightest configuration, then "Yellow", "Orange", "Red", indicating larger groups using larger methodologies. While all cells within the framework advocated strong communication through rich interpersonal communication channels to enable more frequent delivery, but subject to criticality demands and staff size and distribution constraints. The size power law was specified as exponential (power of 2) due to the assumption that communication characteristics call for additional coordination and communication mechanisms when going beyond 2 individuals within earshot, up to those within easy walking distance and so on.

Later subsequent to the release of the Agile Manifesto, Barry Boehm and Richard Turner took a stab at articulating the notion of contextualization [6]. Their goal was to explore and make sense of the tension that existed between traditional plan-based methods and the newly popular Agile methods. As a result of their research at USC they arrived at an articulation of "home ground" for each camp on the basis of five context factors. While the factors and their scales seemed to blur the boundary of what was outside the project boundaries and attributes of the internal project ecosystem itself, it did highlight the critical aspect of culture as somehow being involved in determining fit-for-purpose. Figure 3.4 illustrates the Boehm and Turner factors:

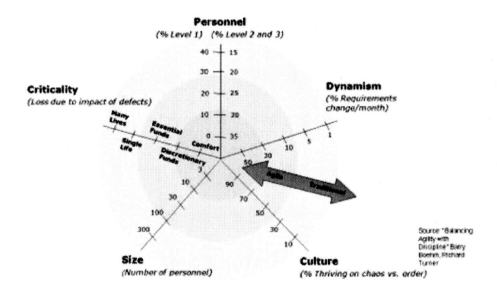

Figure 3.4 – Balancing Agility with Discipline [6]

Later, through experiential evidence within IBM's global Agile adoption, a series of context factors was identified by Scott Ambler, Chief Methodologist for Lean and Agile. The resulting Agile Scaling Model and the Agile Scaling Factors [7] identified six dimensions that were deemed critical for enabling the scaling Agile to the broad array of projects undertaken by IBM. Figure 3.5 illustrates the context factor portion of the model:

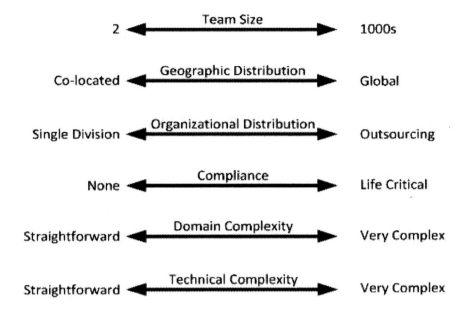

Figure 3.5 – Agile Scaling Factors [7]

With the Agile Scaling Factors model, regardless if it presents itself as being tied to only an Agile mindset, it represents by far the most meaningful set of factors to contextualize all software development approaches and cultures from prior attempts. The main thing noticeably absent are details surrounding the graduations for the scales which are left in subjective form for the most part.

The most recent synthesis of context factors comes by way of Philippe Kruchten and his Frog and Octopus model [8]. The "Octopus" portion of the fable represents the 8 proposed context factors for software endeavors. This model highlights *rate of change, governance, age of the system, size, criticality, business model, team distribution* and *architectural stability*. Figure 3.6 illustrates the Octopus context model:

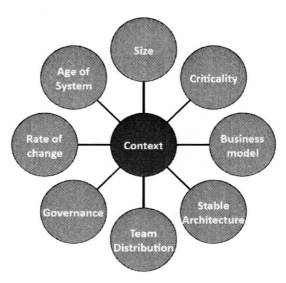

Figure 3.6 – The Octopus and the Frog [8]

In all of the historical approaches, contradictions are evident as to the meaningful dimensions that serve as discriminants to fitness-for-purpose. Even when there is concurrence of the necessity to include a specific dimension, past efforts have varied widely related to the meaningful scales that characterize their range. One would think that an integrative approach from the body of literature should guide the construction of the context factors that matter.

While the aforementioned approaches represent research and empirical efforts spanning almost 20 years, limited application in industry is still the norm. Perhaps the limited attention to contextualization is because the problem is hard. Alternatively, a more skeptical view is that commercial or market pressures drive a continual market disruption through polarizing brand differentiation and the subsequent inertia to maximize investment return. Instead of attempting to optimize project outcomes, a sub-optimal compromise has been struck between investors of software who are basically innocent of the issues at play, and the latest shiny object to arrive on the scene that may represent mediocrity, but at least it's something. Nonetheless, the issue of determining fitness-for-purpose of the various ingredients used to incubate software projects needs to be addressed if the industry is to address the root cause of wasted software development investments.

3.2 – One Size does <u>not</u> Fit All

Software projects come in all shapes and sizes, and therefore no two projects should use exactly the same method or approach. What might work for one type of system may not work as well in another. Aside from some universal principles that are always present due to the domain and nature of software development, no two software projects will receive the same value from either a canned approach or more granular practice. That is to say, even though software development endeavors are all knowledge intensive, and always involve both tacit and explicit knowledge at any point in time, and the fact that learning across the organization is required to converge on a solution, sufficient variability exists to warrant tweaking and tailoring to address specific needs. For example, much is made about the universality of Scrum [10] within Agile circles, and general advocacy is for an "all or nothing" adoption. eXtreme Programming (XP) can also be said to be "open for extension, closed to modification" as XP was designed to work as a whole [11]. However, each of these approaches implicitly assumes that the software development is going to immediately launch into cutting code. What if the output of an increment of value is actually the identification of gaps between a Commercial Off-the-Shelf (COTS) product and the current As-Is business processes? Such gaps would preferably entail modifications of the enterprise business process area in question to conform with the market-targeted view of the world instead of building customizations. What happens if these changes require more time than 2 weeks to implement? What does the Potentially Shippable Increment (PSI) look like? How do you pair-program a business process? Clearly the all-or-nothing rigidity sometimes exhibited within the industry is like attempting to jam a square peg into a round hole. The following examples illustrate this point and raise serious questions about the appropriateness of adopting vanilla off-the-shelf methods in their purist form.

3.2.1 - Embedded Satellite Systems Development:

An embedded system such as embedded software on satellites is a system which performs a dedicated function integral with hardware. Embedded systems are price and size sensitive, have power limitations, are frequently real-time, involve custom hardware, have limitations in tools, robustness and safety requirements, and are long lived and in service for decades. It should be no surprise that software development in this context requires retrofitting of popular off-the-shelf methods.

Clearly, in an example such as satellite systems, testing at full system scope is extremely challenging. Therefore, the ability to iterate towards anything other than simulations or prototypes is impossible. At full system scope, you get one shot to get it right. There is no way to reduce uncertainties beyond what can be simulated or prototyped, and prototypes are very high in cost. These uncertainties are not removed through grinding out code but rather testing designs, which is much like the often reviled "Big Design Up-Front" [12]. Therefore the mantra "working software is the true measure of progress" principle from the Agile Manifesto is not quite a good fit when it comes to the satellite context because the true measure of progress is validated decisions in the face of uncertainty, and this certainty is mostly reduced from prior launch empiricism. The frequency of the effective feedback loop is far lower than any popular Agile interpretation. Similarly, the definition of done for the software aspect of the system is not conducive to delivering any potentially shippable increments in absence of the "done-done" overall system. Finally, blindly following TDD as a practice to predict operational behavior and prevent defect injection is divorced from the critical real-time dynamics that determine pass or fail.

Due to the extensive constraints and broad spectrum of stakeholders, it is highly unlikely that a single *uber* Product Owner or even Scrum Master can handle all the complex political dynamics and subject matter depth. A purist interpretation of the 17 page Scrum Guide through application in a 7+-2 team framing is totally inadequate when a multi-billion dollar program is in play. Even the Scaled Agile Framework, while a small step in the right direction, would find it hard to pull off even the simplest aerospace or satellite program on the basis of leveraging *Emergent Architecture* and Business/Architectural Epics and Features as a basis to structure the high-stakes design reasoning or understanding program constraints and parameters.

Finally, the complexity of these systems requires abstraction beyond that enjoyed by a "the code is the documentation" mindset. With huge code bases and exploding hardware integration and interconnectedness, primitive and overly simplistic approaches to problem solving and knowledge management are clearly not appropriate within 5-10 Million SLOC embedded implementations. Simply put, these systems are not Java or .NET applications.

3.2.2 - Large-scale System-of-Systems Development:

Imagine a program of scale that is mandated by an inability to understand force strength during mobilization of the United States Armed Forces. Imagine a program where developing custom software is not possible due to government mandates defined by the Defense Science Board (DSB) [13], and one that requires all Services and all Components to collaborate in a Joint environment, focused on a single system irrespective of sub-culture, history or subtle differences in Functions, Processes and Activities (FP&A). Imagine being constrained by Government Accounting Organization (GAO) and Office of Management and Budget (OMB) mandated practices [14], which may be subject to change depending on the election cycle and the fight against political earmarks. Now add to that the fact that 6 million members are the potential users of the required system, each who take the morale issue of getting paid and taking care of their dependents very seriously from wherever they may be stationed like under the polar ice cap, or flying the dew line in a B-52 Stratofortress. Obviously this does not fit the 7+-2 co-located team advocacy of popular methods today.

This example represents a software endeavor of unprecedented scale and organizational complexity. Such a program has the potential for extremely large order waste if blindly following practices like Earned Value Management, divorced from a scope-based WBS [15]. Imagine publishing a GANTT view of the schedule that is task/activity/work oriented that is elaborated to low levels of detail and updated daily as a "wall of wonder". Actually that wall is really 4 walls running the circumference of a whole floor of a rather large building. This definitely is not an Information Radiator, and does nothing to implement the kind of swarming behavior that can enhance collaboration and coordination.

Regarding identification of the structure of the program and estimating the capabilities of the to-be architecture, I would be hard pressed to explain to a 3-star General that the roadmap and sequencing for decommissioning around 100 mainframes running Personnel and Payroll functions across the very large and indoctrinated Services and the Defense Finance and Accounting Service (DFAS) will "emerge". It is unlikely that advocating that a "high-trust environment" will enable *"the solution to emerge after we code everything up and do a series of sprint demos"* would result in anything but a dishonorable discharge from the engagement. The first question out of the Generals' mouth is "what is the difference between a PeopleSoft *Transfer* and a Uniform Code of

Military Justice (UCMJ) [16] *Order'*? You wouldn't even get to the pending arguments as to which Service goes first or negotiation of interfaces and boundaries on the necessary changes to business processes. Even this latter challenge requires a heavy dose of pragmatism, as it is likely that a fleet of Product Owners or equivalent Business Analysts are required who are politically capable to understand the local member of congress' constituency. Yet you don't want the program to end up 10 years and $1Billion in without a single ratified "joint requirement" [17], when unfortunately what you need is many ratified "compromises".

Finally, it should be noted that the membership are trigger pullers, not software developers. Therefore, how one gets a sense of velocity requires burn-down of gaps in business process versus COTS business processes. This requires documentation of as-is business processes and comparison with the vendors to-be view of the world. There is no code that is accessible to "self-describe" the product and address the knowledge management risk. Where configuration is possible, documentation is required to capture data modifications. Where glue-code is created to weld on additional COTS components, that is where we can rely on the code to self document, as long as we know why the component was added on to the core platform in the first place.

3.2.3 - Legacy Cobol/CICS Sustainment Developments:

Over fifty years later, COBOL/CICS powers 70 percent of all business transactions – from ATMs, to point-of-sales systems and healthcare prescriptions [18]. COBOL/CICS is present within 85 percent of the world's business applications and is woven far too deeply into the business world to simply tear out and throw away. As many as 75% of all rewrite projects have resulted in failure. IBM owns 90% of the Mainframe market, with around 3,500 mainframe customers. This cash cow is entrenched in some 23 of the world's top 25 retailers, 92 of the top 100 banks, and the 10 largest insurers. An example of a typical large mainframe customer would be running around five-to-ten IBM System z10s supplying upwards of 50,000 MIPS of compute power and handle $1.5 trillion in transaction processing each day. The Cobol codebase that powers those systems has grown from 343 million lines two years ago to 357 million lines today, adding 2,500 new programs along the way.

With such scale and legacy, clearly we are faced with a sustainment problem that requires optimizing flow and achieving compressed cycle times. Unfortunately, every so often, business demand placed on these legacy platforms tends to stretch the entrenched architectures to the breaking point resulting in nasty repercussions like high-level terminations and massive investment outflows due to very public incidents. Take for instance the recent examples of security breaches in some of the world's largest retailers [19]. Simply *refactoring* their way out of the security breaches is not a simple matter when faced with a code-base of many millions of lines of code. Similarly, reliance on emergent architecture can run into severe problems in a telecom provider context when faced with integrating front office order management, billing and accounting functions with back office service provisioning. Without thinking through the timing considerations and concurrency leveraging more formal architectural practices, situations such as an absence of record locking and continued reliance on file-level locking instead of leveraging newer technologies like VSAM-RLS [20] can result in total service outages. Similarly, allowing JCL job-streams [21] to simply emerge as opposed to leveraging visualization support can result in a convoluted and incomprehensible mess.

Often the development environments in most legacy COBOL/CICS shops constrain which popular method practices can be employed. For example, TSO macros [22] are typically preferred culturally and due to their lengthy period of usage. Evolution to more modern IDE's with refactoring and more robust debugging capabilities like Eclipse based environments is difficult. Added to this, version control is often via the ISPF (Interactive System Productivity Facility) SCLM [23] component (Software Configuration and Library Management). A project hierarchy design is common, with physical isolation achieved through groups and physically segregated environments such that code can be changed in parallel for different releases. However, reconciliation of conflicting changes between different data-sets is only possible through the on-demand access to other SCLM Group files. Therefore, noting that member promotion and the use of concatenation are inherent with SCLM, it is likely that developer discipline is relied upon to proactively prevent parallel code change conflicts in advance of promotion. Inherent in these infrastructure choices is a strategy to shield developers from changes in other code branches, rationalized on the basis of being "for their protection". Merging is the corollary of the branching that must be performed at a pace consistent with business-side demand. This favouring of isolation over integration, shielding versus openness and transparency negatively impacts productivity when parallel development complexity of the magnitude of most COBOL/CICS code bases is considered. This is a far cry from the ideals of *Continuous Integration*, and negates the ability to perform unit-level TDD as advocated within core eXtreme Programming (XP).

****

Obviously, from the above examples, various forces or influences on a project determine which practices will make sense and which would be foolish to attempt. Achieving a perfect fit and therefore an optimal delivery from taking an off-the-shelf method is unlikely. The good news is that the selection of practices and techniques proven effective within popular methods is not an either-or (XOR) issue but an AND issue. Meaning we need to leverage some of X and some of Y, and it is the context of the endeavor which will determine which parts are a fit. Fit is an interesting and critical word in the idea of Situational Method Engineering. The question naturally arises: *what is fitting into what?* To explore this issue, we will turn to the same discipline as we use to design systems. When designing systems, we often attempt to define the context boundary of the system so-as to define interfaces to humans or systems, delineate scope and decouple the system-of-systems in robust ways. This allows us to define strategies such as service-orientation versus ETL (Extract-Transfer-Load), and identify meaningful *Personas* that will use our system. Techniques such as Use Cases define the context boundary through identification of Actors (outside the system in question) and the association with the functional value propositions of the system (interfaces into the system), the Use Cases. A little known extension to this object-oriented approach to framing logical scope and specifying requirements is Business Use Cases and their applicability to Object-oriented Business Engineering [24]. Business Actors can equally define the context of a "business system", of which a software project is an example. The core business use case of a software development project ecosystem is to "Deliver Software". Any external force, some of which are intangible, that interacts or influences how the business system will function in delivering system, can be understood to be a Business Actor. Figure 3.7 illustrates the context factors related to making fit-for-purpose determinations.

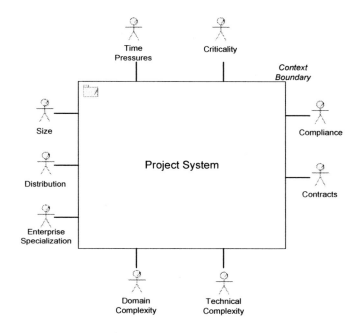

Figure 3.7 – Business Actors of a Software Project

In the figure above, one can view each actor exerting influence or interacting with the project context in question. With system Use Case diagrams, time for example is a common actor which leads to events or triggers that instantiate behavior in a system. Similarly, time events related to market pressures may invoke project behaviors. Others like Compliance or Criticality may mandate outputs required from the project system. Still others like Domain or Technologies and their complexity may act as constraints on the project system that can be instantiated, as well as dampen productivity or introduce disturbances. Finally, the Size of the required ecosystem, the Geographic Distribution, Enterprise Specialization and Contract requirements may influence and constrain how the project interacts with the broader organization. The natural question to ask is what is the magnitude of these Business Actor influences, and what risks or uncertainties do they introduce on the investment. To understand this and leverage contextual drivers for some useful purpose, we must first explore meaningful scales for each dimension.

3.3 – Discretization of Continuous Features

Building upon and harvesting the prior attempts to contextualize software projects (and therefore the appropriateness of approaches, tools, technologies and resource tactics) requires not only an understanding of which forces influence the associated risk profile of a project, but also requires that a useful scale be created for each. The purpose of the scale is to digitize or "discretize" what is in the real world a continuous spectrum for a feature or context factor. There is an large spectrum of values available to choose from for each of the context factors. The question for any enterprise is how to create a robust and finite set by which to characterize their software delivery investment vehicles. This is not a trivial issue, and requires that we delve into *Digital Signal Processing (DSP)* [25] theory to understand statistically meaningful ways to create the scales. DSP represents an interdisciplinary body of knowledge for representing the analog world in digital or discrete form. Creating a discrete set of context values for each business actor for a software project system involves defining the number of increments to include (the sampling rate), and the values to establish (the quantiles). The term "cut-point" refers to a real value within the range of continuous values that divides the range into two intervals, one interval is less than or equal to the cutpoint and the other interval is greater than the cut-point. The term "arity" means the number of intervals or partitions. Quantization [26] should ultimately conform to a power law, defined as a functional relationship between two quantities, where one quantity varies as a power of another. Figure 3.8 illustrates the concepts addressed within Digital Signal Processing:

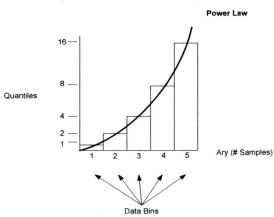

Figure 3.8 – Discretization and Quantization

Various algorithms exist for discretizing continuous features. One simple and pragmatic approach is referred to as *Data Binning* [27], which is commonly used in Artificial Intelligence (AI) applications and Machine Learning algorithms. Data binning uses simple cut-points to create categories of continuous features or attributes. Continuous-valued attributes are transformed into nominal ones by splitting the range of the feature values in a finite number of intervals. Since a large number of possible attribute values slows and makes inductive learning ineffective, one of the main goals of a discretization algorithm is to significantly reduce the number of discrete intervals of a continuous feature. At the same time, the algorithm should maximize the interdependency between discrete attribute values and class labels so as to be able to learn about power laws, as well as minimizing information loss due to the discretization process.

The dichotomy that the industry faces is that to arrive at known power laws for each of the context factors, statistically significant data must be available to provide the evidence of universality. However, to get the data, enterprises must get started with some meaningful scales that add value for reducing risk and uncertainty. Absent of this data and proven power laws, only heuristic-level data binning can be attempted. To look at some good starting points for these scales, consider existing heuristic-based laws that have been around for some time within software development. One is Parkinson's Law, which states that *"work expands so as to fill the time available for its completion"* [28]. We can use this to surmise that such a phenomenon relates to the Time Pressure context variable, and the starting hypothesis is that it represents a power law following a Log-Normal distribution. As such, the data binning we attempt should roughly establish cut-points that conform to this mathematical relation. Figure 3.9 illustrates the concept of a power law through the TIME context variable and Parkinson's Law:

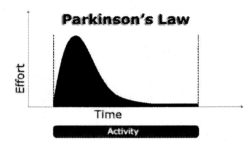

Figure 3.9– Power-laws - TIME and Parkinson's Law

With respect to SIZE, the best anecdotal suggestion presently comes from Crystal, whereby the scale is defined using a basis of the common scenarios of how people might need to interact or collaborate. This is a good starting point, but one might expect that a power law relating to social network dynamics like Small World phenomenon [29] or Scale-Free networks [30] might emerge from the data over time. Figure 3.10 illustrates the power law for a Scale Free Social Network:

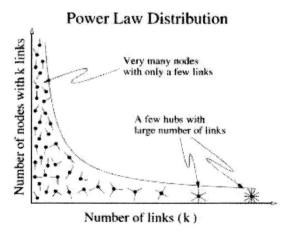

Figure 3.10 – Power-laws - SIZE and the Scale-free Social Network

Each context factor that is quantized in anticipation of an emergent power law acts as a progressive filter of risk. The ordering of the data bins reflects increasing risk or impact on the project ecosystem. The low end of the scale acts to filter out risks as not being applicable to a project, but as selections increase more and more risks are allowed through the filter and are presented to the team. Figure 3.11 illustrates the concept for the progressive filtering type of context factor:

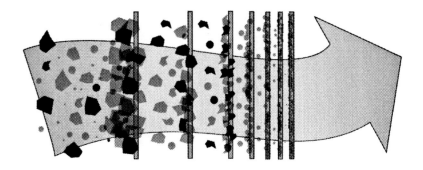

Figure 3.11– Progressive Filtering

Not all context factors will yield the emergence of power laws at the same pace. Due to the many definitions and associated confusion related to complexity, the context factors for Domain and Technology complexity are likely to require much research and consideration as to why certain domains are riskier than others. The essential complexity of various technologies is often misunderstood due to the pace of change in the industry. Similarly, context factors that represent constraints like Compliance or the other legality oriented factors like Contracts likely have highly convoluted power laws related to the state of the Common Law that may never be fully understood. For these factors, and in absence of known power laws that can be leveraged for defining quantiles, the type of filtering we must leverage is "multimodal selective pass filtering". With this approach, we are interested in associating known risks with binary selection of one or more scale graduations for a context factor. Figure 3.12 illustrates the selective filtering related to non-power law scales:

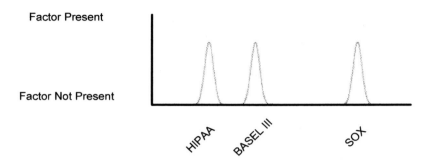

Figure 3.12– Multimodal Selective Filtering

3.4 – Keeping it Real

As will become evident throughout this book, ideas are great but yield limited utility until put into practice. At the scale of the industry or even a single enterprise, this requires concrete manifestation in software. *Advisor* represents such a concrete realization. Contextualization of software development approaches requires the collection of large amounts of empirical data such that robust patterns can emerge. Through automation, such collection can be aggregated due to the reach of the *Advisor* cloud-based expert system. To date, limited research data has been available industry wide due to the fragmentation of corporate experience, and the reliance on tacit knowledge and folklore regarding the makeup of projects. Obviously even if this level of characterization was all that was performed, this would be valuable data to enterprises when reflecting upon which software projects are succeeding and which ones are failing.

The first step in driving towards a contextually appropriate software delivery value stream is to assess and explore the context in which the investment is to be made. This entails having a team, usually through facilitation by a software delivery expert like a coach or other type of change agent, begin the **self organization** process by declaring the context for the endeavor. Through the *Advisor Hybrid Approach Builder* component, teams carefully reflect upon the 9 context factors, making selections which will be associated with the project or endeavor and stored for later usage to make determinations of fitness for purpose of their way of working. Subtle visual cues help teams understand the rough fit for the various lineages of approaches such as Lean, Agile or Unified Process based approaches. Feedback on progress for the assessment is provided that shows the emerging reflection of the teams context using a radar or spider-web chart. The various graduations reflect the currently useful data binning for each factor in the system, and two types of filtering is represented within the selection options - progressive filtering, as in the case of progressively larger endeavors as captured in the SIZE context factor; and set-based selectors, which enable multi-modal selective filtering of context factors that reflect a mixture of normal distributions. Figure 3.13 illustrates the first step in the *Advisor* Hybrid Approach Builder, the Context step:

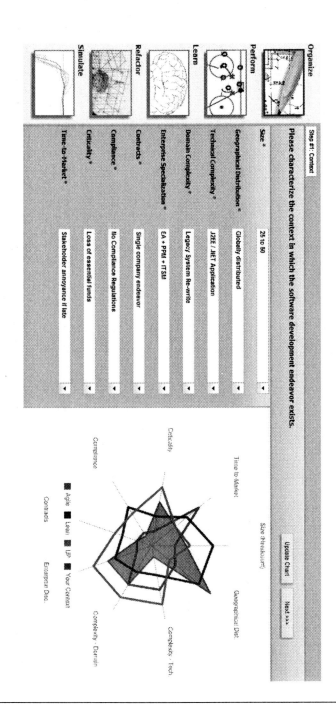

Figure 3.13 – Context Factor Capture for the Endeavor

Later in the self-organization process as facilitated through the *Hybrid Approach Builder*, the selections made for the context factors are matched up with the various practice choices that comprise a way of working, as will be discussed in Chapter 5. The *Advisor* Expert System rule base executes using these inputs to determine risks and offer advice in the form of alternative practices to consider. The context factor graduations are sufficient to act as a meaningful filter to identify when risk is present. Figure 3.14 illustrates the Advice that teams are working towards as result of the declarations performed:

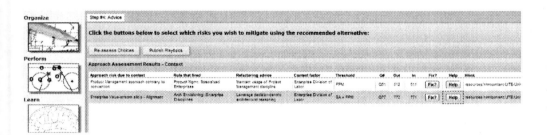

Figure 3.14 – Identifying Risky Practices based on Context

Teams are free to explore what the refactoring advice means in greater detail using the contextual help for each risk identified. If the team agrees with the assessment, they can accept the advice and refactor their approach by clicking the "Fix" button for the risk in question. Once complete, the team achieves a contextually appropriate approach. As will be described in Chapter 5, other than capturing valuable data regarding the marriage of approach choices and context, the output that is produced is a dynamically generated "Playbook" that reflects the approach.

Chapter 4: Influencing Culture through the Management System

"Culture eats strategy for breakfast" - Peter Drucker

Easily the most important enabling condition for successful transformation is attention to corporate culture [1]. We obviously know that bureaucratic practices do not fare very well within startups, and vice versa. Regardless of which "12-step program" one attempts to leverage [2] , or no matter how many *carrots and sticks* one puts in place, some desired changes are doomed to failure. It feels as if the change initiative is swimming against a tide, sometimes very subtly at first with various forms of passive aggressive behavior being exhibited. But later, when the establishment and existing tribes become emboldened, change initiatives get run out of dodge at breakneck speed. Why is that? What invisible force are we constantly fighting against when we attempt to change "the way we do things around here" [3]. The answer is the sociological phenomenon known as organizational culture.

Industry data, such as that from ProSci [4] or the annual VersionOne State of Agile Survey [5], support this assertion as they both cite key adoption success factors for significant change management initiatives as being attention to culture.

A definition of organizational culture is as follows:

> *Organizational culture is the behavior of humans within an organization and the meaning that people attach to those behaviors. Culture includes the organization's vision, values, norms, systems, symbols, language, assumptions, beliefs, and habits. It is also the pattern of such collective behaviors and assumptions that are taught to new organizational members as a way of perceiving, and even thinking and feeling. Organizational culture affects the way people and groups interact with each other, with clients, and with stakeholders.*
>
> *Wikipedia*

A number of elements within this definition stand out that enables us to devise a strategy for how we might address the inherent risks related to software development improvement initiatives. Firstly, **meaning, values, beliefs, norms, habits** and **assumptions** refers to those deeply tacit levels of organizational culture, those elements that are unseen and are unconsciously exhibited by the organizational membership. Accordingly, these are the hardest to identify, understand and manipulate and represent the cognitive level of the culture that far outlasts the near-term state of the entity [6]. Indeed, to attempt to directly influence this level of cultural indoctrination requires connectedness to the innate *mindset* or *ideology* that is shared instinctively among the organizational participants. It also requires trust for any change influence to be achieved, and building this awareness and instinct and trust takes a lengthy amount of time.

Secondarily, **vision,** mission statements or creeds, **systems, symbols,** and **language** all represent the more superficial level that is reflective of culture. These artifacts are the tangible physical aspects of the organizational culture. This level also includes the **rituals, ceremonies, practices** or the ways that individuals interact that operationalize and socialize these culturally sensitive artifacts, and teach the *organizational way* to new members. This level is the tangible level of culture that is observable. As such, these physical objects are reinforced through *stories, myths* or through *rites* of enhanced or degraded standing, or rites of conflict mediation or integration. This latter level is the level that change agents have access to and can therefore alter so as to exert influence. The idea of levels of culture manifestation was originally articulated by Schein in "Three Levels of Culture" [6], as illustrated in Figure 4.1:

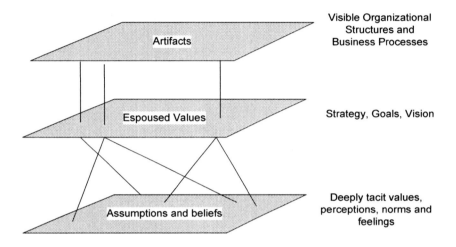

Figure 4.1 – Levels of Culture

The changes of state related to ideas, practices or strategies in the organizational culture are transmitted through the social network through *memes* [7]. The word meme stemming from the Greek word *mīmēma* meaning "to imitate", is defined as *the unit for carrying cultural ideas, symbols, or practices that can be transmitted from one mind to another through writing, speech, gestures, rituals* [8]. The persistent host for holding memes is the human brain. The meme's that are successfully transmitted are those that are easily described or remembered, are interesting and not boring but rather stand out and those that will persevere within the hosts memory [9]. Only those that closely align with the deep tacit cultural identity are likely to propagate through the important hub intermediary nodes; those with weak affinity die and are terminated. Meme's typically travel in sets - that is to say, multiple self-replicating ideas that go together, noting that memes typically replicate better as a group [10]. Figure 4.2 illustrates the lifecycle of a meme:

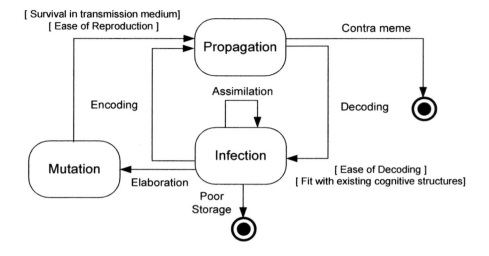

Figure 4.2 – Meme Lifecycle

The fundamental challenge faced by organizational change agents in attempting to adjust culture or introduce new ways of working is that the levers in which one has access to are associated with the underlying cultural kernel in complex ways. Attempts to myopically address any single artifact in hopes of shifting mindsets, values or behaviors is a high risk strategy, with the likely consequences being erosion of trust within the constituency, false starts, frustration and loss of loyalty. Mere window dressing when it comes to adjustments of the deeply ingrained status quo will generally meet skepticism.   The default position held by the people of the organization will be that "this too shall pass". A relentless cycle ensues, with a hitting of the reset button being the typical outcome on a cycle of 18 months in the software development space.   Clearly a more credible, systemic approach to change that is holistic in nature and addresses all of the levers of change related to accessible artifacts is required to avoid failure. We must materially improve transformation success rates which historically only average a mere 30% [11].

4.1 – Competing Values

The first step in influencing the culture of an organization and its impact on change initiatives is chart the landscape. Without knowing our starting point, our baseline culture type and profile, we have no way to know which direction we may want to evolve the organizational culture. We also won't know the risks that we will encounter on our voyage between the as-is status quo and the to-be shaped reality. Knowing our starting point is necessary to get our bearings and plot a course for change. One very well established framework for doing this is *The Competing Values Framework*, developed through many years of research and refinement at the University of Michigan [12]. Figure 4.3 illustrates this cultural assessment framework:

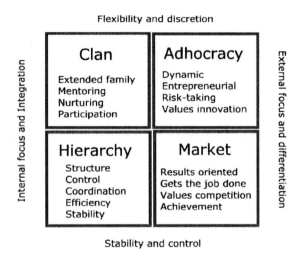

Figure 4.3 – The Competing Values Framework [12]

We can diagnose the cultural profile of an organization, plotted on the two dimensions: the **Internal/External Focus** dimension, and the **Controlling/Discretion** dimension. From the graph above, we can identify 4 different culture-type quadrants - the *Adhocracy, Clan, Market* and *Hierarchy* quadrants. Organizations have a profile that is centered within a quadrant although typically spans into an adjacent quadrant. Organizations that are cross-quadrant are polar opposites and the individuals between these organizations usually conflict. As an organization grows from Startup to established firm, they will evolve counter clockwise through the quadrants, typically starting at Adhocracy. The following tell-tales and traits exemplify the various organizational culture profiles discovered through this research.

4.1.1 – Adhocracy

An organization that fits the Adhocracy cultural profile has a strong focus on their customers and are driven by differentiation in their eyes. To achieve an orientation of creativity, an environment of flexibility and discretion is created by leaders who possess a style akin to innovators or entrepreneurs. Such an organization believes the path to effectiveness is through visionary thinking and creation of innovative new products that are better and are brought to market faster than their competitors. The values instilled throughout such an organization are agility and rapid change. Investment values take a decidedly risk tolerant stance within their fast paced competitive environment. Notable examples of this type of organization includes Apple or Google, which prides themselves on being the most innovative organizations out there. Notable practices that foster the ideals and habits of the adhocracy culture includes open workspaces, self organization and selection of teams, and innovation days whereby teams are encouraged to work on anything they choose. Rather than drive towards "maximum utilization", these organizations focus on nurturing the spark of invention and innovation.

4.1.2 – Market

Market culture organizations are fiercely competitive players within cut-throat industry sectors of the economy. Typically mature in nature, these organizations also have a relentless customer focus, but take a more controlled stance favoring stability and predictable market results, often the reality for "blue chip" publicly traded corporations. Leaders within these organizations are type A personalities who drive their organizations to achieve market-share, stretch goals and maximize profitability on behalf of shareholders. Within financial services organizations like Goldman Sachs or other Investment Banking firms, motivational practices are very evident, usually of the explicit form like *Gamification* [13]. Hard deadlines are evident typically surrounding wall street reporting schedules and quarterly results. Project oriented structures with moderately deep management hierarchies relentless track business cases and typically start more projects than can be completed with a view towards survival of the fittest.

4.1.3 – Clan

The family-like or "clan" organizational culture takes a more inward-looking perspective and focuses on cohesion and integration of the people within its structure. While encouraging flexibility and discretion, long lasting relationships and social structures are nurtured so as to instil employee loyalty and work satisfaction. The orientation of the firm is one of collaboration, with leaders and management exhibiting strong facilitation, mentorship and team building skills. Open conflict is usually taboo, and strong communication skills are actively encouraged to ensure harmony within the ecosystem. Internal development of staff through generous training allowances are indicative of the level of investment in the people of the company. Insurance firms geographically clustered in the Ohio River valley such as Nationwide or Progressive Insurance exemplify these values, as does southern US firms like Lowe's Home Improvements. Change initiatives within these organizations increases in difficulty by "outsiders", and internal change agents that are trusted and well respected is absolutely critical. Accelerated change requirements often result from merger and acquisition activity and often results in overtly passive aggressive behaviour.

4.1.4 – Hierarchy

The most hardened and mature cultures that transformation experts face are the bureaucracies or Hierarchical organizations. Most notable in this quadrant are government and large multi-national behemoths. These super-tanker organizations do not turn on a dime, yet various levers of change are available that might not be available in other cultural profiles, most notably legislation. Orientation is one of controlling, with certainty, prediction and risk aversion being core values. A focus on internal structures results in rigid long lasting management layers focused on coordination, monitoring by highly organized individuals who want to know as much detail as their time will permit. Command and control anti-patterns become prevalent when low-trust environments that are highly political, or where catastrophic loss is highly possible. Defense contractors are likely to exhibit a hybrid of hierarchy attributes blended with market features due to their highly competitive environment which interfaces at multiple levels with governmental entities. Changing these organizations typically happens when geo-political events or national crises occur that result in macro policy changes.

4.2 – Cultural Affinity of Modern Practices

When change frustration and fatigue sets in, diagnosis by software development transformation experts and consultants often pins the blame on "the system". The impediments highlighted usually include "the management layer", or practices that impose too much overhead and bureaucracy on the software delivery teams. Indeed, the industry is now starting to realize that *Individuals and Interactions* can be hampered greatly by the system in which they participate. If you trace the thread far enough, you find that exacerbating the situation is always the endless introduction of *next big things* and *silver bullets* that are foisted upon teams and their existing culture. It is as if the organization is in a constant state of inflammation due to the endless cycle of *regime change* and related pet change initiatives. Each member in the organization constantly exhibits an allergic reaction to each new foreign body, which is basically anything that runs counter-cultural, or is just not "the way we do things around here". Eventually, the organization develops anti-bodies to combat these annoying periodic events. Even if the change were culturally acceptable, usually any change occurs at a pace that is too rapid and therefore too much for the organizational entity to accommodate and digest.

Revisiting the concepts presented in SDLC 3.0, we know that common ground does exist within software development ways-of-working. Reasonable people can agree that at worst common ground practices represent pseudonyms which are named differently having come from different community-specific bodies of knowledge. Yet they are effectively the same practice and serve the same function within the software delivery ecosystem. You could say that common ground practices represent moderate, "centrist political viewpoints" of effective tactics for implementing parts of the software delivery ecosystem. When these practices are introduced to a particular cultural setting using the language and vocabulary that is well aligned with their cultural value drivers, orientation, leadership style and theory of effectiveness, they are likely welcomed with open arms. Even if the practices look foreign and trigger an allergic response, they are different in name only, and adoption difficulties will likely be overcome because the difference is small and only represents jargon. Obviously, it is advantageous to accentuate these centrist practices that represent general consensus so as to establish change momentum. Figure 4.4 below illustrates the cultural affinities of various popular practices through a mapping onto the Competing Values Framework:

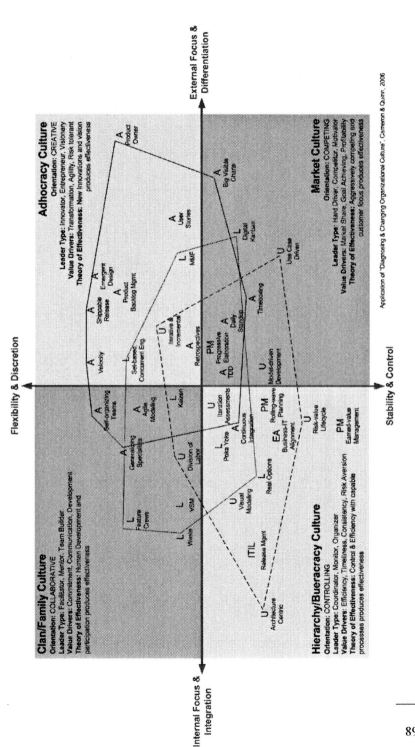

Figure 4.4 – Mapping Modern Software Development Practices onto the Competing Values Framework

As can be seen in the previous figure, the various methodology lineages of Lean, Agile and Iterative & Incremental Development each have a "home-ground" cultural profile. A method of a certain profile will have a strong likelihood of adoption due to the cultural affinity of its practices. It is easy to see where the sweet spot exists for various method communities, with the A's mapped onto the Competing Values Framework to illustrate the region of likely cultural fit for Agile practices (*Adhocracy* quadrant); the L's showing the same for Lean approaches (*Clan* quadrant); and the U's showing cultural affinity for various Unified Process practices (*Hierarchy* quadrant). It is also easy to see why there exists so much friction between the communities attached to these practices, as each naturally sits within different opposing quadrants of the framework. Each body of knowledge (BOK) or method within each lineage is notably different culturally. As mentioned earlier, within the practice sets of each lineage, cultural overlap exists. Only when you decompose the aggregate method containers or bodies of knowledge in to their practice components can you find common ground in which each community can agree.

We know that each popularized industry practice/pattern of success grew up from various enclaves of corporate experience over the past 40 years. These experiences were contextual, whether a method came from a corporate delivery environment, or whether study within communities or groups led to aggregate experience in the form of a BOK. Similarly, each of these organizations manifested unique cultures. Indeed, "the way we do things around here" became embedded with the IT corporate sub-cultures in order to be successful. In other words, these approaches became "adopted". Instead of maintaining the exact method or BOK composition that was reflective of a specific cultural context, we can break these sets into their constituent parts and plot them on the cultural spectrum. This allows us to understand their cultural affinity once we assess whether an organization's cultural center of gravity is reflective of an *Adhocracy, Clan, Hierarchy or Market* culture. The distance between the two will indicate the relative risk to adoption. The magnitude of the gap will also indicate the suggested sequencing of introduction when multiple practices are considered for adoption. Moving beyond common ground practices, where the potential cultural gap is gradually larger, if one understands the magnitude of the gap between a practice to be introduced and the cultural setting, one can understand the risks that will be present if one is to introduce them into the system in which the people coexist.

4.3 – Nudging the Culture

What we seek is a way to incrementally and gently evolve an organizations culture in an environment where complex human forces are at play. Based on the aforementioned politics that exists within Enterprise IT, we must find a way to get at a minimum two very polarized and potentially dogmatic and hostile constituencies to seek out commonality rather than dwell on their differences. Rather than accept these two bipolar extremes in the organizational political spectrum, I advocate a "third way" to be leveraged for realizing software delivery change, one which is centrist in nature and instills balance among the various "freedom" perspectives and the more "controlling" perspectives. This political ideology has been termed "Libertarian Paternalism" [14], and serves as basis for implementing a state-of-the-practice change management strategy. The Libertarian aspect embraces the notion that humans, as fallible as they are in making sound decisions, need the freedom to choose. Presented with a broad spectrum of practice choices, teams can identify with and choose their ways of working in an uninhibited manner. The Paternalism aspect addresses the fallible nature of humans by leveraging broader knowledge than that possessed by small teams or individuals to gently guide teams towards better choices, which in the case of successful change management is sensitive of culture.

Choices between alternatives are presented in such a manner that nudge an evolution of the organization's cultural DNA in the directed manner based on what is believed to be better for the enterprise. Better means more efficient and effective. Better decisions means better outcomes. As we will see in later chapters, nudging teams to make better decision is achieved through "choice architecture" and the presentation of the necessary software delivery choices leveraging influencing tactics such as defaulting, ordering and locality designs. The critical differentiation with this change strategy however is that freedom to choose is not inhibited. This requires the presentation of all possible practices so the chooser is not disenfranchised in their selection process.

Figure 4.5 illustrates the power of Nudge and focusing ones attention and improve human decision in such a way so as to influence an outcome by improve the decision; in the case of Amsterdam Airport the outcome was an 80% improvement in "accuracy" [14]:

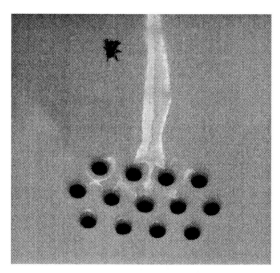

Figure 4.5 – A subtle "Nudge"

Let's say you are a CxO and have a mandate from your board of directors to implement a new business strategy, perhaps focused on Disruptive Innovation [15]. Your strategy entails a shift in the firms' theory of effectiveness. You have a pretty good grasp on the leadership re-alignment necessary to achieve the desired cultural profile. You have performed all the prerequisites for change to occur like establishing awareness for the need to change. You have created the conditions that establishes a sense of urgency and have a guiding coalition of the willing at the top-most levels of your organization. This sense of urgency is filtering down to the troops. You have launched various initiatives to communicate the *Vision* of the change. You have done everything textbook. But you sense passive aggressive behavior is taking hold and can't quite put your finger on it. You are running up against deeply ingrained values and belief systems among the masses. The harder you push, the harder the system pushes back [16]. Clearly to execute you need a different approach because the status quo and all the wishful thinking will not sway the participants in the change.

To successfully change the mindset of the participants in the transformation requires respecting their freedom to choose. Rather than issue directives, humans have an uncanny desire to the right of self determination. This does not mean that they should be empowered to run amok. Instead by presenting simple choices, one can "nudge" the culture in the desirable direction through choices about the management system, and in the case of software delivery, the way of working that teams leverage to get the job done. Radical redesign of an organization's culture is a pipe-dream unless the people that manifested that culture are no longer there. This is very destructive and quite expensive in terms of lost knowledge, trust and momentum. Instead, cultural change has to be evolutionary. Incremental nudges can be facilitated such that the participants are given options that only represent a small gap from their current culturally acceptable practice. In this way the management system, as an accessible artifact of culture albeit a superficial and shallow one, can be leveraged as the subtle mechanism that transforms the deep innermost values and beliefs held by the organizational culture. Such a transformation takes many invocations as the organization learns new ways of working that result in differing theories of effectiveness. By leveraging the generally accepted universe of practices, one can incrementally influence organizational change in an intelligent manner, avoiding the typical culture-clash risks that result from blindly applying approaches in a "bull-in-the-china-shop" manner.

4.4 – Keeping it Real

To enable true and successful change, it is critical to embrace the cultural diversity that exists within the modern enterprise. Geographical differences, national cultures, language differences and social traditions all influence the net corporate culture that must be contended with when embarking on any change to the way-of-working of the software delivery teams. Immediate change resistance results the minute that any one constituency is disenfranchised by an attempt to push ways of working upon teams that have deeply held cultural values. The first step in avoiding such resistance is to surface and bring to light a team or sub-organization's perspective on their cultural values. Different parts of the organization will have potentially differing cultures. Assessment of the various perspectives of what the firm values via the Competing Values Framework enables an incremental, culturally sensitive approach to introducing changes to the various ways of working for the teams. Capturing the cultural context in which the software development endeavor exists represents the tenth contextual variable that can indicate risk associated with practice choices. Figure 4.6 illustrates the cultural assessment within the self-organization wizard of *Advisor*.

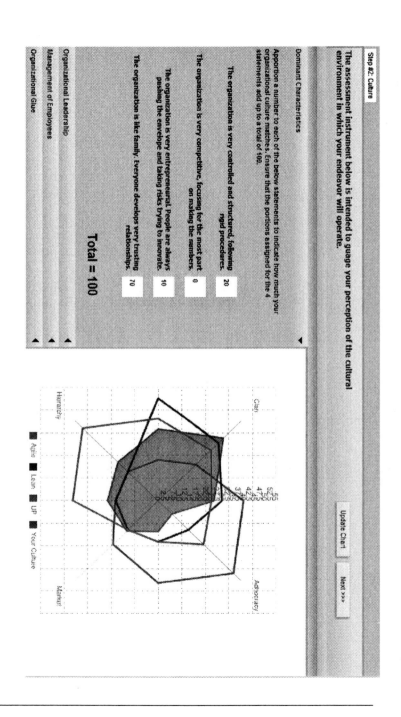

Figure 4.6 – Cultural Profiling in Advisor's Hybrid Approach Builder

With a team's cultural perspective captured, risks are identified and presented as part of the self-organization process. These risks are determined through execution of the rule base within the *Advisor* expert system. Teams can choose to accept the recommended advice and substitute more culturally appropriate practice options, or can ignore the advice and revisit the risk profile at a later date. Figure 4.7 illustrates the results and advice that are presented to the team after completing the contextual and cultural analysis and completion of the practice selection (to be discussed in Chapter 6):

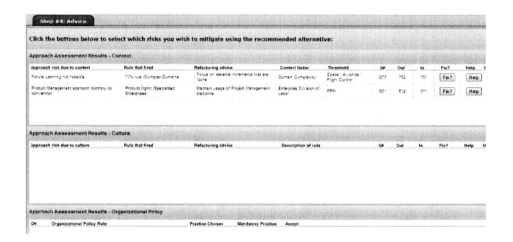

Figure 4.7 – Practice Risk Assessment based on Cultural Affinity

Assessing culture also indicates practice introduction sequencing, with incremental sequencing of changes recommended based on the likelihood of adoptability based on the value-structure of the team and the organization. Practice sets in concentric rings around the center of gravity of the current-state culture are recommended with increasing difficulty due to bigger affinity gaps. In a very concrete way, the freedom to choose within a guiding environment such as *Advisor* supported by the knowledge required to help team members make better choices ultimately results in an evolution of culture towards a more effective value structure.

Chapter 5: The Universal Truths

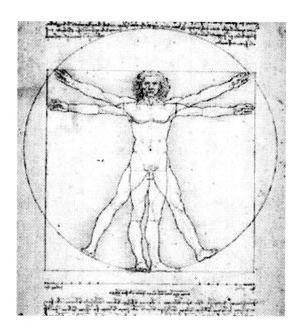

"The whole is greater than the sum of its parts." - Aristotle

One might have wondered why so much variability exists when it comes to software delivery methods. Obviously no two projects or products are identical in terms of the people involved or the tactics leveraged. Yet surely, each project has similarities in terms of context and culture, and commonality in terms of practices that appear to be universally applicable, perhaps subject only to some tweaking or parameterization. Is it possible to arrive at an understanding of software developments that enables us to explain why succeeding projects succeed and failing projects fail? The answer is yes, and exploring our recent work in this regard is a major objective of this book.

5.1 – All Models are "Wrong", Some are Useful

You may often hear rhetoric that questions the value of models in relation to software development methodology. It is as if there is a desire among some to *maintain the mystery* of software development projects so as to elevate the standing of those who "just know" how things work. I take the stand that models help us reason about the world around us and explore why things work the way they do. It is astounding that for all the talk of learning that models somehow are left at the door. While they are only models and are "wrong" in terms of only being approximations of the actual entity, they are useful for such purposes as establishing context for a concept in which we seek understanding; allowing us to group like concepts so as to perform apple-to-apple comparisons; and enabling cross-disciplinary insights and knowledge transfer. Researchers call these issues *Epistemological Contextualism*, in which knowing must require the context of the concept; *Etymology and Taxonomy*, which are the origins of terms and their classification; and *Interdisciplinarity*, which is combining two or more academic disciplines into one activity. It is my perspective that each is necessary to forge new ground and enhance the state of pragmatic knowledge, with the latter being the most overlooked aspect in achieving knowledge breakthroughs.

In the case of software development methodology very little progress to date has occurred in terms of establishing the context for the various practices we leverage. While some limited attention has been given to contextualizing whole movements like Agile or whole methods like Lean Startup, far less attention has been given to contextualizing the smaller components of these approaches in isolation of the container in which they sit. To date, due to the lack of a universal model that can establish the context and function of practices intra-ecosystem, there has been a noticeable void of contextualization at this level of granularity. This has perpetuated the consumption of wholesale methods or bodies-of-knowledge en masse, regardless if it isn't quite a perfect fit. It is the best we have had until now.

We will start to explore such a model for software delivery endeavors by first highlighting and explaining a few universal truths when it comes to knowledge intensive work like software development. This model is the missing ingredient that will enable contextualization and cultural affinity to be of practical use.

5.2 – The Waterfall is Iterative

This universal truth may strike you as odd given that so much has been made as to the dichotomy between Agile or even Iterative approaches and the dreaded Waterfall. Many in recent years have noted that the original 1970 paper by Winston Royce advocated 2 iterative cycles in the interests of learning [1]. While the frequency of iteration that was articulated was far too low a frequency for modern day learning requirements due to the uncertainty and complexity of modern projects and their technologies, the method was clearly a very simple "iterative" development approach. Perhaps the reason why the fallacy of the single pass, serialized Waterfall devoid of any feedback loops persists today is the need to vilify something in the interests of enhancing a communities cohesion. Regardless of the motives, we need to debunk this myth, and firmly state that this waterfall doesn't exist in its negligent form and conception.

Figure 5.1 illustrates the common perception of the Waterfall approach, and the reality that ensues when one factors in the entire lifecycle of the delivery of software:

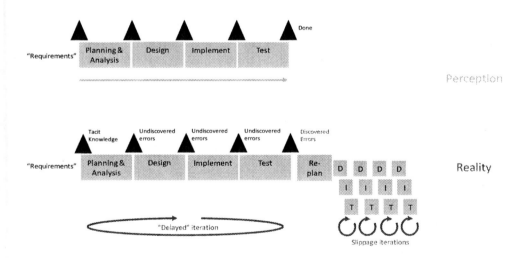

Figure 5.1 – Delayed Iterative - a.k.a "Waterfall"

In the previous figure, the perception of the team is that they will be successful in achieving perfect knowledge within the time-based phases associated with various specializations of Requirements, Analysis and Design, Coding or Implementation and Testing. The perception is that once done a phase in piecewise linear fashion, these activities will not be revisited. In actuality, loss or error occurs during each phase that is not detected. The amount of error varies from project to project depending upon the practices employed to detect these gaps. Much backlash and scepticism has been lodged against such things as stage-gates and formal reviews like *Fagan Inspections* [2]. This scepticism is not without merit, as the root issue is not the diminishing returns that mount as more and more ceremony is attempted to bring the loss in fidelity of knowledge to zero. The core issue is the obfuscation of reality. While on paper it appears that perfection is being achieved in terms of achieving perfect knowledge, the reality is something entirely different. Worse, the team doesn't know that reality differs from perception until it is too late. The effect on the overall dynamics of the project is instability. Some, notably Walker Royce, have articulated this as "late integration and breakage". What transpires at the point where true gap is uncovered is that more rapid iterative cycles ensue. The natural resonance of the feedback cycle necessary for organizational learning is delayed and prevented from occurring until the system rights itself. More formally, in research titled *The Effects of Feedback Delay on Learning* by Rahmandad, Repenning and Sterman [3], the effects of delays in receiving feedback (the payoff) are studied related to the sub-organization (the allocation) performing work (the actions) based on different heuristics including *Reinforcement Learning, Myopic Learning, Correlation Learning* and *Regression Learning*. The results show that the former case, which would be akin to implementing a software product using a serialized Waterfall approach, leads to much delay in convergence on the desired goal, and has the likelihood of instability. More importantly, according to Rahmandad et. al. *"the introduction of delays, and particularly misperceptions of their duration, causes error in the association of actions and payoffs and results in the organization's inability to learn the true relationships between actions and outcome and hence improve performance through experience."*

Intuitively, this explanation makes common sense and matches practical experience and empirical observation. But sometimes, as in the case of the dreaded Waterfall, this is not enough. Reiterating the point made in the previous section, it is only through models and research that such myths can be debunked, in this cited example the use of both Agent-based and Differential Equation mathematical modelling.

5.3 – Software Development is Dynamic

How many pretty pictures do you observe daily related to methods, practices, or org charts. How many of these have accompanying illustrations of the dynamics that are associated with these structures? While there are endless processes espoused, they rarely if at all illustrate what happens to them as time progresses during the lifecycle of a project. Specifically, certain liberties are taken to suggest that the nature of the various elements of the software delivery ecosystem are fixed and the advocacy within various practices holds true during the entire flight of the development effort. These attempts at modeling and communicating effective tactics are far oversimplified. The reality is that as each segment of time is traversed or each "waypoint" is achieved, things change. Changes occur in the system under development, the people involved, the technologies being leveraged and emerging within industry, and the organization surrounding the team. With all this change occurring, leveraging a static, fire and forget set of tactics is far from optimal. In fact, constant steerage and adjustment of the levers available to the team is required to provide the investment the standard of care demanded by those who pay for them.

As an example, take the simple practice of *Iteration*. While it is tempting to fix the frequency for the entire duration of the "flight", it makes sense that achieving certain objectives will require a different dynamic during the early going than the latter stages of the project or product lifecycle. Not all legs of the journey are created equal. During the initial iterations, while time-boxing is advantageous to enforce a feedback loop so as to achieve the necessary learning, these cycles are likely focused on proving out the high-stakes decisions that can make or break success. The so-called risky or architectural iterations may require more time to achieve feedback on Performance, or achieve concurrence among multiple humans regarding Usability. Later iterations are likely more deterministic and emphasize completeness rather than first-order learning, and therefore yield value in quicker, tighter feedback loops. This idea is known as *Adaptive Structure* [4], and is common within Control Systems Engineering and design of such systems as flight control and autopilot within avionics. Figure 5.2 illustrates the nature of Adaptive Structure as applied to software development efforts:

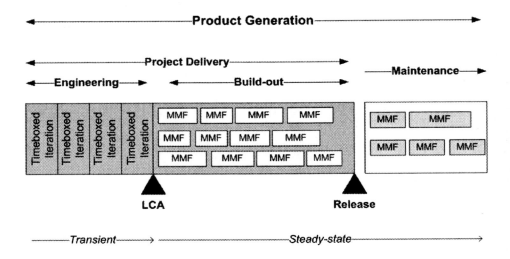

Figure 5.2 – Adaptive Structure and Feedback

From the above, one may note that introducing dynamically different practices that implement iteration or feedback may also suggest alterations to the structural aspects of the overall project or product context. For example, during the "hard engineering" period of time, small 7+-2 teams may make sense due to the skill-sets required of the team or availability in the marketplace. The batching of scope into time-boxed iterations may be necessary to provide enough scope for visibility into risk mitigation surrounding high-stakes solution decisions. As time proceeds, more optimal queue-oriented tactics will likely make sense with lower WIP limits and therefore tighter feedback loops by more parallel crews possessing more generalized and cross-functional skill-sets. Later still, geographical distribution may occur during low-risk sustainment or maintenance iterations which may require more lengthy feedback cycles yet leveraging less costly individuals.

One key take away from this universal truth is that change is always occurring, and only when one accepts this do attempts occur to improve outcomes through more dynamic "steerage" of the endeavor. This was one of the key tenets articulated within the Agile Manifesto.

5.4 – Software Development is Stochastic

The observation that software development is uncertain goes back to at least 1981 with Barry Boehm's original COCOMO parametric estimation model [5]. Later articulations of this model stressed the reduction of uncertainty over time by introducing a "cone of uncertainty" which illustrated error to be as much as +- 4X the actual investment outcome at the onset of a software development project. This model informally stressed that achievement of the system's architecture represented an inflection point for investment uncertainty and that the future can be predicted only so far into the horizon. Figure 5.3 illustrates the COCOMO II model [6]:

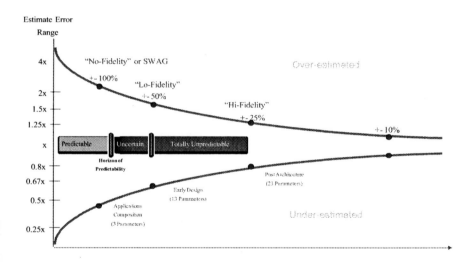

Figure 5.3 – Estimation Cone of Uncertainty [6]

While the aforementioned model does not include time as an independent variable, nor does it introduce the more complex mathematics related to probability including Monte Carlo Simulations [7], Analysis of Variance (ANOVA) [8] or Stochastic Differential Equations [9], it did popularize the probabilistic essence of the management problem. Entire methods resulted from these early works, including Model-based Architecting and Software Engineering (MBASE) [10], the early precursor to the Rational Unified Process. In each case, a risk-confrontive lifecycle model was advocated whereby risk would be driven out through focus on the riskiest or most uncertain parts of the system through build and test such that forecasting and convergence on reality could occur at the earliest.

In recent years, more robust models have emerged that embrace the essence of uncertainty and the stochastic nature of software development decision making, most notably Real Options approaches. With these models, focus is on decisions in the face of uncertainty through the discounting of cash flows into the future as likely events unfold. Notable methods in this regard include Datar-Matthews [11] and the Fuzzy Payoff Method [12]. Figure 5.4 illustrates the Real Options that accrue value upon successive iterations within a software endeavor:

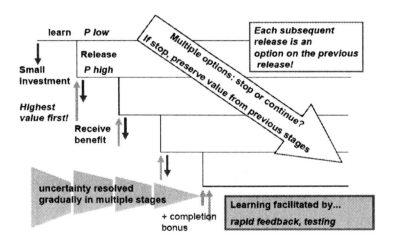

Figure 5.4 – Real Options Theory [13]

In each methodological case above, strong advocacy is given to debunk the perception held by some managers that the future can be predicted as a point solution. The reality is that due to the inherent dynamic process of humans making decisions with imperfect knowledge, prediction will be at best a near term possibility. Piecewise linearity of the project is possible, but the further out in time you project, the more non-linear the dynamics and therefore the more error prone the prediction.

5.5 – Software Development is Knowledge Intensive

You often hear that software development is knowledge intensive. The question you might ask is what exactly does this mean and how is such an observation useful? If you view everything that happens on a software development project as requiring knowledge as input and the change in state of the product as output, then it is decisions made by one or more humans that represents the trigger and guard condition for the activity that transitions a product from State A to State B. Figure 5.5 illustrates this atomic state-change unit that is always occurring in software projects:

Figure 5.5 – Product Development State-machine

The emergence of the software product results from the totality of product state changes. For some state changes, decisions require more knowledge and distillation. The guard condition for performing work is more stringent than for other activities which are triggered by simpler, more automatic decisions. Yet two different types of decisions of varying significance are made for various parts of the product. These decisions that block or enable activity to proceed to change the product state are also more or less sensitive to timing considerations. Some decisions require a large lead time due to procurement complexity. Other decisions can only be made during a limited window of opportunity. The challenge with software development is to make good decisions as fast as possible within our risk tolerance for the investment within an environment of imperfect knowledge. In effect our decisions are subject to uncertainty because our knowledge is uncertain - as the old saying goes, garbage in, garbage out.

When thinking about improving outcomes, one must recognize that the speed at which humans can make good decisions is limited in both time and space. To optimize our decision making abilities that enable the product to transition state and progress towards the final end state, we need to create **flow in decisions**. If we plug up our pipeline with erroneous or voluminous knowledge (in the form of documents or other high-ceremony artifacts) we run the risk of backing up the system and creating an inventory backlog of decisions.

To make decisions, humans rely on **"two different cognitive systems"** within our brains [14]. Speedy judgment is passed using the *Automatic System*, which is automatic, associative, and effortless and fast. Decisions made using this mode of reasoning are also subject to all forms of human imperfection including bias and logic errors. Figure 5.6 illustrates what can happen when we use our Automatic system and make quick judgments:

Which line is longer?

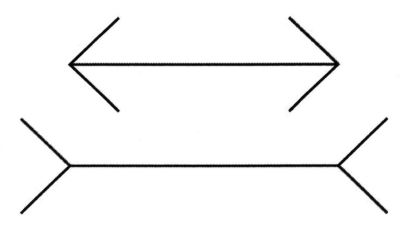

Figure 5.6 – Issues with the Automatic Cognitive System

In the above, the lines are exactly the same length - the arrow directions trick your brain into thinking this and is one of many flaws in human cognition. You relied on your Automatic system rather than leveraging the slower, methodical and analytical processing that is typically used to mitigate the risks of such errors in judgment, like getting out a ruler and measuring them. This mode of reasoning is usually what we refer to as "thinking" and uses the *Reflexive System*. Depending on which approach a software delivery team leverages to arrive at decisions also affects the speed at which decisions can be made. If decision making is made by gut instinct by an individual leader, the decision is likely to be very fast, but unfortunately must rely on the single individuals knowledge and experience which may or may not be sufficient. If decision making is made through consensus, which is usually heavily dependent on the culture of the organization, then decision are likely to be much slower. In either case, it is the decisions that need to be made that are the limiting factor in the progress that is made in transforming the product using the raw material of knowledge. We can track the quality of our knowledge by the performance of our decisions making and therefore the performance of the transitions of the product state machine. Normally, decisions are not captured effectively and therefore the sources of poor knowledge remain unknown and likely to be relied upon in the future. Whether it be knowledge of how to build the product efficiently and effectively, or knowledge about the technologies in use, or even knowledge about who possesses high quality knowledge, only through the capture of decisions do we have a lens into the knowledge input to the software delivery ecosystem.

One critical factor that affects which cognitive system we can rely on and therefore the performance of our decision making is complexity. Complexity in decision making has long been seen as one of the leading cost drivers in software economics [6]. Software is increasingly complex and research into how humans deal with complexity is longstanding. Examples include simple paradoxical references like psychologist George Miller's 1956 statement *"An individual can process seven give-or-take two items of information in their correct serial order in his or her short term (15-30 seconds) of working memory"* [15]. Going back further, "Factor Analysis" from Charles Spearman in 1906 states that *"multi-dimensional systems thinking requires holistic multi-factor thinking, multi-future thinking combined with causal feedback thinking. A crucial link between practical consulting, applied cognitive science and applied system science is the use of visual facilitation which increasingly makes use of the power of interactive visual representations of mental models behind decisions.* "[16]. Figure 5.7 illustrates the representation of how humans can leverage systems thinking to deal with complexity:.

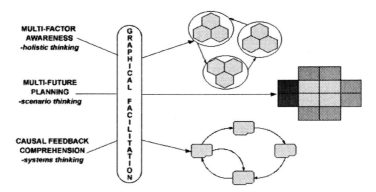

Figure 5.7 – Essence of Visualization [16]

From this we can understand why Visualization and Visual Modeling is so important when dealing with complexity in the face of decision making. When complexity increases beyond the point where we can rely on our Automatic System, we must leverage such visualization tools and models to enable the holism of systems thinking - multi-factor, multi-future and feedback causality. Without such a tool, we are left with the only other tactic available to us - driving towards simplicity. This is the basis for the Agile philosophy of "doing the simplest thing that could possibly work". The challenge is that complexity comes in two forms - *essential complexity and accidental complexity* [17] . While we can and must do everything possible to reduce accidental complexity, avoiding the essential complexity of our problem or chosen solution space eventually catches up to us in the form of hidden *technical debt* [18].

5.6 – System's Thinking Beyond Mere Buzzwords

Nowadays you will hear the term "System's Thinking" used with increasing frequency. Unfortunately, these words are often dropped by consultants eager to justify their favorite wares or jump on this emerging direction in industry to make a quick buck. To determine if this is the case, enterprises would be well served to evaluate the credibility of the work that backs up claims in this regard. It takes some pretty heavy lifting to truly be practicing System's Thinking and the associated engineering and mathematics discipline that accompanies it. If the consultants haven't "done the math", they likely do not have the knowledge or experience and background to play in this space. Various modeling tools are required to understand the behavior of systems, and system's analysis goes far beyond the pretty pictures and purely structural views of the project ecosystem.

With all the universal truths discussed this far, we arrive at the most important truth of all in relation to software development. This fact is that software delivery projects or product lifecycles are **systems**. Specifically, they have a number of interacting parts or components which work together to achieve a desired outcome. The system is more than the sum of these parts, and exhibits emergent properties as a result of the interplay amongst them. The parts of this "ecosystem" are subject to time as an independent variable - in other words they are dynamic and can be modeled as functions of time. More accurately, because these components are modeled as **changing functions of time**, and because there is a **high degree of uncertainty and non-linearity associated with each component**, they are modeled using *Stochastic Differential Equations*. Due to the fact that software development is knowledge intensive, loss and error is present throughout the system. Wherever knowledge from one human brain must be transferred to another human brain, regardless of formats like real-time face-to-face communication or persisted documents, only that which is surfaced as explicit knowledge from tacit knowledge gets conveyed. Gaps remain until enough repetition and trust is built to extract all the required knowledge. This repetition in system's thinking terms is feedback. Feedback occurs microscopically among various combinations of the people or agents within the system as well as macroscopically between the output of the system mechanisms used for comparing that output to the desired output in the form of a reference signal. Figure 5.8 illustrates the system's thinking model as described above, first articulated in SDLC 3.0:

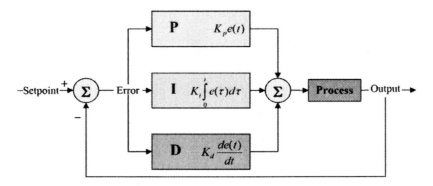

Figure 5.8 – System's Thinking for Software Development Projects

From the above, we recognize this configuration as a system which includes negative feedback in a closed-loop configuration - so called *Feedback Control Systems* [19]. It is universal in that all software projects are of this high level configuration. What varies is the details of how we realize such a system. This is the topmost universal, and enables us to leverage this cross-disciplinary knowledge to gain critical insights into software project behavior. Finally, because software development is human intensive, it is said to be a "Socio-technical System".

Firstly, the tracking variable of the system is "scope", not work. Our current time varying perception of scope or "intent" for the software product is the reference signal, which is "where we are going" based on the long-term vision. The reference signal is expressed in such a way so as to be actionable within the system whole and achieve optimization of the whole if we are taking a System's Thinking perspective. Feeding back a measure of the meaningful time varying output of the system for software development means testing it against the input intent or scope. The gaps between these two signals represents the error, which we can react or adapt to by exerting influence on the system. This influence is usually in a simple proportional form through the application or removal of people. The fundamental and most primitive input into the software ecosystem from these people is knowledge. However, other forms of influence are possible to cause acceleratory effects like reuse, or quality effects like through refactoring and defect remediation. These main components form the "management system" which surrounds the core system of humans interacting together using tools and techniques of various disciplines and specializations.

The above conceptual model enables us to reduce much of the us-versus-them rhetoric that occurs regarding methodology. It is the first essential ingredient that allows us to begin exploring more than just what is visible empirically on the surface. Studying the various practices and patterns that comprise and decorate our system provides us the interface to explore the inner workings of projects. Figure 5.9 illustrates the System's Thinking knowledge engineering concept, as articulated in Peter Senge's *The Fifth Discipline* [20]:

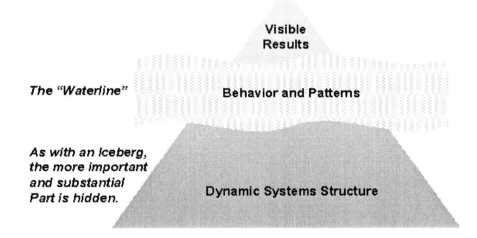

Figure 5.9 – Hidden System Dynamics [20]

Where the observable components of the system serve as the "waterline" for creating knowledge of the System's Thinking iceberg, only through such a system's model can we understand the hidden dynamics that can provide clues to the cause and effect of our choices for configuring projects. Overall, this model is similar to that of Domain Specific Language (DSL) [21] which facilitates the integration and explanation of all software development methods and bodies of knowledge. Taking a systems thinking strategy whereby practices are woven together in the context of the system parts that they realize empowers enterprises to understand their purpose, when they should be utilized and how to be effective in their usage.

Another framework stemming from a differing mindset that purports to have practical application to software development is the *Cynefin* [22] framework..   Agile advocates of this framework generally leverage it for its beneficial features when engaging in agenda-driven rhetoric with the objective of obfuscating the study of software development ecosystems. Figure 5.10 illustrates the complexity science viewpoint on categorizing systems, with the typical assertion that software development is within the "Complex" domain:

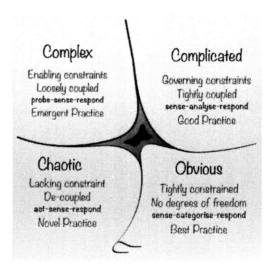

Figure 5.10 – Cynefin Framework [22]

In contrast to this view, all the empirical research and system's thinking science to date suggests strongly that software development is more appropriately categorized as a **Complicated Adaptive System** rather than a *Complex Adaptive System* [23]. Specifically, the notion that projects are exclusively "retrospectively coherent", and can only leverage "emergent practice" with no ability to reuse prior experience assumes that absolutely no cause-and-effect understanding is possible. While the human brain is typically associated with CAS, the assertion that a 7+-2 software delivery team ecosystem of loosely coupled brains is "without doubt" a CAS is without merit or empirical credibility. This is a continuance to the rigid orthodoxy rhetoric that attempts to de-contextualize the field of software development.

5.7 – The Universal Kernel

The model of how software projects work has been elusive to date [24]. The closest we have come as an industry are the System's Dynamics models created by researchers at universities such as Massachusetts Institute of Technology (MIT) [25] or the University of Southern California [26]. While they represent high fidelity mathematical simulations, they are absent of the overarching structure that enables one to quickly grasp what is going on in the ecosystem. They are also intractable to understand absent of simulation engines which render the likely dynamic response as a result of the parameter settings in the model. Finally, they are solely time-domain models reflective of a process versus practice orientation.

The innovative step in the model that follows is that the system is of the form of a *Proportional-Integral-Derivative Control* in a *Cascaded* configuration. Practices realize the various universal components of this system, constrained by the various contextual drivers or factors of the endeavor and impacted by the forces of uncertainty and change. Similar to "control tactics" as found in *Feedback Control Systems*, practices are the analog. Such an interdisciplinary perspective enables us to rapidly understand the context and locality of practices against the various attributes of the universal components of the system. This allows us to begin to collect empirical observations as to the coefficients of the governing equations that describe the dynamics of such systems. Bounded by the 7 *constraints* and 2 types of complexity *disturbances*, the software endeavor forms an ecosystem which contains the *organization* structure in the form of a social network of *individuals interacting* with each other while they perform *work* using *tools*. The raw input of the ecosystem is *knowledge*, and the output is a time varying *software intensive system*. *Convergence feedback* is implemented through tests and evaluated using various forms of *evaluation* or measurement practice to form an aggregated gap or *error* signal. *Comparison* is performed on this signal such that informed changes to *influence* over time can ensue. The *reference signal*, also a *time varying* signal that is highly *uncertain*, is created through the upstream identification, assessment and *alignment* of *opportunities* as they emerge from *stakeholders*. A way of working or *approach* guides and *governs* the ecosystem, and is informed through the feedback signal. Finally, downstream *releases* occur to stakeholders on a cadence that is external to the *Endeavor*. In this model, it is the Endeavor which forms the context boundary, which may be a Project, Program or holistic Product lifecycle. Figure 5.11 illustrates the model:

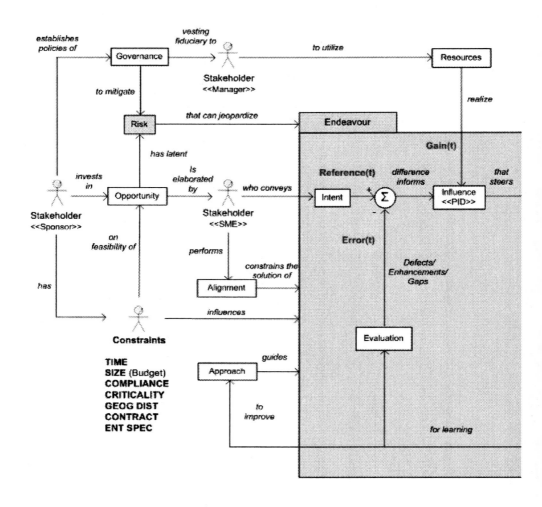

Figure 5.11 – The Software Development Universal Kernel

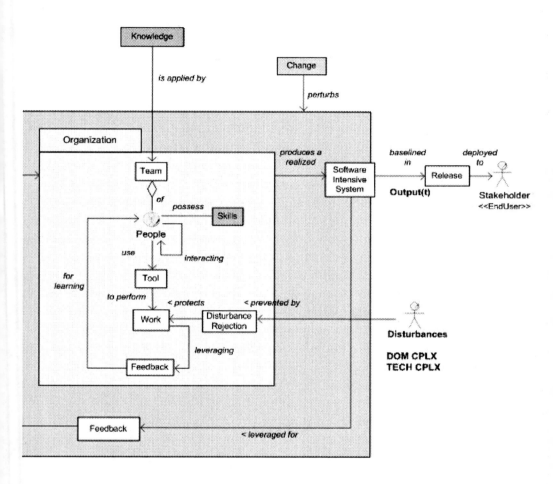

Figure 5.11 – The Software Development Universal Kernel

5.8 – Practices are Aspects

Ever since situational method engineering arrived on the scene in the mid-1990's, the unit of chunking up methods has been explored. At one end of the spectrum is breaking up methods functionally, as reflected in the notion of "disciplines". At the other end of the spectrum is the decomposition of methods through the use of structural components. Various standards like the Software Process Engineering Meta-model (SPEM) [27] and the Unified Method Architecture [28] are examples of the latter. The typical legacy process-ware that treats methods as "lifecycles" are likely to exhibit a functionally decomposed bias. In recent years, the notion of a practice has been leveraged to divide up what constitutes a holistic method. The natural question to ask is "what semantically is a practice?" The answer is that a software development "practice" is an **Aspect** - as in *Aspect Orientation* [29]. Aspects have been described contextually within the Business Use Case View as *Extension Use Cases* [30], as illustrated in Figure 5.12:

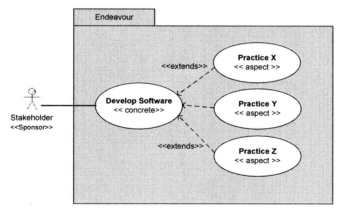

Figure 5.12 – Modeling Practice Aspects as Extension Use Cases

Aspects in software engineering are formally defined as follows:

An Aspect is a feature or concern of a program which is linked to multiple core parts of a program, thereby violating encapsulation and separation of concerns. The concern forms a set of advices that are scattered across the program at specific join-points and are woven or tangled at run-time to form a point-cut. - Wikipedia

The key concepts from this definition that relate to how we can use practices as our chunking approach are **tangling** and **scattering**. We can tangle practices together into a method if we know the "join-points" in which they insert themselves into one or more universal components as they scatter across the Universal Kernel.. This means we need to know what their context is within the ecosystem, and because Aspects are multi-dimensional in relation to concerns, they instantiate potentially multiple structural components in ways dependent upon the specific practice elements. Formally, this concept has been articulated as "hyper-slices". Figure 5.13 illustrates the meta-model of the Universal Kernel and the inclusion of Practice Aspects and their core practice element decomposition. The various aspectual attributes (concerns) of the 19 Universal components are described using a well known design pattern, and serve as the *Abstract Factory* [31] for the concrete practices (Concrete Factory):

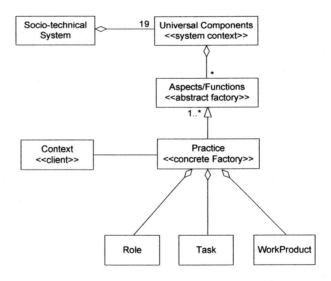

Figure 5.13 – Abstract Factory of Practices

The process of assembling a method reflective of the system being instantiated can be thought metaphorically as being similar to the assembly of integrated circuits. Integrated circuits are created by differing layers etched out or applied to silicon wafers to build up the entire chip including semiconductor layers, insulating layers like SiO_2, conductor layers made of various metals like Tungsten and Aluminum. The function of the system is the totality of the various layers that realize the various functional modules of the integrated circuit. These functional modules are not made sequentially, but by the various layers of "concern" like semiconduction, power routing vias, insulation, and external contacts. Similarly, the software delivery "chip" or ecosystem is instantiated by multiple layers of practice that overlay across different universal components and their various sub-concerns. Together these practices result in an integrated workflow "circuit". Figure 5.14 illustrates this assembly approach pictorially:

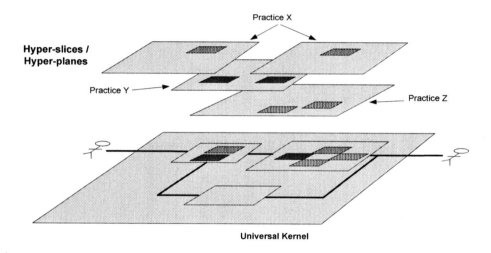

Figure 5.14 – Practice Hyper-slices

To illustrate the application of this meta-model for the Universal Kernel, consider the example given in Figure 5.15 for a very popular industry method, Scrum. As can be seen, the practices of Scrum manifest themselves as different combinations of either Role, Task or WorkProduct elements that scatter across the software delivery ecosystem:

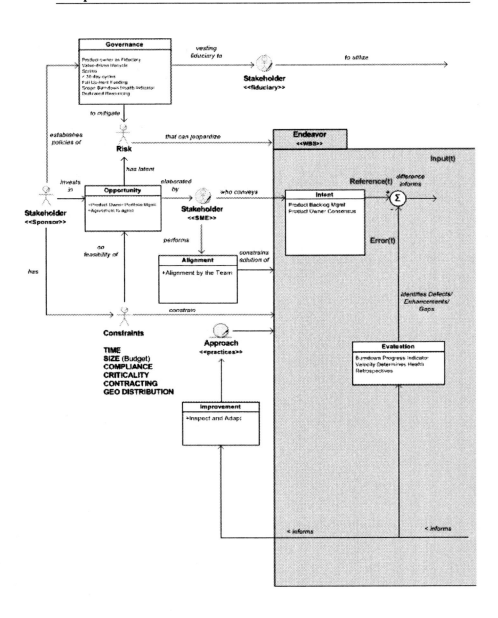

Figure 5.15 – Applying the Universal Kernel - Scrum

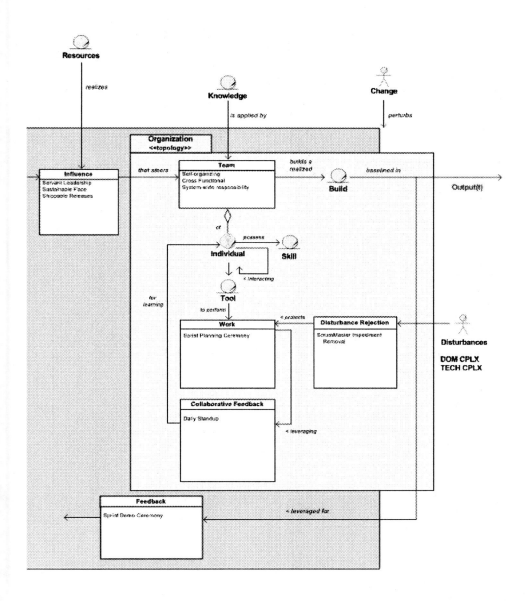

Figure 5.15 – Applying the Universal Kernel - Scrum

5.9 – Practice Choice Architecture

When you decompose methods into their constituent parts, it is possible to map them in a coherent and high fidelity fashion into the universal kernel from the previous section. That is to say, for the kernel to hold as "universal", each existing and future method must pass the test of fitting within the model. Empowered by Systems Thinking, a choice architecture can be devised that takes these mappings and presents them in the context of system components and their respective attributes and function. By combining the strategy of breaking down the industry's methods (basically containers of practices) into parts and then empowering teams to reassemble them into a management system, *Responsible Autonomy* is achieved as described in the book Nudge. Such a decomposition ensures that the freedom to choose is upheld. The organization is also exercising due diligence by ensuring that decisions are made in an informed manner due to their association with the contextual purpose within the system. It also provides the power of Nudge to the organization to exercise influence and emerge policy guidance to the teams in a responsible fashion.

Figure 5.16 below illustrates a powerful nudge and choice architecture which frames and guides the decision making process through a presentation that invokes the emotions and ethics within the participant.

Figure 5.16 – Nudge and the Power of Choice

Not all nudges are created equal. Without designing a choice architecture based on a model of how things work, the alternative would be to let teams choose, but not understand the implications of those choices on the overall ecosystem and would have no basis to explore and understand why they are declaring those particular practices. By just posing simple questions that have no correlation to how things work on software projects, we would have no way to perform causal analysis for future learning. Bad choices would likely repeat themselves, and organizational learning would be impossible. There would be no way to ensure completeness, nor make credible arguments as to the basis for classification and taxonomy, something important if you are to build credibility with the choosers.

To date mappings have been done for all major methods onto our universal kernel model. With this maturing and stable model in tow, many interesting research and learning opportunities are possible. We can begin to contextualize practices into their locality of the various ecosystem kernel parts. We can then simulate their likely effect upon the overall system in concert with the complete set of practice choices. We can also calibrate the parameters of the model related to the universal components through the collection of data related to usage and associated causality data from actual software delivery results. With practices representing aspects, each practice scatters into various attributes of one or more universal component attributes. With the universal component as the abstract factory, the realization of the concrete factory is the aggregate of the tangled practice aspects across all universal attributes. Figure 5.17 presents the decomposition of various industry practices against one component within the systems thinking kernel, referred to as the *Evaluation* universal:

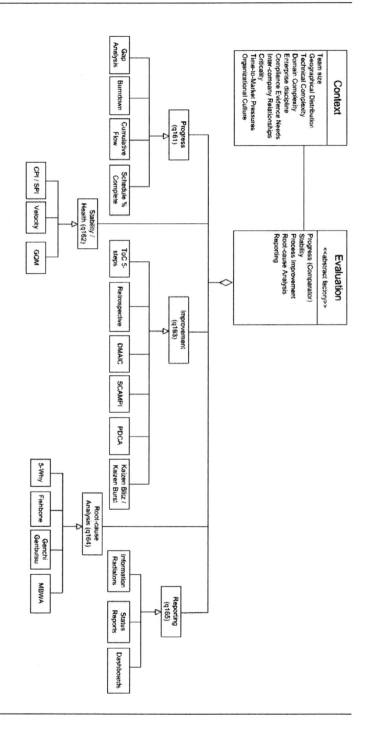

Figure 5.17 – The Evaluation Universal

The subtle and powerful nature of devising a choice architecture using the system components of the universal kernel is that teams can identify with the alternatives, as they are presented such that an apple-to-apple comparison is quickly made. The sequencing of the questions is based on the sequencing of instantiation of the software project ecosystem. A spectrum of options for the decision tree presentation exists. Choices within the kernel-driven decision-tree can be presented clustered by universal component, with the sub-level questions being tied to the various attributes of the kernel. Each kernel cluster of questions can be either presented individually in a natural order of sequencing, or can be presented in a flexible and flat manner to enable teams to jump around in the decision tree. The degree of Responsible Autonomy can be altered by either leaving all combinations possible during choice selection, or can be implemented with stronger forms of influence by narrowing the scope of potential choices in the forward chaining of the questions as choices are made. Finally, the scope of Responsible Autonomy can be adjusted by hiding various choice architecture segments due to their lack of variability across the enterprise or the historically based policy making and standardization. An example of this modification would be to not require teams to make choices related to fuzzy front-end practices related to *Opportunity*, *Alignment* or *Governance*.

Figure 5.18 illustrates the tree-like structure of the kernel based choice architecture for software development practices. Each node in the tree represents one of **19 universal components** that are part of the Systems Thinking based universal kernel. Each "universal" has various questions associated with attributes that have sets of practices available as alternatives. Such attributes have resulted from emergence by categorizing practice aspects together based on pragmatic equivalence. This equivalence is driven by function. The realization of the function can be variable with respect to the resultant workflow elements of task, work product or responsible role. Enterprise scope, up-front and trailing universals present choices related to the *Customer*, the *Opportunity*, *Alignment*, *Stakeholders* and SMEs, *Governance*, *Release* management and improving an *Approach*. Core system universals present choices related to *Intent*, *Influence*, *Organization* structure, *Work*, *Teams*, *Individuals*, *Tools*, *Collaborative Feedback*, *Disturbance Rejection*, *Convergence Feedback*, *Evaluation* and the *Software System*.

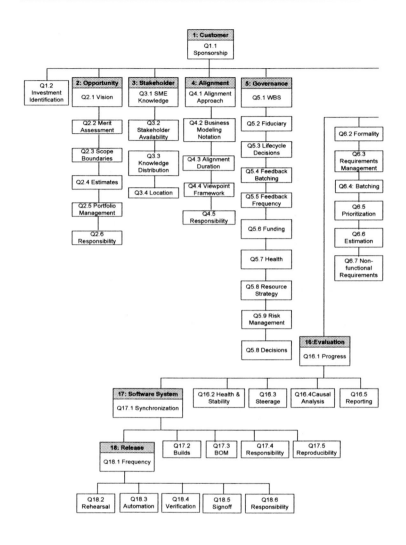

Figure 5.18 – Systems Thinking Practice Decision Tree

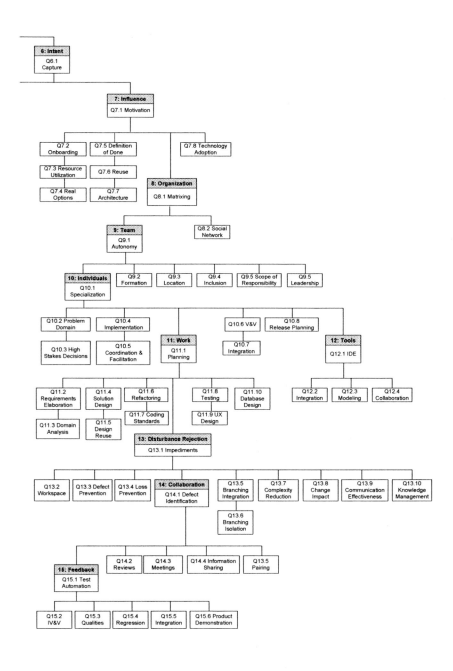

5.10 – Keeping it Real

Empowered by an inventory of practices mapped into the context of the various components that comprise the software delivery ecosystem, organizations can afford a degree of autonomy to teams with minimal oversight. Instead of prescribing a branded method on large parts of the organization, the "boots-on-the-ground" can choose the best course of action for the endeavor. Without encumbering the teams by rhetoric associated with the consulting market or dictating "standards", teams are given the right to self determination. The organization however has the right to oversee and capture this intelligence from the front lines. To achieve both requires automation if value-added oversight is to be provided in a timely manner. Similarly, without automation, mitigating risk and guiding or coaching teams would require a small army to ensure that teams didn't go off the rails being faced with the inherent complexity. A lack of automation would also lead to large delays and errors introduced into the startup of the enterprises' projects. Finally, rather than ignoring many of the aspects and universal components that comprise all software delivery ecosystems, automation can ensure that no issue is left unaddressed. Such openness and transparency is essential to allow this new Responsible Autonomy relationship to flourish.

Figure 5.19 illustrates the Practice Choices step within *Advisor's* Hybrid Approach Builder. It is structured to allow teams to quickly make their selections and dynamically update their approach. As suggested previously, different presentations are possible, including a full or robust questionnaire or a simplified version. Other variations possible within an enterprise might include a progressive narrowing form of the questionnaire. As teams organize their way of working by selecting choices, their approach is updated to later enable the dynamic construction of their playbook, discussed later in Chapter 6. Throughout this step, teams can hover over the decision tree to recollect the choice made for the various universal component. Progress of completing the decision tree is illustrated through color coding the dynamically updated tree. Finally, if teams want to understand how their favorite named method maps to the choice architecture, they can leverage the mapping reference at the top of the iFrame by clicking the appropriate button. Each method or body of knowledge shows the list of practices that result when decomposition into their constituent parts, along with the choice architecture mapping.

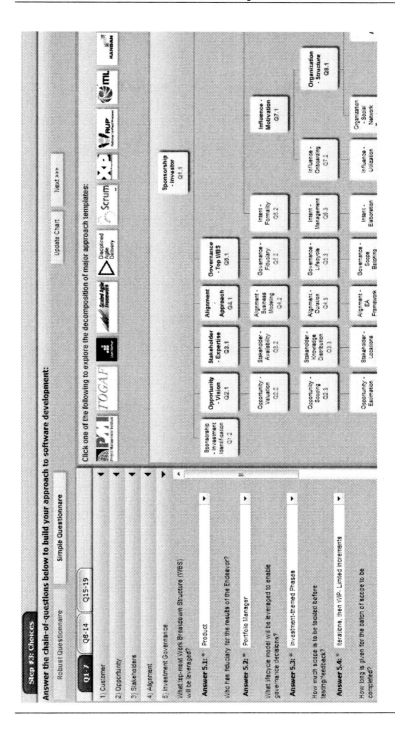

Figure 5.19 – Practice Choice Completeness

Once a team has declared their way of working using the practice choice architecture, the final step in building an approach is to execute the expert system rule base and determine the risk profile of the selections based on contextual and cultural declarations. Each risk that is triggered is presented in the Advice step, along with a suggested refactoring and help for understanding why the risk is present. The team can either decide to accept the mitigation advice, or can accept the risk and retain their choices. If the risk mitigation advice path is undertaken, the alternative practice is substituted in place of the original choice. The approach is updated and the newly integrated practice choice will be reflected in the teams playbook. Figure 5.20 illustrates the results of the Hybrid Approach Builder in terms of the different types of risk captured by *Advisor*.

The overarching value of leveraging a System's Thinking choice architecture in driving the independent declaration of hybrid approaches is that teams are implicitly informed of equivalence of practice choices through their locality in the choice architecture. Such a presentation, while reflecting the true complexity of software delivery ecosystems, also encourages facilitation and learning such that teams come together and gel quicker as a group. The approach that results is their approach, not some other team or person's approach to software development.

Step #4: Advice

Click the buttons below to select which risks you wish to mitigate using the recommended alternative:

Approach Assessment Results - Context

	Rule that fired	Refactoring advice	Context factor	Threshold	Q#	Out	In	Fix?	Help
Approach risk due to context									
Failure Learning not feasible	70% rule: Complex Domains	Focus on testable increments that are done	Domain Complexity	Space: Avionics / Flight Control	Q73	752	761	Fix?	Help
Product Management approach contrary to convention	Product Mgmt Specialized Enterprises	Maintain usage of Project Management discipline	Enterprise Division of Labor	RPM	Q81	812	811	Fix?	Help

Approach Assessment Results - Culture

	Rule that fired	Refactoring Advice	Description of rule	Q#	Out	In	Fix?	Help
Approach risk due to culture								

Approach Assessment Results - Organizational Policy

Q#	Organizational Policy Rule	Practice Chosen	Mandatory Practice	Accept

Figure 5.20 – Practice Risk Assessment and Facilitating Substitution

Chapter 6: Integrating the Enterprise Software Value Stream

"The emphasis should be on why we do a job" - *W. Edwards Deming*

We finally arrive at what this book is all about - configuring the enterprise software delivery *Value Stream*. We have all the necessary ingredients to integrate the various practices required to identify, align, develop, acquire, and release software intensive systems in a contextually smart and culturally sensitive way. This title was not chosen lightly. The business stakeholders to software development identify with this term, and live it every day. From the early days of the strategy work by the likes of Michael Porter [1], a strong focus on the customer is necessary to optimize business outcomes. Software development should be no different.

Until now, *Lean Software Development* [2] and more generically *Lean Thinking* [3] have relied on simplistic Value Stream Maps to reason about flow and the different types of waste that can affect the throughput of value. This modeling technique was derived from early structured analysis approaches, specifically the Jackson System's Method [4]. Unfortunately, this approach represents a functional decomposition paradigm in which the object of value, obviously due to its outgrowth from manufacturing circles, flows through the various functional disciplines that transform the raw material into product form. This fundamental assumption is flawed when it comes to the dynamism related to knowledge intensive work and software development. Figure 6.1 illustrates the Value-Stream Mapping technique:

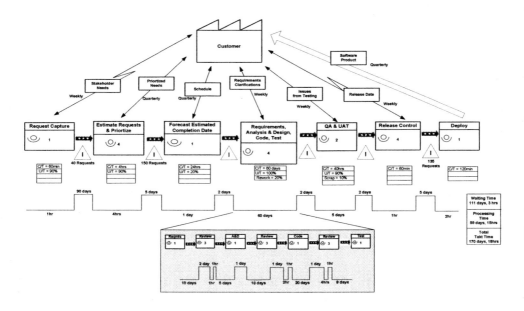

Figure 6.1 – Value-Stream Maps

The above approach relies on an oversimplified linearized process configuration. We know from Chapter 5 that software development incurs much more parallelism and feedback. However, the idea that modeling the flow of work is not without merit. It enables us to reason about ways in which our current "standard work" approach may be further improved, whether it be reduction of unnecessary activity, rearrangement of process configurations, or better holistic value-stream integration. Through the introduction of object-oriented *value-stream networks* which are the result of an integrated systems of practices, we may facilitate such analysis and work design. Figure 6.2 illustrates at the highest level the Enterprise IT Value-stream as representative of an integrated set of practices.

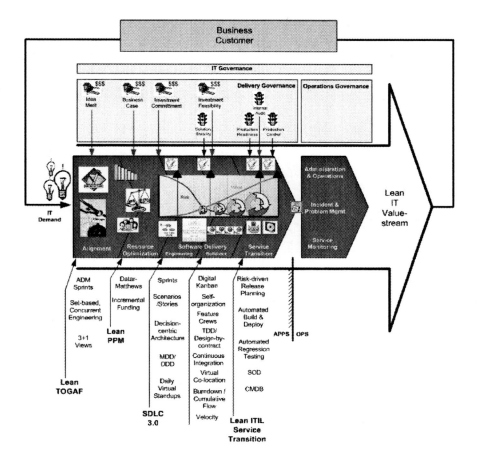

Figure 6.2 – Value-stream configured using Practice Systems

The metaphor that should be invoked is that of an **integrated circuit**, with many layers assembled to form the functioning enterprise circuitry that fulfills the end-to-end transformative pipeline between inputs (IT Demand) and the outputs (IT Value).

6.1 – The Optimization of Flow

When we look at any segment of the value stream, our practice choices tangle into a network of tasks and work products configured within various skillset combinations called roles. Each role has responsibility over a swimlanes which either splits or merges with efforts within other swimlanes in so-called V-Plant, A-Plant or T-Plant configurations [5]. As an example, Figure 6.3 below illustrates drastic network configuration changes driven by the practice choices made.

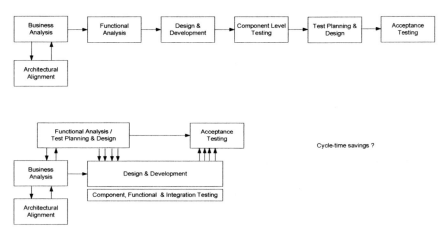

Figure 6.3 – Value-network Configuration

The first order effect that can be made on improving value stream performance is reconfiguring the workflow. In the above example, we can see the drastic shortening of the overall process configuration by introducing Acceptance Test-Driven Development, also known as *Specification by Example* [6]. Such a strategy shows that elevating constraints within the value stream is entirely possible This contrasts the process improvement assumptions made within the Kanban Method, which stresses that exploitation of constraints through Work-in-Progress (WIP) limits should be undertaken because elevating the constraint is too costly or impractical [7]. My view is that simple alterations of the value network based on innovative practice choices and associated skillset implications is far more effective. It also reflects the fact that work within the value stream is far more concurrent than the simplified I-Plant configuration, the only configuration in the Kanban approach for optimizing flow.

The second way to optimize flow is to address the issue of batching within the value stream. Lean has long advocated limiting WIP through pull systems like *kanban* or other signaling techniques. The governing management science behind this is Little's Law [8] and is associated with queuing theory. Most of the techniques popular within software development approaches to date has been focused on "hunting" for *Critical WIP*, the point at which cycle time drastically increases due to batch size. In fact, the Scrum practice of Sprint time-boxing represents an attempt to zero in on this critical WIP threshold. Placing too much scope within a time-box during Sprint Planning results in blowing the iteration or leads to burnout. Figure 6.4 illustrates Little's Law and the relationship between cycle time and WIP:

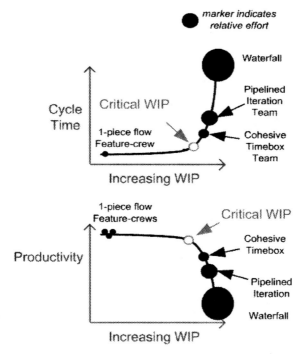

Figure 6.4 – Critical-WIP

The implications of increased cycle time matters because it directly relates to productivity, as described in Figure 6.5 below:

$$Productivity = efficiency \times effectiveness$$

$$= \frac{output}{input} \times \frac{desired\ output}{all\ output}$$

$$= \frac{throughput}{input} \times \%\,valuable\ output$$

$$= \frac{WIP}{Cycle\text{-}time\ x\ input} \times \%\,valuable\ output$$

Figure 6.5 – Productivity as a function of cycle-time

Looking at the productivity curve in Figure 6.4, the poorest performance is that of a full serialized batch of a "Waterfall" approach. It not only produces the lowest productivity, but is the highest cost in terms of resources, a compounded effect of the poorest efficiency and the inherent scrap and rework of poor effectiveness. Moving back the utilization curve, iteration pipelining actually has the opposite effect than optimizing cycle time. Beyond this point, as long as a time-boxed iteration has the critical amount of scope, productivity will be optimized for that organization and practice structure. To move beyond this potential productivity point on the curve, one that minimizes cost and enables maximal productivity, requires changing organizational structure and the introduction of parallelism by small teams or *Feature Crews*. With the increase in parallelism, an increase in skill-sets per individual is required to achieve the same realization of scope.

The previous discussion illustrates the complex interplay that exists between process configuration, skill-set cohesion or division of labor choices, and scope batching. Differing contexts within the enterprise will naturally allow some combinations and preclude others. Whether it be the constraints on skill-sets, or the nature of the technology or domain that preclude certain configurations, an enterprise will have multiple parallel value streams within the product portfolio. The overall Enterprise IT organization will look like a bundle of multiple pipelines of differing shapes and sizes. Assuming that any one configuration is universally applicable to all situations will result in sub-optimization and is the likely cause of total train-wrecks and project cost or deadline overruns.

6.2 – Investment-centric Governance

Often the rhetoric within IT relates to the so-called anti-pattern "command and control", a nod to the term coined by Henry Fayol [9]. Several mental leaps are made when the word governance is attached to this phrase, and images of sweat shops or Theory X [10] low-trust management are immediately thrust into the mind of the recipient. However, governance has nothing to do with controlling or micro-managing individuals, except under circumstances of extreme negligence. More importantly, it is for the investor to decide how they wish to manage or "govern" their investments, not methodologists or the proxies executing their endeavors; in each case, this would represent a conflict-of-interest.

We define governance in the mature, investment-centric sense as follows: to **govern means to steer**. Effective governance steers the investment towards favorable outcomes. The mechanism for governance and therefore steerage is decisions - all decisions are related to steerage, but those that can have material effects on our investment outcome are the ones that are held to a higher standard-of-care. These decisions are governed by those that have what is termed a "fiduciary duty", those individuals entrusted with making the decisions but with commensurate accountability if those decisions do harm to the outcome. Note that governance does not mean deliverables, nor documents. These are merely persistent stores of information. Some decisions must be taken to improve the likelihood of a favorable outcome. Making these steerage decisions requires timely access to the information; otherwise the effects of the steerage or course corrections will be lost. Formally, the ability to exercise our real options will expire if not acted upon in a timely manner. Therefore, instruments of governance must be pragmatic to keep up with the stochastic, dynamic nature of the software endeavor.

Exploring what governance looks like from a holistic value-stream perspective and a systems thinking mindset, we can build up a view of the ecosystem that addresses the fundamental fiduciary concerns. As discussed in Chapter 5, time and uncertainty are critical variables within our software delivery ecosystem and therefore if we break up the entire journey into *piecewise linear* segments, certain themes of effort will need to be performed so as to address the concerns in each period. Early on, in the "fuzzy front end" of the value stream, the themed period of time is that of either "discovery" or "alignment" depending upon whether IT Demand is speculative or defined by a justifiable business need. In the case of Alignment, we must make decisions and govern the expenditure of resources to only those investment opportunities of merit. This often entails reasoning about complexity as in the case of large enterprises, and therefore governance decisions typically consume as-is and to-be visualizations as well as transition roadmaps of how such a journey will take place. Figure 6.6 illustrates the meaningful themes of investment activity related to software delivery:

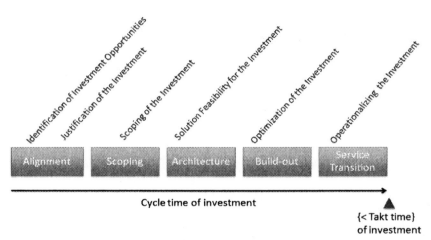

Figure 6.6 – Value-themed Periods of Time

From the above figure, we can see that discrete periods of time address investment-centric concerns rather than IT jargon. What we are interested in with such a value-stream set of activities is demarking the points where we will make steerage decisions and potentially accrue value in the form of either exit or learning options. If this condition does not exist, then the discreteness of the value-stream activity is in question and likely inserting a break in the flow that is non value-add. If bona fide decisions that could materially affect the outcome will occur, then their end points naturally result in go no-go decisions tied to funding. Without such a gate, discontinuous activities or "phases" are meaningless.

It should be noted that within IT, the value-stream governance view is known as a "lifecycle model", whereby the phases are often synonymous with the type of deliverable to be produced rather than the investment centric implications of their existence. If the lifecycle model advocated is truly value-stream oriented, the milestones that delineate the phases will have names that suggest what is being achieved in terms of investment health. This litmus test will further be supported by the types of Toll-gate Questions [11] that investors will ask of the fiduciary of the project or endeavor. If these questions are of the form "do you have a *<<pick favorite document here>>*", then it is likely that a non-investment-centric approach is being leverage. Needless to say, checklists of this form do nothing to improve outcomes, mitigate investment risk or improve cycle time. They are indicative of large order waste, and likely result in "deer in the headlights" milestone review meetings whereby project sponsors are not given crisp answers to very fundamental investment questions. Figure 6.7 illustrates the second component of effective investment-centric governance - meaningful milestones and investment health questions:

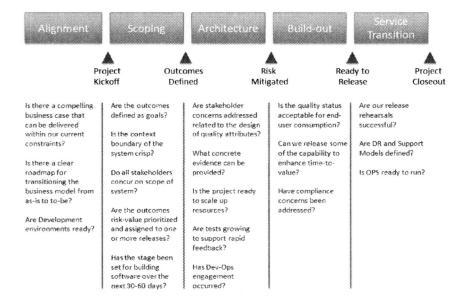

Alignment	Scoping	Architecture	Build-out	Service Transition
▲	▲	▲	▲	▲
Project Kickoff	Outcomes Defined	Risk Mitigated	Ready to Release	Project Closeout
Is there a compelling business case that can be delivered within our current constraints?	Are the outcomes defined as goals?	Are stakeholder concerns addressed related to the design of quality attributes?	Is the quality status acceptable for end-user consumption?	Are our release rehearsals successful?
Is there a clear roadmap for transitioning the business model from as-is to to-be?	Is the context boundary of the system crisp?	What concrete evidence can be provided?	Can we release some of the capability to enhance time-to-value?	Are DR and Support Models defined?
Are Development environments ready?	Do all stakeholders concur on scope of system?	Is the project ready to scale up resources?	Have compliance concerns been addressed?	Is OPS ready to run?
	Are the outcomes risk-value prioritized and assigned to one or more releases?	Are tests growing to support rapid feedback?		
	Has the stage been set for building software over the next 30-60 days?	Has Dev-Ops engagement occurred?		

Figure 6.7 – Milestones address Investment Uncertainty

The next issue to address in constructing an efficient and effective governance view of the software delivery value-stream is how much and by when. In other words, how much investment should be roughly allocated to be spent answering the fundamental investment centric questions by what percentage of the overall expected timeline. These heuristics, while probabilistic or stochastic in nature, should be roughly what is achieved nominally. Different investment types or contexts will result in different performance indicators, but the general concept is that software development projects should not be a sunk cost if we are exercising our fiduciary and performing effective governance. Exercising our real options requires exercising them before all the cash is burned or it is too late. Attempting to have perfect knowledge for a decision or set of decisions runs into diminishing returns, and even the perfected decision is of no value if too late. Figure 6.8 illustrates the key performance indicators that derive from the Unified Process risk-value lifecycle:

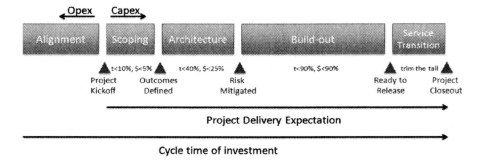

Figure 6.8 – Investment-centric Performance Indicators

The next issue to consider is who is in the best decision to make timely, quality decisions. While the fiduciary usually lies with the Project and Portfolio Management discipline, too often this swim-lane attempts to acquire all information rather than delegate to authorities that can more efficiently and effectively interpret results. Moreover, all investment gates and toll-gates are not created equal, with themes shifting from the problem domain to the solution domain and then to operations over time. This implies that different stakeholder groups should be the primary facilitators for adjudication of investment health over time. Ultimately it is for the customer, sponsor or investor to decide if their investment is healthy, but different specialized skill-sets can distill the differing perspectives of project activity. Figure 6.9 illustrates the discharging of intelligent project fiduciary:

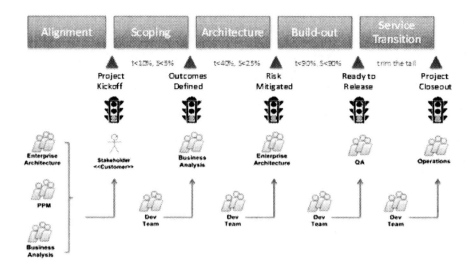

Figure 6.9 – Intelligently-vested Fiduciary

Finally, it is the result of the practice choices that are made within an endeavor that determine the inputs to the toll-gates that will be assessed by the various delegated fiduciaries on behalf of the investor. While it is tempting to prescribe these inputs on the basis of convenience, such an approach runs counter-culture to all but *Hierarchy* organizations. More importantly, focus drifts from the processing of information for making critical decisions to the document container that houses that information. A far better strategy is to be able to render views of data that address the complex governance issues at each gate. Such a data-centric versus document-centric stance enables far more delivery intelligence due to the temporal and dynamically changing nature of the project ecosystem than the batching that occurs within documents. The general function of the workproduct output of a practice should be the focus, not the form, and practice equivalence and variability should be embraced for reasons that will be discussed in Chapter 10. It should be noted that evidentiary standards in various compliance mandates do not require document centricity. While the quality of evidence is an issue with such standards as Statement of Auditing Standard - 70 (SAS-70) [12], nothing suggests that data that achieves the same intent of a control is inferior. In fact, reducing information to documents can materially introduce risk into the endeavor rather than mitigate it.

Finally, as effective practices and cultural affinities start to emerge, practice usage policies will result in standardized inputs to the governance milestones over time. Figure 6.10 illustrates an example of the resultant inputs for the various governance steerage points due to practice choices:

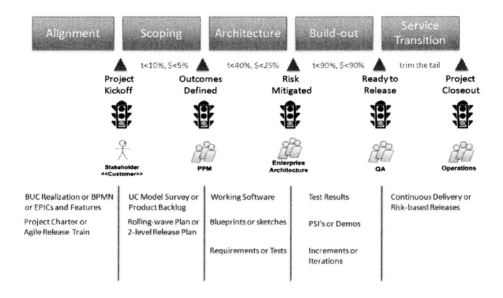

Figure 6.10 – Focus on Decisions, Agnostic of Practice

As is typically the case, the above reasoning is glossed over and ignored in the case of Agilists, or is self-serving and overburdening in the case of hardcore Traditionalists. In the former case, the community and body of knowledge holds a decidedly risk-tolerant perspective on efficacy. In the latter case, the body of knowledge and community have a decidedly risk-adverse perspective with respect to efficacy. Neither extreme in these mindsets serves the investors. The above pragmatic governance approach for the value stream is akin to managing to the interface, not the implementation. As long as the "command intent" is met, the organization can take a descriptive versus prescriptive stance with all the organizational change management and motivation benefits that such a strategy brings.

Tying all of these issues together, it should also be evident that the configuration of the various aspects of the governance view is contextual. This means that the investment situation should drive the utility of the various themed periods of time, the meaningful toll-gate questions, the various key performance indicators, the intelligent fiduciary delegation and the efficient and effective practice choices that realize these various aspects of the management interface. The implications are that value streams and their governance are not a one-size fits all; holding such a view is extremely wasteful. For example, if a certain class of IT investments are governed by a higher order policy leveraging a constrained technology solution space, a strategy of solution risk avoidance rather than mitigation means there is no "Architecture" activity and themed period of time. That is to say, there are no high-stakes solution decisions to be made and including such a governance structure would only serve to insert delay into the all important feedback loop. The architectural iterations already occurred on previous projects and is being reused, so no distinct, let alone lengthy theme of risk mitigation is necessary. Similarly, taking a product management lifecycle for N+1 generations of a product may not require the scoping activity due to the Opex/Capex boundary and the projectization of the Endeavor. Trying to treat all software development as batched projects also yields a sub-optimal value stream configuration. Finally, in purely speculative developments, discovery may require a differing stance on discharging fiduciary as mandated by Venture Capitalists, and key performance indicators are likely tied to a Startups pitch deck, with toll-gates representing different rounds of funding.

In summary, Figure 6.11 illustrates one possible holistic value-stream configuration, the themed periods of time that result from the lifecycle choice, the key decisions to be made, the KPI's, the workproducts that are consumed for adjudication, and the stakeholder communities who will perform the assessment:

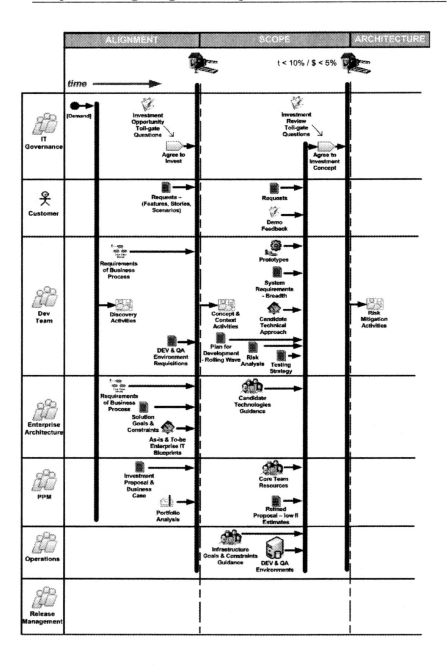

Figure 6.11 – Holistic Investment Governance View

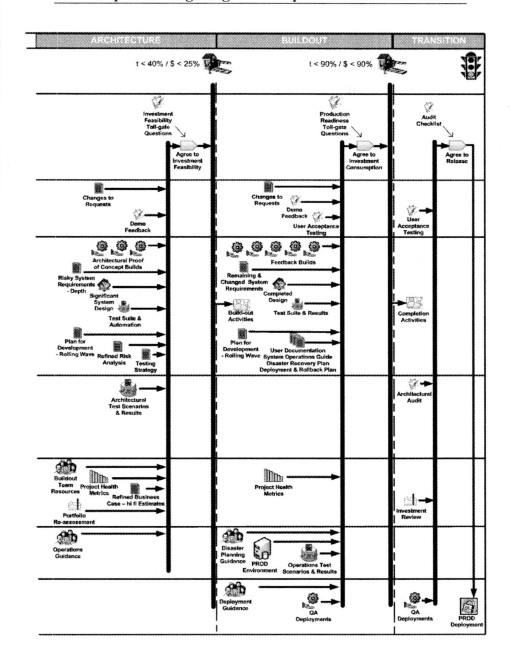

Figure 6.11 – Holistic Investment Governance View

6.3 – Lean Business-IT Alignment

The first activity that is part of the core Enterprise Software Value Stream is that of Business-IT Alignment. Alternatively, if a purely speculative venture is undertaken, this activity of the Value Stream is typically called "Discovery". This themed period of time serves to identify demand for IT service changes and product development that will support reconfigured and improved business processes. These activities are typically fulfilled by organizational units referred to as Enterprise Architecture (EA) in the former case or an Innovation Center of Excellence (COE) or Research and Development center in the latter [13]. Elaborating on the former case, EA organizations support this core mission through developing specialized-generalist capability around business architecture (business modeling, business process improvement, business process "whatever"), and around application and infrastructure architecture. The scope of EA is broader than that of single system architecture (sometimes called Technical Architecture) due to the fact that alignment to business processes usually crosses business organizations (or companies) and involves the integration of sometimes many business systems. As such EA deals with the alignment of business process change as realized by *systems-of-systems*.

While most Agilist's view the EA function as waste, it does serve a useful purpose in that business process opportunities are identified in what could be termed a complex business system. The controversy typically hinges around immature EA organizations that launch into "boil-the-ocean" modeling exercises. The rationale usually given for these grandiose visions is that the business needs "blueprints". Unfortunately, this usually devolves to include the assertion that the business also needs detailed system-of-system blueprints at fine-grained levels of detail, just-in-case. With this latter point, "just-in-case" is the key to resolving the tension between the perspectives of value-add vs. total waste or *Muda* [14]. The answer regarding the differing views on the subject of EA is that they are both right. The business is willing to pay for innovative business process ideas that are identified through reasoning and approaches to reduce complexity. Achieving innovation results in direct value in terms of efficiency and effectiveness, customer satisfaction or increased market share. As such, it fits within the definition of value-add as required by *Lean Thinking*. But the fact that Business-IT Alignment deserves a place in the IT Value-Stream does not mean that it should be performed in a manner contrary to the ideals or lessons of Lean. Performing big-bang alignment activities that cause delay in the downstream realization work/projects is waste and drastically affects the overall flow. Instead, Lean Enterprise Architecture focuses on creating flow through pull by limiting the alignment work-in-progress.

The Open Group Architecture Framework – TOGAF [15] is arguably the most common EA body of knowledge that exists in industry. Importantly, the constituency associated with this alignment approach is unlikely to depart wholesale towards an ultra-lightweight approach like *Emergent Architecture* [16] and replace all forms of reasoning about enterprise complexity with loosely formed statements of coarse-grained demand - *Epics* [17] in the Agile community. The critical issue to address is to prevent application of the entire bloated piece of process-ware at face value. A pragmatic perspective must be introduced which attempts to always question the efficacy of the various elements of the value network. Figure 6.12 illustrates a TOGAF Architecture Development Method (ADM) [15] Iteration at a high level, and Figure 6.13 illustrates the "leaning out" of the workflow:

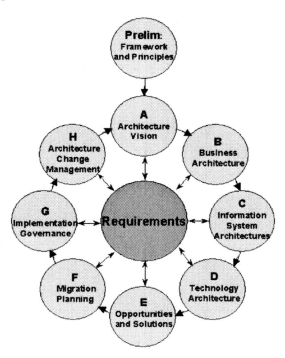

Figure 6.12 – TOGAF Architecture Development Method [15]

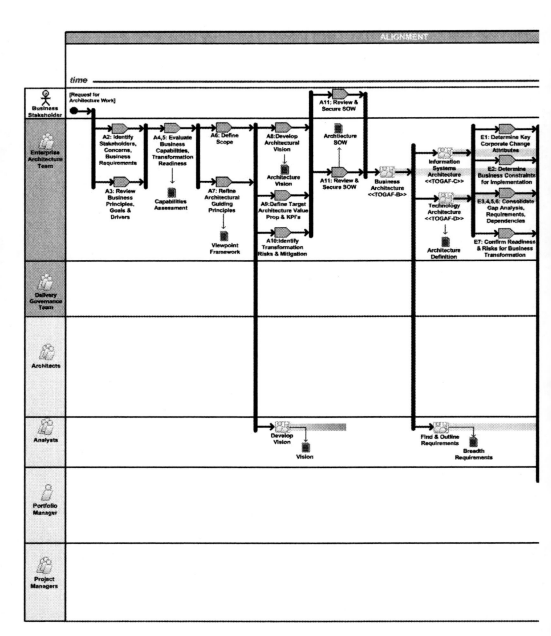

Figure6.13 – Lean TOGAF Workflow

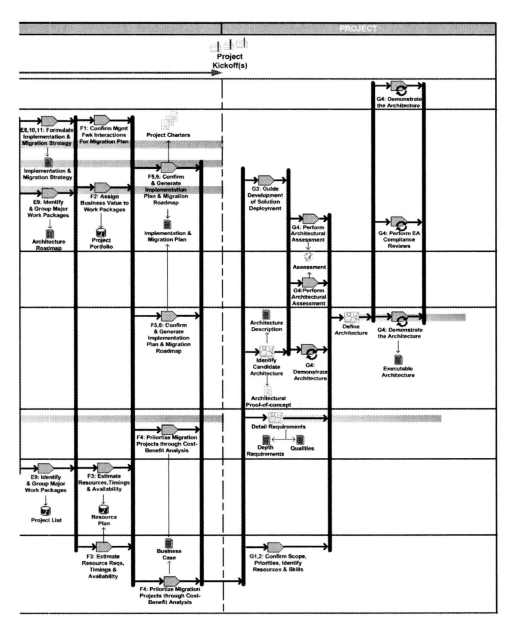

Figure 6.13 – Lean TOGAF Workflow

As we see in the previous model, there is a tight interplay between the value-stream activities of Business-IT Alignment and resource optimization. IT Resource Optimization is all about ensuring that an expensive resource is leveraged in as optimal way as possible. This means that where the Enterprise Architecture function identifies IT Investment opportunities based on alignment reasoning, the Project & Portfolio Management (PPM) capability should be brought to bear to match supply with demand. Management and investment analysis skills that are common within Project Management circles should be leveraged to their fullest extent such that the identified demand is realized in a value-centric prioritization. That is to say, the first value proposition of Project Management is in determining through cost-benefit analysis what investment returns should be expected. From this assessment of "the biggest bang for the buck", the PPM organization then matches demand with available IT supply. Such resource optimization adds value by pulling IT supply to realize the demand based on problem domain, required solution domain skill-sets and resource availability.

Once demand has been discovered for IT Delivery, one or more Product Backlogs of some form are established, or in the case of sustainment demand, existing Product Backlogs are updated. The natural question to ask is how much demand should be batched within the up-front alignment and resource optimization effort. From Lean Thinking, we know that the highest productivity is established by reducing cycle times. To do this we leverage pull-systems to limit WIP. This means that the Business-IT Alignment activity performed by an Enterprise Architecture organization, and the Resource Optimization activity, performed by the PPM function should work in a one-piece flow rather than a batching mode. Instead of batching demand, Product Backlogs should be seeded for each discrete "business change request". This enables the just-in-time pull of IT supply resources. Rather than launching into discrete multi-year batched planning exercises that coincide with budgeting cycles, single Business-IT Alignment requests should continuously flow downstream. Whether the demand results in one or more project's or existing products require adaptive maintenance, demand should flow as fast as possible without incurring the waste of waiting/delay.

Another area within the Business-IT Alignment activity that requires some *Lean Thinking* application is in the area of associated Viewpoint frameworks that supports the ADM and defines the recommended work products to be produced. While TOGAF defines a generic Viewpoint framework within its almost 800 pages, the common Viewpoint framework chosen within EA circles is the Zachman framework [18]. One of the reasons for the perspective within Agile circles that EA is wasteful is probably due to this framework. Whether you agree with the basis for the meta-model or not, it is kind of hard to disagree with the perspective that 30 Views and diagrams is a little over done. The framework is good in that it articulates the notion of levels of abstraction, such that reasoning can progress towards more detail. The problem is that there is not guidance as to how to navigate the cells, or the semantic relationships between the views. This is important because it is this navigation process that reflects the ADM. Also, one would be hard pressed to establish a system's theory basis for the choice of "what, how, when, who, where and why" as the decomposition of the views. Noting that this framework originated in 1987, Figure 6.14 illustrates John Zachman's framework.

Figure 6.14 – The Zachman Framework [18]

One could easily argue that this framework represents the kind of "just-in-case" philosophy everyone has lived through in their past companies or engagements. And because of the scale and complexity of the *system-of-systems* under study when dealing with any non-trivial business, it is no wonder that numerous "boil-the-ocean" scenarios have unfolded. Requiring that all 30 views be produced in the odd chance that some stakeholder somewhere may consume the work product to address some lingering concern represents not only over-processing waste, but inventory waste.

One Viewpoint framework that reduces waste and represents a systematic ADM is the 3+1 Views Viewpoint framework [19]. This amplification and simplification of the 4+1 Views of Architecture approach [20] advocated within UP projects reduces the number of necessary Views/Viewpoints to only eight. It is minimalistic and sufficient to address all concerns that stakeholders may have, and provides a systematic model-driven development approach for business-IT alignment, including Service-Oriented Architecture (SOA) reasoning and service identification. Figure 6.15 illustrates the EA extensions within the 3+1 Views approach.

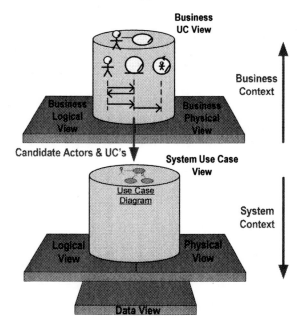

Figure 6.15 – "3+1 Views" EA Framework [19]

In this picture, a model-driven approach for the realization of business processes starts with understanding the context of the business and its core business processes. The Business Use Case View captures this context and identifies who the customers are through the use of business actors. Business-IT alignment activity continues through the reasoning of the business processes. These Business Use Case Realizations articulate the business worker roles, business entities and business system services that will make the operational value propositions within the business context come to life. It is from these process models that identification of required services, systems and interfaces is achieved. Without such a reasoning technique, it would be left to the business to attempt to articulate IT need. Once required system interfaces are identified, these become candidate system Use Cases, each potentially requiring realization modeling in the event that they are complex or cannot be acquired and must be built from scratch. This system level of model driven development is what is commonly associated with the CASE tool era mentioned earlier.

Figure 6.16 that follows illustrates details of the relationships between the stakeholders, their typical concerns, and the diagrams that are useful in addressing these concerns. It also shows the correlation among the views and the UML diagram types that are typically leveraged. In the above figures, a model driven development iteration starts with identification and communication of system value propositions captured for a system under consideration. Typically performed graphically through what is known as a Use Case Diagram, this viewpoint is focused on breadth and establishes context through the identification of interrelated systems and what is out through "actors". Textually this same information has historically been captured in a Use Case Model Survey, which is supposed to be minimalist, and akin to a Product Backlog but without the queuing overtone. Iterations are planned by selecting instances of Use Cases to realize or build (not entire Use Cases). These instances are scenarios, and are equivalent to User Stories with fully elaborated acceptance tests. Scenarios are dynamic, and therefore are orthogonal to the static type oriented Use Case Diagram. Through first identifying analysis or "what" abstractions that make up the scenario the logical structure of the system can systematically be discovered as represented as "what" classes — technology neutral abstractions. This is followed by deeper realizations of the scenarios, where lifelines in the scenario visualizations (sequence diagrams) are "pulled apart" using design patterns such that design or "how" classes emerge. These design classes are then realized within components behind interfaces based on analysis of coupling, cohesion and likelihood of change in the Physical View.

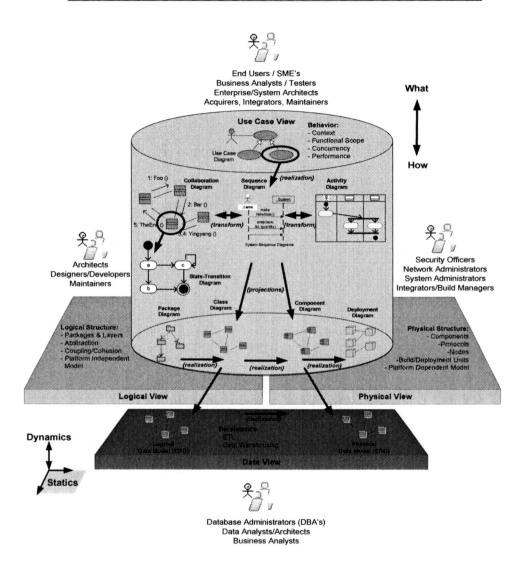

Figure 6.16 – 3+1 Views of Architecture [19]

The critical value-add of this framework is that it enables flow through the well defined path that is articulated. This mitigates the risk that often materializes where teams get stuck in any one view and attempt to gold plate the diagrams, losing site on the overall objective of realizing them in software.

6.4 – Core Development

It is all too easy to simplify the Value Stream to just those tasks and work products that are close to where the rubber meets the road - coding. Whether self serving or not, or resulting from the social undercurrents described in Chapter 1, many methods and communities take certain liberties or make certain assumptions of how this core activity integrates with the broader enterprise. It is no wonder that grass roots capability improvements like "Agile Transformations" run into serious difficulty when they step outside their 7 +- 2 sweet-spot. Mystery and mystique surround such simple issues like the timing and emergence of product backlogs, how software investments get capitalized, or what happens to software once it has been developed and needs to find its way into production. The devil is in the details as they say.

Development as a core Value Stream activity is the primary value contributor in the stream, and is separate and apart from Governance, which interfaces with the core stream but is off to the side. Lifecycles of various forms represent governance structures, not core development work. Due to the universal kernel discussed in Chapter 5 and the need for feedback, attempts to convolute a lifecycle with the core development activity artificially sequence work that would otherwise be highly concurrent. Without the obfuscation of the overall product delivery lifecycle getting in the way, we can see 3 distinct segments or periods of time related to the software development ecosystem as a team traverses a single iteration through the feedback loop to produce a product increment. These distinct segments are 1) the continuous fine-grained demand capture, triaging, approval and prioritization into release increments; 2) the work actually being performed, including planning and facilitating work, elaboration, design, implementation, integrating, building, testing and preparing for deployments; and 3) evaluating the results and learning/improvement.

In the case of the first segment, the creation of the "reference signal" for the project or endeavor is created and constantly tuned and refined. The typical and generally accepted practice for realizing this is *Product Backlog Management* [21]. Once scope is put in-progress, *Use Case Driven* work is a common suite of practices that still to this day offers a balanced set of choices. *Workflow-centric Configuration Management* and *Continuous Integration* support the performing of work in all segments. Figure 6.17 and the following sections describe these common core development practices:

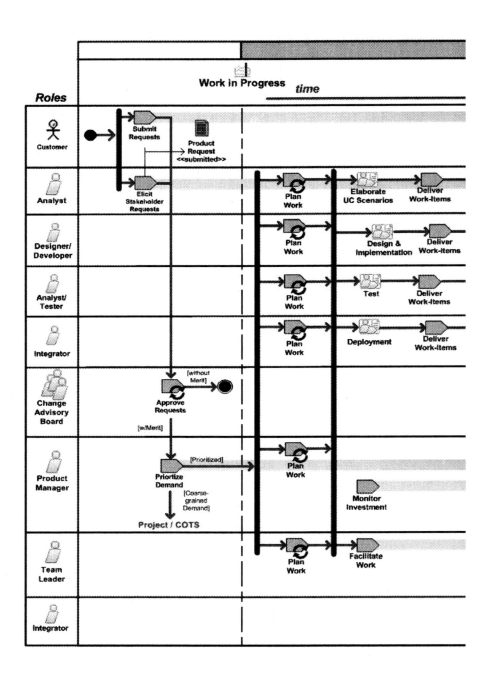

Figure 6.17 – Core Value Stream Activity - Development

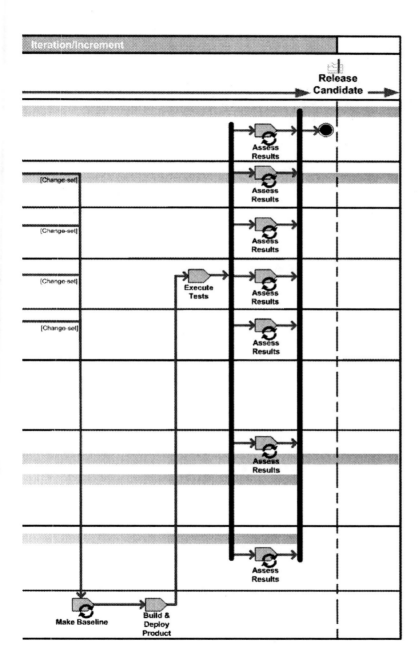

Figure 6.17 – Core Value Stream Activity

6.4.1 – Product Backlog Management

A very simple concept based on queuing theory, a *Product Backlog* is simply a constantly re-prioritized mechanism for collecting and managing product requests. It serves as the interface to the customer and represents all demand for IT service for a particular product. There can be many physical forms of a Product Backlog, from low-tech yellow Post-it notes on a whiteboard (the usual Agile practice), a stack of 4-by-6 index cards in queued stacks, or electronic versions from various vendors. When leveraging Use Cases, the Use Case Model Survey serves the same purpose, but using a much more static form of a document. If one replaces a document-centric strategy with a more lightweight or data-centric form, you achieve the same intent. One key concept of the Product Backlog is that it is the Customer or *Product Owner* who is responsible for managing the backlog – including submission, prioritization and obsolescence of items. This effectively removes the need for a Change Control Board (CCB), and implies that Analysts with subject matter expertise would fit such a role. This fundamental paradigm shift related to scope management favors embracing the reality of changing scope rather than trying to control it. Figure 6.18 illustrates the concept of a Product Backlog. Product requests are collected, prioritized and typically allocated into time-boxed iterations for completion. A similar mechanism called a *Sprint Backlog* is also used for managing the work breakdown for the iteration – the tasks/work items necessary to fulfill the demand. This backlog is used internally by the team for coordination and management visibility and mid-iteration assessments.

Figure 6.18 – Product Backlog Queue Prioritization [21]

The key idea introduced with Backlogs is that the team is forced to "put first things first" and work the highest priority items first. Instead of leveraging an overly detailed and potentially prescriptive task sequencing found in command-and-control style schedules based on Critical Path Method [22], the backlog mechanics reflect the fact that far more fluidity exists in modern software development. Note that the Product Backlog is never likely to be complete or empty until a product is retired. As such it reflects a Product Management versus a Project Management perspective.

6.4.2 Performing Core Work using Use Case Driven Practices

Use Case [23] requirements elicitation techniques are an example of what could be termed generically "scenario-based practices". Scenarios are "instances" of Use Case "types". In other words, scenarios are the objects formed out of the Use Case class which bundles all the possible run-time variances of behavior. The Use Case type is an important, customer-centric abstraction of desired observable behavior which yields a valuable result in their eyes. As such they can be thought of as an interface to the system to be developed. It hides the complexity of all the permutations and combinations of potential behavior which must be considered and is of interest to the internal development team. Figure 6.19 illustrates the relationships between Use Cases and their scenarios.

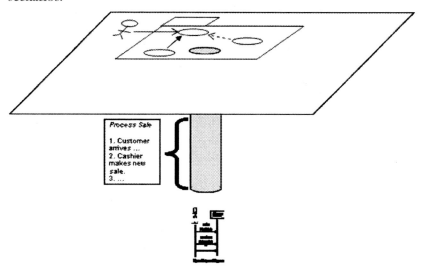

Figure 6.19 – Use Case breadth versus depth

Given the logical scope for a system captured within either a Product Backlog or within a Use Case Model Survey, work proceeds on the basis of selecting some subset of the entire requirements set to elaborate. Elaboration of the details of a Use Case represents the "deep dives" beyond the "mile-wide and inch deep" intent capture within the Backlog. Elaborating each Use Case to whatever degree of formality means working through the complexity of the conversation between the actor and the system and the bundles of scenarios that comprise the functionality. Definition of the normal flow of events (the "happy path") and the various alternative flows and exceptional flows is akin to putting the flesh on the bones beyond the basic functionality of the system. Prioritization of which Use Cases to elaborate and which scenarios to build out at any point in time is dependent upon the prioritization approach to the backlog or the lifecycle. It should be noted that scenarios are also applied to other forms of requirements like quality attributes / non-functional requirements. In this case they are known as *Quality Scenarios* [24].

A common misconception is that Use Cases are heavyweight and wasteful. This is probably due to the examples of "documentation for the sake of documentation" that have occurred from time to time, which is symptomatic of deeper problems like a lack of appreciation of iterative development practice. Use Case Elaborations and their scoping Use Case Model Survey are essentially equivalent to the Agile practices of User Stories and User Story Mapping. The main difference is the cohesion that each Use Case provides and the semantic relationships with other modeling viewpoints. User Stories have no semantic relevance and are essentially flat without any nesting or packaging. Due to the fact that they are intended to only facilitate conversations between developer and customer, their persistence only arises in regards to the acceptance tests, which emerge as more and more stories are built.

6.4.3 Workflow-Centric Configuration Management

Support for the storage and accounting of workproducts created as result of a team performing work is through configuration management practices and infrastructure. If we combine Product Backlog Management and basic file oriented configuration management with workflow technology, the result is process-centric or workflow-centric configuration management. Such an approach supports the collection of meaningful workflow metrics in a pragmatic fashion due to the fact that instrumentation of the process is implicit and only requires the usage of the system and production of "natural artifacts". If customer demand capture is constrained in such a way as to represent similar granularity across product requests, then automatic timestamps can be leveraged to yield cycle-time metrics and therefore indicate productivity – either overall across a program over time, or among the various teams realizing the requests. The state-machine of a Product Request represents the start-to-finish lifecycle of the demand, so capturing the work-in-progress transition event and comparing it to the delivery transition event yields cycle-time. Obviously, when looking for root causes in relation to poor throughput, internal timing data can be leveraged.

Figure 6.20 illustrates Workflow-centric Configuration Management:

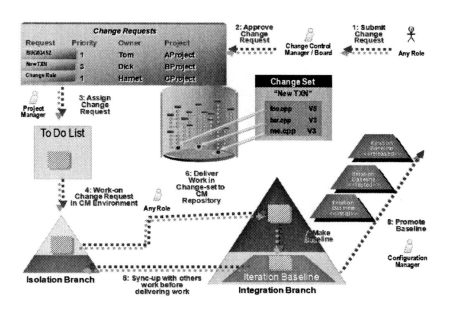

Figure 6.20 – Workflow-centric Configuration Management

6.4.4 Continuous Integration and Test

Continuous Integration (CI) is a practice originating out of the XP community that is commonly mentioned in conjunction with Agile. It could be argued that it was popularized and made practical by Martin Fowler from ThoughtWorks through the contribution of an open source tool called *Cruise-Control* [25]. This practice is now a hallmark of the typical custom development project that is deemed Agile, with most if not all Configuration Management (CM) vendors claiming CI capability. The key concept is to integrate and test early and often (common with all modern software development), but CI takes this concept to the extreme, with a per check-in build being triggered. Issues typically arise when builds do not have time to finish for extremely large developments, or with product-line and multi-generational product management, so various strategies exist to support near continuous integration, with staged builds and variations in build scope. With more robust parallel development strategies and their use of branches, integration build and test triggers occur on a per-demand element (feature, story, scenario, activity), so "effective" integration from the isolation occurring due to branching occurs at a less frequent pace. Along with the build trigger mechanism that ties CM infrastructure with build servers, unit test jobs are also triggered at a near continuous frequency with the key goal to prevent defects from "breaking the build", thereby ensuring project health. Visual mechanisms are commonly leveraged like the always popular *lava-lamp*; specifically, it changes colors when a build is broken, and adds bubbles the longer builds remain broken. This practice is effectively equivalent to the Lean concept of *poka yoke*, which means "mistake proofing".

Continuous/near continuous release is a little more contentious of a practice it turns out when dealing with most complex IT organizations. With the Agile practice of *Potentially Shippable Increment*, the intent is to have a complete increment of a product ready for a customer. The key issue is the ability for the business customer to consume a release. More often than not, the frequency by which demand is realized and is shippable is higher than the frequency of release cycles. This is due to the inherent risks associated with change, and leads naturally to the discovery of a frequency that matches the nature of the demand and the nature of the risks. At whatever frequency realized demand can be "pulled" by the customer, any deployment must be automated and scripted for repeatability and avoidance of human errors, and integrate with Release Management orchestration.

6.5 – Lean Acquisition

One of the quickest ways to improve outcomes and reduce the amount of waste produced within Enterprise IT is to "build less stuff". Establishing an acquisition-orientation which favors leveraging pre-existing assets over custom development is also consistent with the Lean Product Development practices as seen in the Toyota Product Development System (TPDS) [26]. Leveraging standard, reusable parts enables rapid delivery and responsiveness to market demands with little downside. Conscious limiting of technology choices starts with investment in strategic reuse in the form of product lines (in Toyota's case reusable chassis and power trains for yearly models), or more fine grained reuse through off-the-shelf commodity parts rather than one-off design-from scratch components.

The strategy requires explicit attention to these purposeful constraints by architects. To do this, active consideration of Commercial-Off-the-Shelf "buy" options must be performed in parallel with any build fall-back. And this should be governed as part of the Investment Alignment and Feasibility periods of time. In some environments attempting to make strategic large order reuse a systematic part of solution fulfillment is mandated as policy. The most notable example is the US Federal Government. Through study of the Defense Science Board, the decision was taken to establish policy that mandates the use of commercial technologies instead of internal development, which was viewed as not being a core competency [27].

From study of the experiences within the sometimes very large scale acquisitions, knowledge has been captured as to the subtle differences between development and acquisition. This experience has been harvested by organizations like the Software Engineering Institute at Carnegie Mellon University who publish guidance to industry and government as a result of their research funding. Within the COTS-based Software Engineering initiative (CBSE), one body of knowledge has emerged that mirrors Lean Thinking concepts of set-based, concurrent engineering and real-options theory in its articulation. The Evolutionary Process for Integrating COTS (EPIC) [28] presumably leveraged some of the very same concepts from TPDS as applied to software. Figure 6.21 illustrates this body of knowledge.

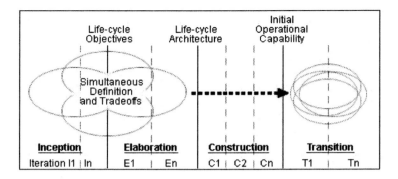

Figure 6.21 – Convergence of decision trade space [28]

The lifecycle framework used to articulate and deliver a governance structure around these concepts was that of the Unified Process. The EPIC body of knowledge is manifested in two forms – a 275 page document that could be argued as being bloated, and as content that is additive to the Rational Unified Process web-delivered product [29].

While some within the Agile community would claim that they "do COTS", the claim is not without skepticism. This is because many of the practices assume a custom development environment. Some of the practices, when strictly interpreted, are inconsistent with the nature of COTS acquisition. Due to the scale typically involved in the large acquisitions that have been studied within the DOD, enforcing a specific frequency of iteration can be problematic. This wouldn't necessarily be a problem if the intent of the practice was embraced, not the prima facie interpretation.

The best way to describe acquisition is akin to Test-driven Development as opposed to requirements driven development. This is something that Agile can rally around, but the tests are more like acceptance tests or test scenarios than the typical TDD unit tests. Figure 6.22 illustrates the distinctly different sequence of events in a COTS Acquisition iteration.

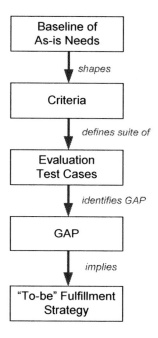

Figure 6.22 – "Test-Driven" Acquisition

When one boils all of the content of EPIC into a practical set of persisted work products and reasoning techniques coherent within an UP-like product lifecycle, one arrives at a workflow articulation like the following in Figure 6.21.

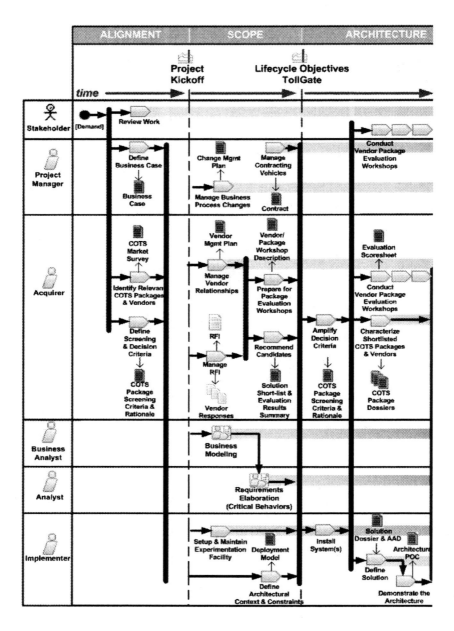

Figure 6.23 – Lean Acquisition Workflow [30]

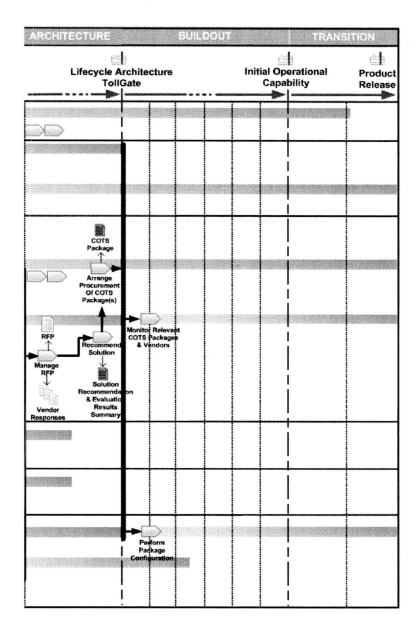

Figure 6.23 – Lean Acquisition Workflow [30]

One criticism with EPIC, which arguably is the best modern software acquisition research that the industry has in terms of reflection within DOD and US Federal Government circles, is that it comes up short in the "how" department. It is left to the practitioner to bring in various experiences and practices to make it actionable and Lean.

Note that placeholder stories will not suffice unless accompanied by their acceptance tests. This is due to the degree of stakeholder concurrence and negotiation that often accompanies COTS acquisition of any scale. This reality occurs because the decision to acquire rather than "require" necessarily involves business process change. And unfortunately Agile is silent on business process analysis and change, as it doesn't amount to code. The upfront reasoning (gap analysis) has nothing to do with coding. In fact, coding of any form is discouraged when an acquisition-orientation is taken, as customization beyond the recommended practice of a vendor has been known to cause large order pain and suffering. This is due to the fact that the Vendor made explicit decisions about what the market requirements were at the outset of building a COTS, and they therefore are in control of not only the requirements but the code that realizes this scope. If they change their mind, or just upgrade, breakage ensues with any customization that is below the radar.

The above discussion implies that tradeoffs are present in relation to the choice to acquire marketplace offerings. This constrains the Lean organization (by design) and requires awareness by everyone involved that full degrees of freedom are a luxury not present in the COTS form factor. Figure 6.24 illustrates the nature of the tradeoffs in play.

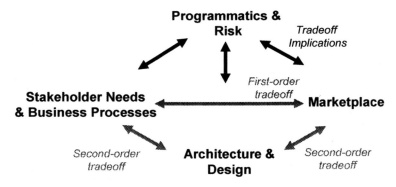

Figure 6.24 – Spheres of influence in Acquisition [30]

The biggest implication of choices made among the various *Spheres of Influence* on the decision making process is along the axis of Business Process criteria and Marketplace offerings. Choices made among conflicts in this first order dimension and the second order tradeoffs with existing enterprise architectural choices leads to implications in terms of cost, benefit and risk. Figure 6.25 articulates this through the asymmetrical shape in the spheres.

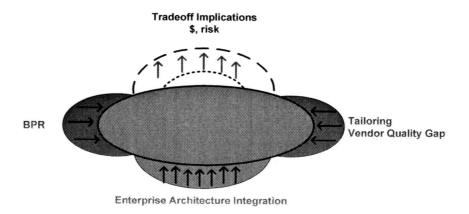

Figure 6.25 – Implications of Convergence on a COTS Solution [30]

It should be noted that not all COTS are equal and there exists a spectrum in which varying degrees of "tailoring" or "configuration" are possible. Here, normal Agile practices find their home. And the focus on working software for feedback is also consistent with the tenets of modern software engineering. Experimentation or test execution is to be established quickly, and the narrowing of the candidate solution space proceeds in an iterative and evolutionary manner.

Due to the fact that COTS acquisition is performed at a business process level, typically high complexity exists due to the sheer scope of the value streams involved. Here, one technique that can and should be leveraged to facilitate an understanding of gap is visual modeling. Figure 6.26 illustrates the usage of visualization in gap reasoning.

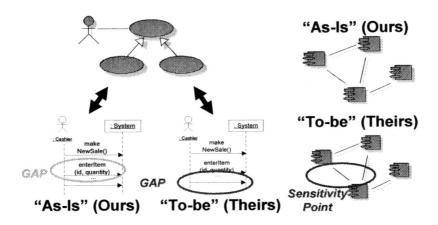

Figure 6.26 – Leveraging Visual Modeling for Gap Analysis [30]

But these efforts cannot degrade into "boil-the-ocean" exercises. One way to prevent this is to leverage pull and one-piece flow from Lean. Visualization is only one tool to leverage in understanding and quantifying gap. Other skills and techniques come from multivariate reasoning approaches such as Multi-attribute Utility Tree analysis [31], Analytical Hierarchy Process – AHP [32] Kepner Tregoe [33] Cost-Benefit Analysis Method-CBAM [34] in conjunction with Architectural Tradeoff Method – ATAM [35]. An example of how to correlate the spheres of influence to a Multi-attribute Utility Tree - MAUT is shown in Figure 6.27:

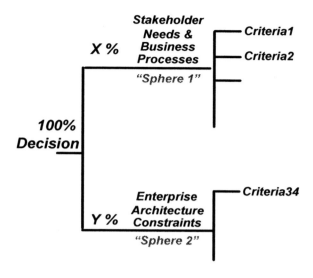

Figure 6.27 – Multi-attribute decision reasoning technique [30]

The results of what are typically open-space testing and evaluation (sometimes called conference-room pilots) are leveraged to enable both visual and economic based evaluation of alternatives through the above techniques, and to enable multi-stakeholder constituency negotiation and collaboration such that convergence on a feasible solution occurs in as Lean and rapid a fashion as possible. In this process, management expertise can play a vital role in delivering leadership. Skills such as vendor management, negotiation and facilitation are critical capabilities of the management specialization.

6.6 – Lean Service Transition

The area where IT Delivery (sometimes referred to as "Apps") meets IT Operations (sometimes referred to as "Ops") is known as Release Management. This is the portion of the Value Stream which encompasses the DevOps Movement, which strives to facilitate better integration and collaboration between these often silo'ed and disjoint organizational units. The purpose of this capability is to reduce the risk of change to the business. One body of knowledge that is typically referenced for Release Management practices is ITIL – the IT Infrastructure Library [36]. This compendium of IT Service Management (ITSM) practices is published by the government of the United Kingdom. ITIL v3 is divided into five "books", namely Service Strategy, Service Design, Service Transition, Service Operations and Continual Service Improvement. While it could be argued that this governmental organization has established a great deal of experience related to IT practices, it would be unreasonable to suggest that the entire value-stream is served by ITIL as the authoritative source of knowledge. Other BOKs have far more insight into certain practices, including for example the three modern software engineering communities or the IEEE SWEBOK [37] when it comes to Service Design. However, when it comes to Service Transition and Service Operations, ITIL is definitely seen as the leading BOK.

Similar to the other activities within the value stream, the practices leveraged are contextual. That means that various context factors will discriminate the risk profile of using one over the other. In the ITIL-based Release Management practice, the contextual appropriateness is where segregation of duties is mandated by a compliance mandate such as Sarbanes Oxley (SOX) and SAS-70 audits. Achieving compliance in these contexts requires strict access controls to segregated environments, and organizational boundaries related to these controls that establish what could be termed "silo'ing". The other critical aspect in such compliance environments is *positive acknowledgement* which requires formalities and evidentiary quality in terms of multi-disciplinary signoffs from clearly defined stakeholder communities. Agilists often claim this to be indicative of a "low trust" culture. Nevertheless, it is reality, as the organizations who pass down audit findings get to be the judge and jury when deliberating on this standard of care. Figure 6.26 below illustrates the relationship of Release Management as it pertains to ITIL v3's view of changes within a business enterprise.

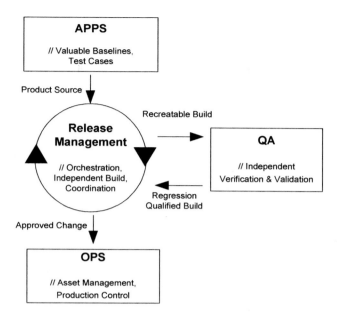

Figure 6.28 –Release Management Orchestration

When it comes to the topic of Lean Thinking in relation to Release Management, Toyota's revolutionary step was to take Piggly Wiggly's supermarket replenishment system and drive it back to at least half way through their automobile factories [38]. Their challenge today is to drive it all the way back to their goods-inwards dock. Recognizing JIT could be driven back up the supply chain has reaped Toyota huge benefits and a world dominating position in the auto industry. When one looks at how Toyota ships finished cars to market however, one sees a different decoupled process dynamic. While automobiles are still "pulled" to market via constrained transportation resources (Roll-on, Roll-off ships) and associated queuing or staging docks, this is done in a batched manner. This is due to the inherent risks associated with the physical barriers of oceans and continents, and the economy of scale that batching yields related to the risk mitigation associated with "deployment".

Applying this metaphor to Software Product Development, one can extrapolate the notion of a Release Plan to that of the Production Forecast. The rough-order number of Requests is forecast within the

Release Plan which is based on known Release "ferry" capacity which reflects current demand trends and customer budget. When Requests are fulfilled, they arrive in the staging area and are "baselined" together; the analogy of this is adding a car's VIN to the ships waybill. Requests that arrive to the "dock" in time are eligible to be included in the baseline, and can therefore be included in the Release. Requests that do not meet minimum lead times for inclusion on the "ship" must wait for the next scheduled departure. One can see that with this analogy, Releases establish a finish-to-finish dependency among Requests, where instead of batching the commencement of work by grouping demand into iterations, batching occurs only when the Requests are fulfilled and are staged.

In Software Development, the parallel to the risks associated with the shipping of product to market in the case of automobiles is related to overall product quality and the risk of regression due to production changes. Regression testing mitigates this risk, but at a cost. Segregated testing resources and the necessary regression suite maintenance add to the total-cost-of-release. Therefore, release frequencies (ferry departures) are selected to balance the risks of change and the risks of delays of product to market. Note that all changes are not created equal. Delivery of defects and non-risky enhancements can occur more frequently due to the smaller risk mitigation measures. The analogy is the use of smaller, more frequent transport ferries. The matching of transfer batches to the just-in-time downstream process needs (regression testing) serves as another waste reduction measure. Over-processing waste should be avoided where higher ceremony releases and their associated controls are not warranted. Waste related to delay and waiting on delivery of product to the broader business process should be mitigated through the ability to release in a right-sized way for smaller batches of demand. In this way, total cost-of-release is balanced with time-to-value considerations using a risk management perspective.

The key practice that supports efficient and effective releases into the production environment has been termed *"Process-centric Configuration Management"* [39]. This practice enables informed decisions as to what is being released to production and what acceptance and regression testing is required. By combining change management / request tracking with configuration management versioning and baseline management, automated "waybills" can be produced. Figure 6.29 captures a detailed workflow model of ITIL-compliant Service Transition:

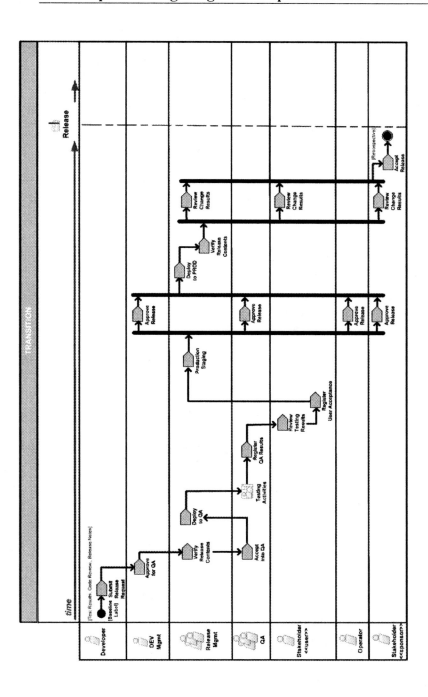

Figure 6.29 – ITIL v3 Release Management

As our focus towards flow and maximizing productivity upstream in the Value Stream evolves as a result of shifting dynamics, so too should adaptation towards smaller and smaller batches during service transition. During this last mile, all of the practice choices made from the entire upstream activities come to bear and shape and constrain our Release Management discipline. Evolving towards Continuous Delivery requires much automation and tight seamless integration among the various toolsets. This begins further upstream with the practice of continuous or near-continuous integration. This implies that configuration management infrastructure is integrated with build and release/deployment automation, and metadata associated with demand is readily available for automated production of the release bill of materials. Automation such as various build engines trigger the storage of the various derived build objects into a repository and initiate the release orchestration workflow, including deployments and the triggering of execution of regression suites, again which are only available if they too are created in smaller batches earlier in the Value Stream. Human involvement is still necessary in all but the most risk tolerant contexts such as startups. Any publically traded company will likely have to have some form of positive acknowledgement signoffs, and likely will have manual User Acceptance testing. Continuous Delivery pragmatically means driving towards the highest degree of automation which in itself removes much of the dysfunction of treating testing and release discipline as an afterthought. It does not realistically imply no gating by humans.

One of the most complex topics related to enabling flow and achieve the ideals of DevOps within Service Transition is Environment Management [40]. Without the ability to seed environments with the test regression suite and data set corresponding to a product baseline, the ideals of Continuous Delivery are a pipe dream. Unless software products are not to be tested effectively, the ability to achieve this degree of automation likely involves virtualization. Technologies in this space include IBM's UrbanCode [41] and Parasoft Service Virtualization [42]. In this strategy, environments are spun up from images that are maintained in sync with the evolving test suite. It should be no surprise that the technologies that enable this degree of maturity are costly. With large modern enterprise portfolios comprising upwards of 200 applications, lack of automation would require the manual provisioning and management of over 600 environments. If these were physical environments, chaos would ensue. Figure 6.30 illustrates the core Continuous Delivery workflow:

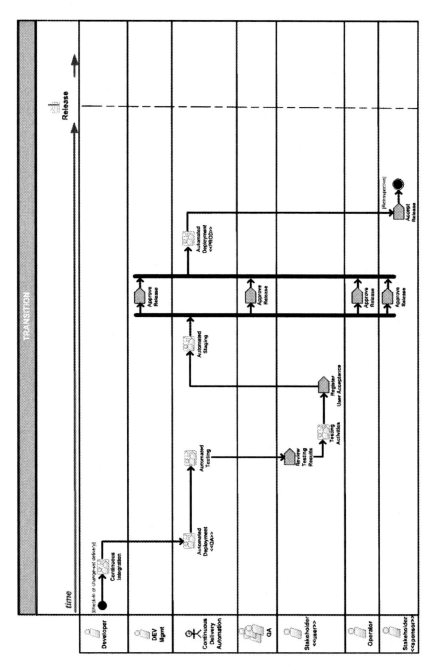

Figure 6.30 – Continuous Delivery Workflow

6.7 – Keeping it Real

The word "process" has been a dirty word for some time within Agile circles. Based on the era when the values of Agile were codified, it's no wonder. The stories of bloated process-ware are widespread. However, if you change the word "process" for the words "standard work", something interesting happens. The persistence of knowledge related to practices suddenly doesn't seem so offensive. This is because *Standard Work* is a key enabler to *Kaizen* in Lean Thinking, and Lean Thinking and Agile seem to get along.

Standard Work is a practice in which the approach for how work is performed is documented. That means the knowledge of how work is performed is persisted. It does not mean that this is a prescription. Nothing in the Standard Work component of the TPS implies that somehow by documenting procedures or practices is this knowledge static. Rather it is intended to represent a baseline of how work is currently performed, and it is continuously evolving. This is because when combined with Kaizen, the organization consistently strives to improve the standard baseline, and encourages improvement in this snapshot of contextual "best practice" over time as more is learned. Standard Work is a necessary component of achieving a Learning Organization, which will be discussed later in Chapter 10.

In the world of software engineering, we know that we cannot prescribe a deterministic process. It is in conflict with the nature of tacit knowledge and the nature of complicated or complex adaptive systems. However, persisting ways of working in a non-prescriptive way can have a stabilizing effect, removing delays due to the learning curve for how "our organization develops software". At a *type* level rather than a specific *instance*, the knowledge of how work should be approached adds value such that further non-linearities are not introduced into the delivery. Approaching method knowledge management in this manner is contrary to the detailed work-breakdown structure approaches of the past which historically have degraded into prediction exercises. Instead, practice-oriented approaches attempt to abstract the general attributes of experience that has proven to yield success.

Advisor realizes the Lean notion of Standard Work by dynamically publishing the results of the team's latest practice choices into their own "Playbook". Figure 6.31 illustrates the currently declared Playbook for a team, showing one Value Stream activity network based on the corresponding button selected, in this case Development:

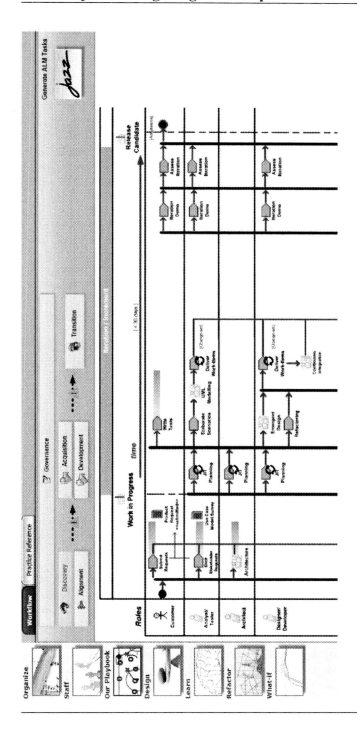

Figure 6.31 – Advisor's Dynamic Playbook (Workflow tab)

Historically, "process-ware" has been in the form of printed documents, typically in sets of binders that sit on shelves only to collect dust. Later approaches replaced this paradigm with online publishing. Modern process and practice management capability typically involved web published content in some sort of structure such that retrieval of knowledge is unimpeded and rapid. Early attempts at this approach include the RUP from IBM Rational and Process Continuum from Platinum Systems [43]. Unfortunately the misapplication of these knowledge assets has resulted in a perception similar to document based process descriptions. Anti-patterns include Ivory Tower process groups who seem to develop process for the sake of process with no real connection to how software is developed. Also contributing has been a lack of understanding of these assets as frameworks to be instantiated.

Moving beyond the publishing paradigm, *Advisor* enables rapid definition of contextual methods as a result of choices made to assemble sets of practices. The resultant workflow visualization provides feedback as to the net result of the team's playbook strategy. One benefit of this approach is that the team's way of working is a dynamic reflection of the underlying decisions rather than a "hard-wired" process. This prevents impediments to refactoring a team's approach as they learn more and capture learning's through retrospectives. This contrasts with the method publishing paradigm which becomes stale in a kind of fire-and-forget mode of knowledge management.

A second benefit of leveraging this approach within modern large-scale enterprise environments is a more cost effective knowledge transfer mechanism. In the absence of persisted forms of knowledge related to software delivery guidance, an over-reliance on coaches or mentors can occur. While the coaching and mentoring of personnel is a required element for traversing the knowledge transfer curve [44], focusing solely on this component of knowledge management can result in reliance on costly "master" level resources. To avoid vendor lock-in, tacit knowledge must be extracted over time at a reasonable pace to eventually replace external real-time coaching with internal mentoring candidates. Coaching is only one component in knowledge transfer and should be supplemented with book learning and classroom training. More importantly, much of the early stage learning has to occur before the leap between Apprentice and Practitioner can occur. Figure 6.32 illustrates the 7-Stages of Expertise model for Skills Acquisition:

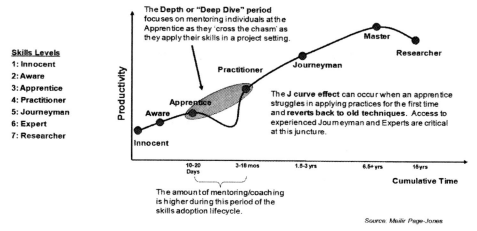

Skills Levels
1: Innocent
2: Aware
3: Apprentice
4: Practitioner
5: Journeyman
6: Expert
7: Researcher

The Depth or "Deep Dive" period focuses on mentoring individuals at the Apprentice as they 'cross the chasm' as they apply their skills in a project setting.

Master

Researcher

Practitioner

Journeyman

Apprentice

Aware

The J curve effect can occur when an apprentice struggles in applying practices for the first time and reverts back to old techniques. Access to experienced Journeyman and Experts are critical at this juncture.

Innocent

| 10-20 Days | 3-18 mos | 1.5-3 yrs | 6.5+ yrs | 15 yrs |

Cumulative Time

The amount of mentoring/coaching is higher during this period of the skills adoption lifecycle.

Source: Meilir Page-Jones

Figure 6.32 – Seven Stages of Software Engineering Expertise [44]

Without such a Standard Work facility as *Advisor*, what typically transpires is a huge amount of waste related to coaches filling in the blanks on the fly. In the worst case scenario, what results is "Cargo Cult" coaching [45], whereby coaches focus on this entry level knowledge transfer, going through the motions and filling up calendars with the various ceremonies and rituals rather than embedding deeply with the team and actually facilitating core value production. Instead, *Advisor* enables targeted, pull-based coaching whereby a team requests coaching on a per practice basis as they need it. This ensures that coaching goes to those individual's who need it, and expensive coaching cycles are not diluted in a "spread the jam thin" mode. All coaching requests are tracked and dispatched to the organization's master level personnel. Instead of coaches being assigned full time to a team, potentially forcing themselves upon the team, the team can raise a hand in the context of their work and ask for help. Asking for help is encouraged, and engagement with coaches on live software endeavors is accounted for in relation to results to determine cause-effect relationships of the knowledge transfer investments being made. Similarly, coaching requests count towards an individuals' learning curve for a practice or skill, which goes to their fitness scoring for assignment to projects. Figure 6.33 illustrates the *Advisor* Dynamic Playbook Practice Reference view of a teams chosen way of working:

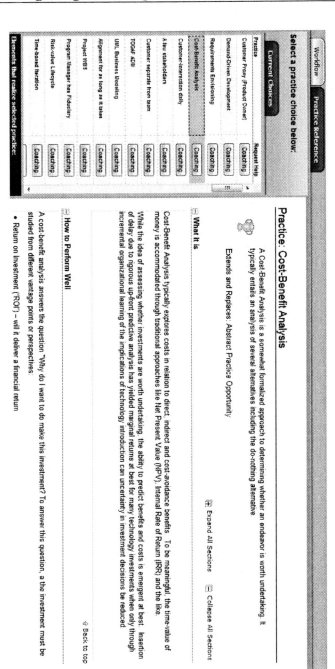

Figure 6.33 –Advisors' Dynamic Playbook (Practice Reference Tab)

Chapter 7: Common Form-factors in Software Development

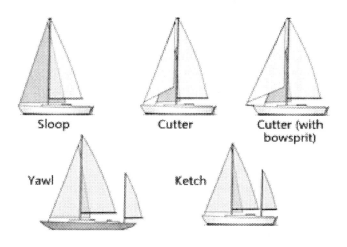

Sloop   Cutter   Cutter (with bowsprit)

Yawl   Ketch

"Form ever follows function" - *Louis Sullivan*

When you get right down to it, fundamentally unique software development projects occur infrequently in practice. While every project is different in the details by definition - different people, different detailed design, different business constraints and the like - only rarely does a radically new *skunk-works* [1] project surface in modern Enterprise IT. Projects typically fit within one of a few "form factors", and evolutionary forces drive specific novel practices to emerge as being useful and provide utility. A finite set of recurring patterns or archetypes exist that guide practice uniqueness within the universality of Generally Accepted Practice. Unfortunately, people tend to treat their management systems as a one-off and entirely novel.

To date, software delivery methods have been almost always constructed in such a way as to claim universality in their application, irrespective of the type of project that is being waged. With popular mainstream approaches, what's good for web or mobile development is good for a 6 million SLOC Cobol/CICS application. Scrum would be one of those methods which claims that due to its minimalistic "pressure cooker" design, it is always appropriate in the pure form. It is left to the teams and practitioners to do the mental gymnastics once problems arise that don't quite fit the rhetoric. When teams stray from populist doctrine, they are labeled "Scrumbutts" or "Faux Agile" [2]. While some bastardization definitely warrants being challenged by business investors, the above petty hazing or bullying does not represent the interests of those that care about optimal returns on investment.

The alternative is to allow teams to define their own "custom tailored suit" when it comes to their way of working. This approach is not without support from the perspective of organizational psychology, as will be discussed in Chapter 9. Instead of buying a popular method "off the rack" so to speak, a more optimal strategy than trying to fit a square peg into a round hole is to either declare new approaches from scratch, or leverage proven experience in the form of templates. Such templates emerge as *reference classes* because they have shown themselves to work on similar endeavors. As improvements occur related to these starter archetypes, an organization can evolve the templates to reflect new learning that work best for their business context. Several common project development types exist that serve as a stronger basis for structuring approach templates. These form factors reflect either the common problem space being addressed, or innovative and emerging technologies where the problems that can be addressed and the business models that are possible haven't been fully explored. The sections that follow will explore the subtle nuances of building software of the following project archetypes: Rich Internet Applications [3] based on Java/.Net and HTML5 [4], currently one of the most popular project types representing the lion share of the $930B spent globally in 2013 [5]; Mobile development, often coupled with RIA developments, growing at a rate of 44% totaling $26B in 2013 [6]; the worldwide market for Embedded Systems is estimated to be 160B euros [7], the software development of which amounts to a spend of $25B per year [8] ; Big Data initiatives that are growing at 30% CAGR [9], which could be lumped together with Predictive Analytics and other Data Warehousing initiatives; ERP COTS Package Acquisition and accompanying services, forecasted to hit $50B of IT spend globally by 2015 [10]; and legacy developments involving Cobol/CICS, adding 5 billion LOC yearly to the base of 200 billion LOC, still representing 60% of the worlds business applications [11].

7.1 – Rich Internet Applications (RIA)

Rich Internet Application developments are characterized by rapid time-to-market demands, a high degree of technology churn, high risk associated with user experience acceptance, and cross-platform integration complexity. Criticality is typically financial, and developments often leverage offshore resource plans. From this profile, the following practices typically deliver contextual value to these types of endeavors:

Steerage and Influence - to positively influence outcomes on RIA developments, a *Risk-Value Lifecycle* [12] within a *Product Management-orientation* [13] is preferred. This means that all demand is not treated as projects, which has a tendency to batch demand and reduce time-to-value and flow. Leveraging a risk-confrontive stance enables *Real-options* to be exercised for learning and investment exits. Introducing such an inflection point in the delivery lifecycle also informs and enables the practice of *Adaptive Structure*, whereby the initial team structure can be scaled up without introducing additional risk on the investment. *Feature Crews* [14] are the preferred organizational structure for achieving scale, leveraging specialist teams in a hybrid service provider structure. Tools that support practices in this area include IBM Rational Team Concert [15].

Acceleration can be achieved during the architectural period of time through leveraging *Decision-centric Architectural Reasoning*. Due to the relative stability of web and RIA frameworks, we can catalogue the various technologies and place them in the context of the job or function that they perform within a classic layered architecture. For each technology stack, we can codify options that are available as they emerge, and allow teams to declare their choices. The set of decisions that are made represent the architecture of the system. Rather than start from a blank sheet of paper, teams are made aware of all the potential options available as they emerge across the typical stacks. This accelerates committal of a solution direction, and provides visibility into progress of the architecting activity. Known benefits and tradeoffs are highlighted such that bias or ignorance of potentially beneficial solution components is prevented.

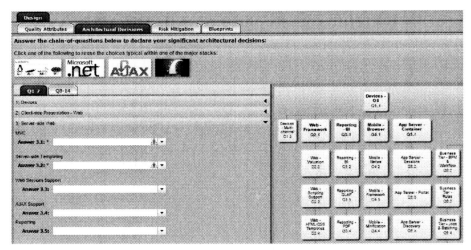

Figure 7.1 – Reference Architectures and Choice

Decisions regarding technology components and patterns need to be assessed in relation to the desired qualities or quality attributes of the system. The industry is notoriously poor with respect to specificity and testability of non-functional requirements. By discretizing the scales of various quality dimensions, architectural risk can be triggered to help determine the goodness of the proposed technology stack choices.

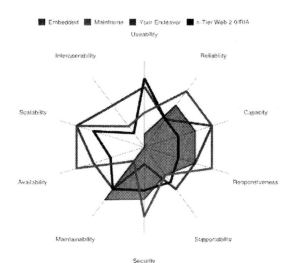

Figure 7.2 – Discretization of Quality Attributes

To prevent delays due to "marketecture" and other anti-patterns, generation of blueprints of the technology stack is possible. This is similar to the same contextualization that occurs related to the software project delivery "business system".

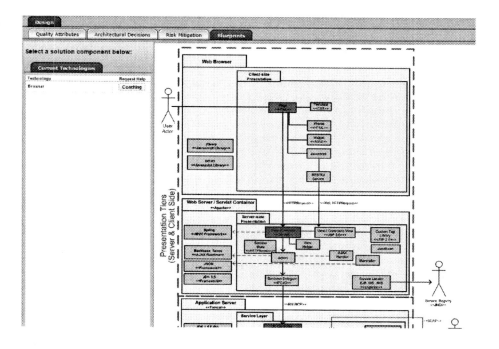

Figure 7.3 – Stack Blueprint Generation

Intent - to capture and elaborate the intent of the software product, *User Experience (UX)* [16] design is essential. This is due to the very high risk associated with Usability qualities of the product. Effectively getting into the head of the market users of the product requires understanding their psychology through usage of *Personas* [17], and leveraging the practice of *Scenario/Use Case Storyboarding* to crisply capture expected interactions. *Information Architecture* [18] as a sub-area of UX Design is increasingly important as richer and broader sources of data need to be leveraged, integrated and presented to users. Tools that support practices in this area include IBM Rational Requirements Composer [19].

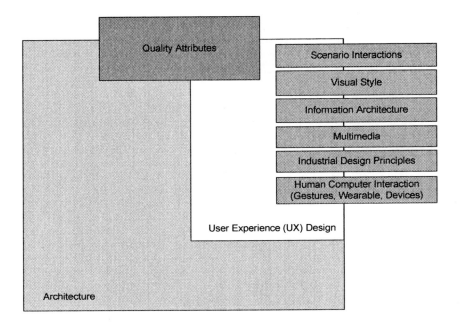

Figure 7.4 – UX Design

Design Work - design in an RIA environment must confront rapid technology churn. Therefore, more rigid forms of sequential modeling-then-coding must give way to more compression in the form of reliance on *Emergent* [20] object model design from code and associated *Data Modeling* [21]. Rarely can this time-to-market critical project type afford to spend any length of time formally modeling in leau of concrete implementation and testing/demonstration. However, equally appropriate is the fact that as the design emerges, the ability to retain data model knowledge in visual form to deal with complexity is important, as the likelihood of requiring *Round-trip Engineering* [22] and R*efactoring* [23] of the database is high. Tools that support practices in this area include tightly integrated database modeling tools like MySQL Workbench [24].

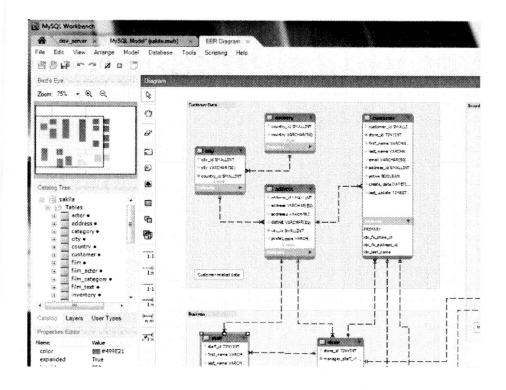

Figure 7.5 – MySQL Workbench [24]

Feedback - differing feedback strategies make sense at differing periods of the product lifecycle with RIA. During the risk mitigation period of time, leveraging a *Minimum-Viable-Product* [25] increments enables a high frequency feedback loop for Usability testing. Once uncertainty related to this quality attribute has been reduced, and the product development team has scaled up to build out the remainder of the product, defect prevention through *TDD* [26], *Continuous Integration* [27] and full *Regression Testing* [28] ensures confidence in the release schedule. Tools that support practices in this area include CruiseControl [29], jUnit [30] and Cucumber [31].

Release - common within RIA developments is the need to deliver incremental value to the customer base. To achieve this, the ideals of *Continuous Delivery* [32] eventually become a necessity. While the point in time for establishing this automation should be near the mid-point of the lifecycle, care should be made to not force risk exposure from customer backlash too prematurely. Tools that support practices in this area include IBM UrbanCode Release and Deploy [33].

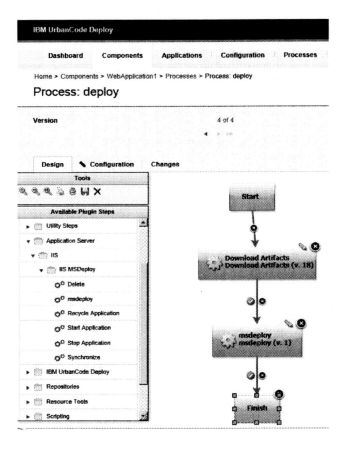

Figure 7.6 – UrbanCode Deploy [33]

7.2 – Mobile

Mobile Application developments are characterized by a high degree of speculation related to market acceptance, rapid technology changes, platform portability concerns and physical device constraints. A changing landscape related to initiation of software endeavors from outside IT increases complexity related to integration of the delivery value stream into the broader enterprise. A shift in emphasis towards marketing organizations and away from traditional EA means Alignment most resembles a startup. From this profile, the following practices typically deliver contextual value to these types of endeavors:

Alignment - *Systems of Engagement* [34] are different than Systems of Record and therefore require alignment with dynamic market trends and customer acquisition and retention strategy rather than with legacy platforms. Establishing a focus as an *Island of Innovation* [35] to discover new ways mobile devices can enrich Customer Experience is a shift for traditional EA organizations. *Product-Line Engineering* [36] exploration of emerging technologies to the point of being *Minimum Viable Products* for Marketing organizations to leverage enables the ability to rapidly adapt to the disruptions in technology strategy.

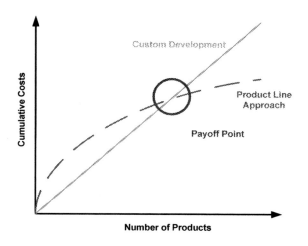

Figure 7.7 – Product-line Engineering Strategy

Steerage and Influence - to positively influence outcomes on Mobile developments, a *Risk-value Lifecycle* is leveraged but focused on the Usability quality attribute. While a *Product Management-orientation* is preferred, it is likely to tend towards smaller batches quicker than with RIA. An emphasis on Validated Learning is required to gauge customer response to the Mobile experience quicker due to the higher impact from the reach of Mobile apps. A high degree of emphasis on *API level Reuse* [37] *and Restful Services* [38] provides acceleratory influence over the project ecosystem.

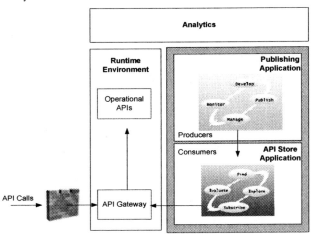

Figure 7.8 – API Management

Intent - the use of *Information Architecture* discipline and skills are crucial to make use of the limited resources available in Mobile devices, with the goals being to mitigate the limited attention of users over a limited set of features requiring a minimum of keystrokes. Mobile requirements also are likely to expand into *Predictive App* [39] customer experience qualities in which dynamic customer experiences are defined through device interactions and sensor data. Capture of Intent in this form factor is best achieved through *Rapid Prototyping* [40], as document based approaches result in too much delay for getting emergent feedback from *Market Focus Groups* [41]. *Product Specification Snapshots* [42] can be *Reverse Engineered* [43] from the evolving product rather than forward engineered. The demands of an extremely competitive marketplace and the highest time-to-market pressures require more focused and integrated prototyping capabilities specific to the mobile marketplace instead of generic incumbents like Axure [44] or iRise [45]. Examples of such mobile specific capability includes Proto.io [46].

Figure 7.9 – Mobile Prototyping [46]

Design Work - with Mobile development, design and development blur, and developers work in environments that are tightly coupled with the framework being leveraged. The legacy approach of selecting a tool per discipline is replaced by a developer centric platform due to the requirement for tighter feedback loops. Firms taking a Mobile First [47] stance to the "Fidelity versus Reach" tradeoff are likely to gravitate towards a Write Once Run Anywhere [48] strategy (an example of *Product Line Architecting*). A Hybrid as opposed to Native-only approach is feasible due to market trends towards HTML5 and Javascript [49] and makes heavy use of technologies like Adobe PhoneGap [50], Sencha Touch Architect [51], or Titanium Studio [52] to realize BYOD [53] (Bring Your Own Device) support. Device-specific templates abstract the details for supported build targets which yields important design reuse due to the large array of array of screen sizes, hardware specifications and configurations.

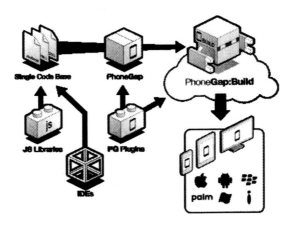

Figure 7.10 – Write-once Run Anywhere [50]

Mobile specialized IDE functionality to address the multiple layers of a Mobile First strategy provides acceleratory effects due to the emphasis on seamless integration. Rather than start with a Web-oriented IDE, starting with a mobile-oriented development environment prevents constraints being imposed by the slower advancing technology stack.

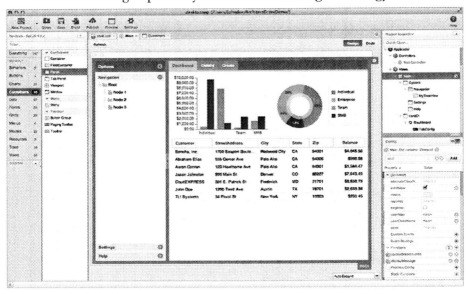

Figure 7.11 – Sencha Architect [51]

Feedback - cycle times for achieving effective feedback on Mobile development efforts are on the order of days to hours, and encompass rich engagement and involvement with subject matter experts, usually marketing proxies representing the *Personas* being targeted by the campaign. Testing Mobile apps requires the use of *A/B testing* [54], also known as Split Testing) , where two or more pages are subjected to consumer tests to evaluate the system's efficacy. *Preemptive Performance Testing* [55] ensures that load beyond that of small sampling will not negatively affect Customer Experience. Tools and SaaS [56] (Software-as-a-Service) offerings that support *Cloud-based Testing* includes Cloudbees [57] and Ship.io from Electric Cloud [58].

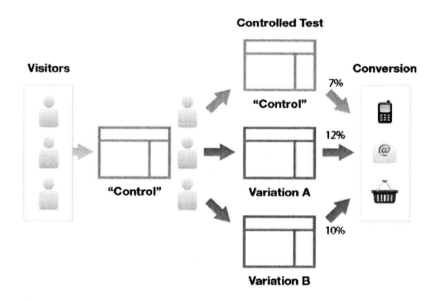

Figure 7.12 – A/B Testing [54]

Release - the constraints that exist with Mobile development requires alterations to typical *Continuous Delivery* [59] practice. Although Mobile represents the context that has the biggest affinity to this practice, it requires that delays of up to 5 days [60] be factored in for access to App Stores from either Apple or Google. To prevent the potential for destabilization of the software delivery pipeline, technical debt is typically incurred through the use of *Feature Toggles* [61] in leau of *Feature Branches* [62] due to the limited ability to quickly patch builds when things go awry. Emerging automation to monitor and manage the activation and deactivation of these "flippers" includes *FT4j* [63]. Where App Stores do not allow for this practice, the alternative of *Canary Deployments* [64] can be leveraged to only expose new functionality to defined *Personas* and market segments. Such a rolling start for releases leverages Load Balancer functionality to partition traffic. Finally, if neither practice option is available due to Compliance requirements, building an *Internal App Store* [65] to mimic the production release process prevents risks associated with limited access to break-fix flexibility.

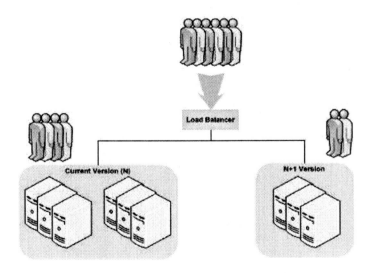

Figure 7.13 – Canary Deployments [64]

7.3 – Embedded & Real-time

Embedded development is characterized by hard real-time and resource constraints, high reliability, safety, security, portability, availability and serviceability requirements, and growing code complexity. Difficulty in final system testing requires innovative approaches to achieving meaningful feedback. For this type of development, the following practices yield contextual value:

Steerage & Influence - due to the fact that embedded software is by definition contained within larger systems, the management structure is that of *Programs* [66], with potentially each parallel track leveraging a *Product-oriented* lifecycle based on *Risk-Value Prioritization*. Generational release train planning is supported through *Parallel Development* support and robust *Branching strategies* . *Reference Architectures* [67] and leveraging commercial off-the-shelf (COTS) components through *Asset-based Development* [68] has an acceleratory effect that can positively affect outcomes.

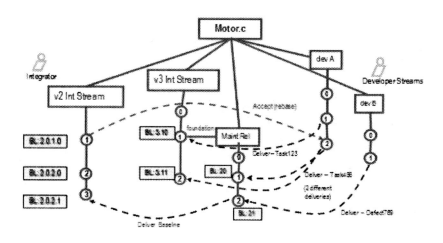

Figure 7.14 – Parallel Development

Team and Collaboration - embedded development programs typically involve a lengthy product life. *Small teams* [69] built around features become familiar with their area of concern. The goal should be to construct a team structure at scale where self-sufficiency is created through *cross-functional* [70] skill-sets and *Pairing* [71] problem and solution domain expertise. Such long-lived teams form social bonds that are valuable for knowledge retention and effectiveness.

Intent - due to the emphasis on architectural quality attributes with this type of project, leveraging *Quality Scenarios* [72] as a form of requirements elicitation ensures the necessary precision and testability throughout the lifecycle. For functional elicitation, product development oriented *Features* enable integration of Marketing and Development organizations. To ensure flow, features should be sized using the heuristic *"Minimally Marketable"* [73]. Practices commonly utilized for elaborating intent related to robustness are *Fault-tree Analysis* [74] and *Requirements Traceability* [75]. These practices are typically required for various compliance certifications in the embedded space.

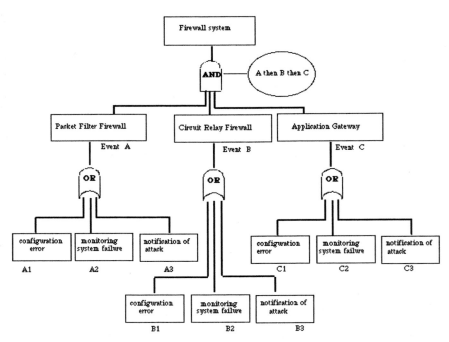

Figure 7.15 – Fault-tree Analysis [76]

Design - due to the real-time nature of behavioral abstractions such as telecom switches or control systems, state-machine modeling provides utility, typically performed in UML Statecharts and sysML [76]. Coupled with this is the practice of *Model-driven Architecture* (MDA) [77] which enables rapid simulation and *Pattern* orientation [78]. *Design-by-contract* [79] or *Operational Contracts* [80] can prevent defects from being injected into the product where a high degree of reliability is required. Tools for performing Model-driven design and simulation includes IBM Rhapsody [81]. Static code analysis tools like IBM Rational Asset Analyzer [82] are also useful for preventing common design flaws.

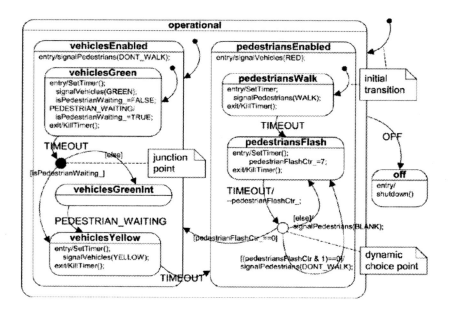

Figure 7.16 – Embedded Design and Statecharts [76]

Feedback - due to the difficulty of testing some embedded systems, simulation is often the only alternative. When one-time deployments or very high cost prohibits the use of sacrificial prototypes, feedback is implemented through *RTOS Simulation* testing and static code analysis. Model-based simulation is included within IBM Rational Rhapsody. Alternatively, *MatLab* [83] is commonly used in real-time applications.

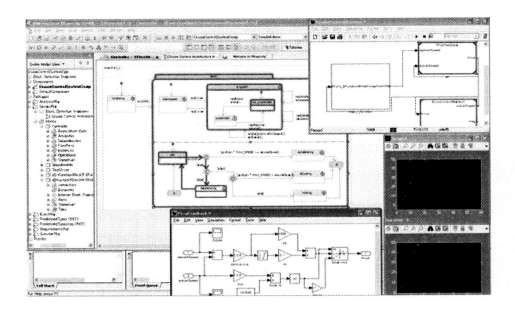

Figure 7.17 – RTOS Simulation Environments [81]

7.4 – Big Data & Data Warehousing

Initiatives categorized as being related to "Big Data" have 5 commonly espoused attributes called the 5-V's: volume, velocity, variety, validity and value. While the first three capture the essence of the technologies and infrastructure required to support the enterprise, the last two are the most important and least understood. Presented with vast quantities of structured and unstructured data, sensed opportunities for insight are discovered rather than predicted; are emerged rather than designed. While infrastructure streams of effort within the program can run leveraging traditional IT management practice, business opportunity related streams should operate in more of a "startup" fashion. The following practices provide leverage when embarking on big data initiatives:

Alignment - because the process of accruing value from big data is akin to discovery, practices related to *Emergent Vision and Strategy* [84] make more sense than those that are leveraged for aligning more certain transitions. *Hypothesis driven development, Minimum-Viable-Product* and rapid *Build-Measure-Learn* cycles enable emergent learning about the data and potential utility contained therein. Tools should enable rapid investigation and analysis of composite data-sets, and should not inhibit daily or even hourly feedback cycles.

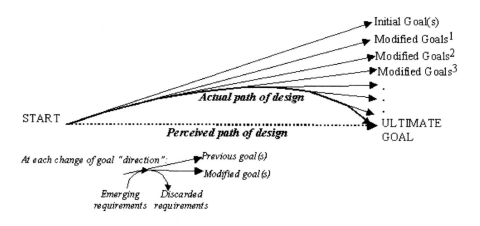

Figure 7.18 – Emergent Vision [84]

Steerage and Influence - once identification of opportunities related to data start to emerge, work can be prioritized and governed through a *Value-driven* lifecycle in the analytics track. For prioritization and governance related to the infrastructure tracks, a *Risk-value* lifecycle should naturally be used due to the architectural qualities in play with big data initiatives. Division of labor and roles necessarily need to change, with special emphasis on skills related to related technologies and data science. But to be successful, this type of project especially needs to leverage specialized skill-sets on teams that focus on *cognitive and behavioral sciences* with people who understand people and their differing mindsets. Measurement of success and steerage must avoid "vanity" metrics, but rather yield understanding of perceived problems and measure results from answers provided.

Intent - once opportunities and understandings from the data emerge, business process reengineering will enter the program. *Business Use Case* technique is especially useful to identify the context of the system changes that will be required to exploit opportunities. Special attention should be given to *User Experience (UX) Design*, as emerging opportunities like *Predictive Apps* are enabled by new, richer forms of contextual data. Especially applicable is the data science of Deep Learning using Restricted Boltzmann Machines [85].

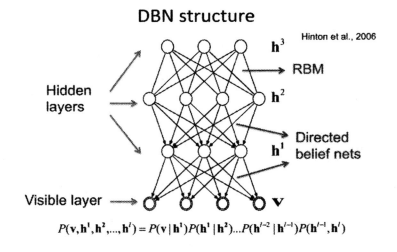

$$P(\mathbf{v}, \mathbf{h}^1, \mathbf{h}^2, ..., \mathbf{h}^l) = P(\mathbf{v} \mid \mathbf{h}^1)P(\mathbf{h}^1 \mid \mathbf{h}^2)...P(\mathbf{h}^{l-2} \mid \mathbf{h}^{l-1})P(\mathbf{h}^{l-1}, \mathbf{h}^l)$$

Figure 7.19 – Predictive Apps using Machine Learning [85]

Team and collaboration - due to the scale of this type of project, a hybrid strategy leveraging *cross-functional teams* for the analytics tracks supported by *specialist service teams* for the infrastructure track is optimum.

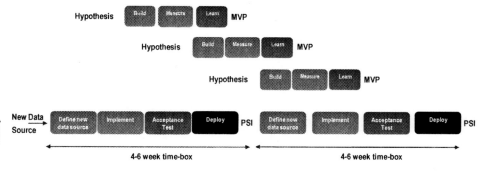

Figure 7.20 – Different Program Cadences

Design Work - the analytics track is focused on the design of experiments based on the sensed opportunities with the data. To test out these hypothesis, insights in the form of questions that might be asked leads to exploring possible answers through *simulations and modeling.* Because big data sets typically involve complex adaptive systems, exploring various aspects of a model of dynamic behavior is best achieved through either *Agent-based modeling* [86] or *System's Dynamics Modeling* [87].

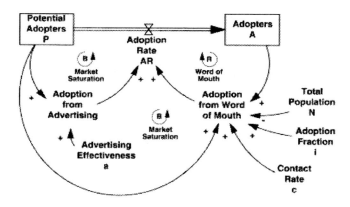

Figure 7.21 – System's Dynamics Modeling

Feedback - due to the complexity and uncertainty related to new datasets that are becoming available, testing hypotheses necessarily requires meaningful experiments if results are to be interpreted correctly. *A/B Testing* is useful to reduce the chances that results will interpreted with confirmatory bias. Instrumentation using Google Analytics [88] must be given enough time to collect enough data from the tests and render statistically meaningful results.

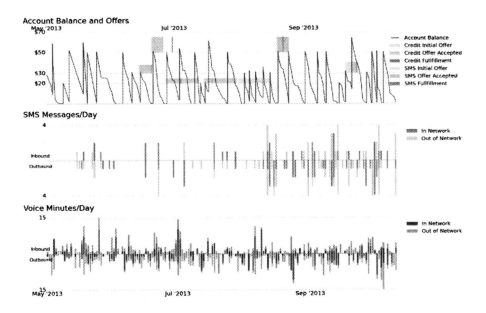

Figure 7.22 – A/B Testing Instrumentation

7.5 – COTS Package Acquisition

COTS (Commercial Off-the-Shelf) Acquisition is a typical project type when packages are considered for adoption by large enterprises. These developments are characterized by very large teams due the pervasive nature of the core business processes that they realize. While implicit in the strategy that a desire exists to acquire business processes manifested within a package and therefore the view of business execution by the mass market, this reality is often misunderstand and therefore introduces confusion and complexity in the development process. Gap remediation is first and foremost achieved by BPR. To address these essential complexities, the following practices are situationally appropriate:

Alignment - the alignment period of time is specifically focused on reducing the uncertainty related to the high-stakes decision regarding how radical the process will be to acquire the vendor's business process and how risky partnering with the various vendors will be in the long term. *Set-based Concurrent Engineering* as an application of real-options theory enables the avoidance of vendor lock in, in addition to emergent strategy.

Steerage and Influence - effective governance of a COTS acquisition necessarily involves utilization of a *Risk-Value* lifecycle, with the critical go-no go decision point for the package representing a Lifecycle Architecture (LCA) milestone. Where prior to this point effort is focused on narrowing options through the identification and valuation of gaps, post LCA is characterized by closing gaps through tailoring where possible, integration and as a last resort, customization. *Feature Crews* are the best way to scale for the various gap remediation efforts in a lean, *one-piece flow* manner through the use of *Digital Kanban*.

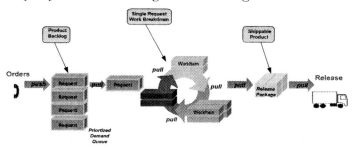

Figure 7.23 – Digital Kanban

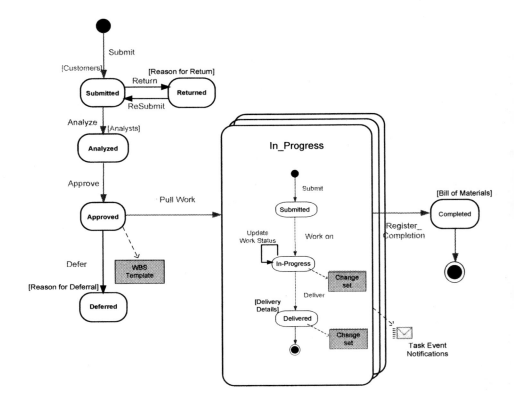

Figure 7.24 – Digital Kanban Nested State Machines

Intent - because COTS represents the acquisition of core business processes, identifying gaps between the as-is and the candidates to-be business processes is best achieved through leveraging *Business Use Case* practice. This is because of the seamless transformation that is possible when elaborating business use case realizations, and the subsequent identification of system use cases and system interfaces. Such *visualization* allows quick identification of candidate system behavior in the context of the business processes that leverage them. Also, because system use cases are a structured form of requirements that bind clusters of scenarios, the practice lends itself to *"specification by example"*, whereby test cases are a natural extension and typically provided by COTS vendors. This enables the compression that *Acceptance Test-driven Development* yields.

Exercising the COTS capability through acceptance tests yields gap identification. Gaps will occur between the offering and the three independent spheres. The forth sphere of influence on the package decisions is dependent upon the others. Through either first-order compromises between the Business Need and the Marketplace offerings, or second order tradeoffs with changes to the existing Enterprise Architecture, gaps can be remediated.

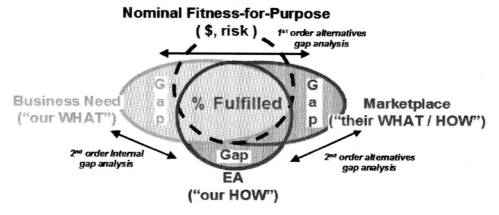

Figure 7.25 – First and Second-order COTS Tradeoffs

Application of differing remediation strategies for gaps yields differing implications for risk and cost. Each strategy may also yield differing fulfillment percentages that are acceptable for the acquisition.

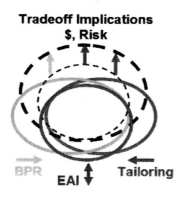

Figure 7.26 – Gap Analysis and Remediation Tactics

Design - due to the abstract nature of business processes, and their potentially timing-critical details, visualization through various types of UML or equivalent is a preferred approach for performing design cycles. *Sequence and Activity diagrams* are especially useful in localizing potential gaps between as-is enterprise processes and the to-be processes as contained within the COTS package. Scoring typically can be best achieved by leveraging *Multi-attribute Utility Trees (MAUT)* to understand the various sources of potential gap from the "four spheres of influence" related to COTS, including programmatics, enterprise architecture, marketplace dynamics and functionality.

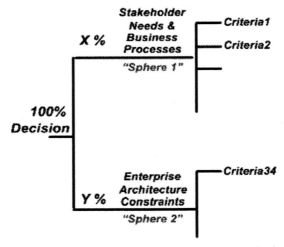

Figure 7.27 – Multivariate Decision Analysis

Feedback - due to the desire to keep decisions fluid for as long as possible, and the fact that the application of real-option theory underlies risk mitigation for COTS acquisition, leveraging a *Conference-Room-Pilot* [89] as a practice to uncover gaps between the as-is business processes and the to-be product capabilities is desirable. The ability to rapidly walk through scenarios is desirable such that as much learning is made possible in as short a time as possible.

7.6 – Mainframe (Cobol/CICS)

Mainframe developments, typically built using the Cobol/CICS pattern of technologies, is characterized by very large code bases of legacy code in which few fully grasp. Similarly, limited knowledge of past decisions exists with a high degree of difficulty in maintaining, let alone extending system functionality. An aging workforce related to this skill-set, antiquated terminal editor tools, and monolithic architectures each contribute to complexity, which shows up in the limited ability to test effectively to any modern standards of regression or coverage. For this type of development, the following practices yield contextual value:

Alignment - due to the overwhelming scope and complexity of many mainframe developments, the risk of launching into lengthy alignment and planning cycles is high. Leveraging *Portfolio Kanban* [90] can constrain these activities such that smaller increments of change ensue, and more ability to deal with the complexity is achieved. *Limiting WIP* can be achieved through IBM Rational Team Concert through more advanced schema/template design.

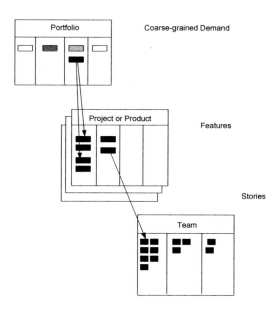

Figure 7.28 – Portfolio Kanban

Steerage and Influence - to ensure large teams can be leveraged in a successful way, scaling should occur once uncertainty/risk is reduced. Leveraging the *Adaptive Structure* practice ensures that scaling doesn't occur prematurely. *Feature Crews* can pull requests in parallel if properly supported in *Parallel Development* infrastructure like IBM Rational Team Concert for z/OS [91] and the associated Jazz Source Control meta-model.

Intent - due to the typical delays that are inserted in the feedback loop due to complexity and attempting to build large specifications as commonly found with traditional requirements engineering practice, it is beneficial to engage in "specification by example" or *Acceptance Test-driven Development* in an effort to compress the value-stream. Doing so ensures that full regression suites are possible if given the automation support for their execution.

Design Work - to deal with complexity, typically seen in copybook structure or JCL (Job Control Language) [92] Job streams, *visual modeling* supports risk reduction in this area. Additionally, IDE's like those based on Eclipse help provide a cross-generational environment to encourage younger developers to take up this business critical language. Tools such as IBM Rational Asset Analyzer enable assessment and visualization of the codebase along with support for refactoring.

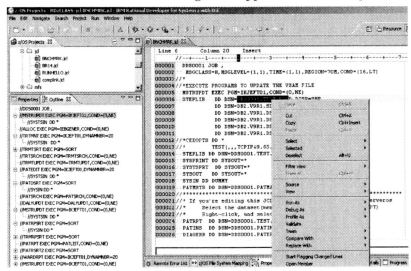

Figure 7.29 – Cobol/CICS Code Analysis

Feedback - with the large scope of legacy systems, *6-week incremental cycles* are necessary to achieve flow. Forcing too rapid a feedback loop can create instability, just as is common with too low a frequency akin with the waterfall approach. A critical constraint on mainframe platforms is the high cost of purchasing CPU cycles on the LPAR [93]. This typically negatively affects the amount of testing that can be undertaken, with full product regression almost never achieved. Tools like IBM Rational Developer for System Z - Unit Test (RDz-UT) [94] enable establishing virtual mainframe partitions on PC hardware such as towers or laptops which enables *distributed build and testing* activities in a cost effective manner.

Figure 7.30 – IBM Rational RDz-UT

Release - achieving coordinated releases with legacy Cobol/CICS codebases is achieved through correlation of component and module baselines. Coupled with a trend to unify developer tools like Eclipse for both distributed and mainframe developers, integrating release practice through heterogeneous SCM platforms like that provided by IBM's Jazz approach allows movement towards parallel development and prevents the type of serialization seen with legacy SCLM infrastructure.

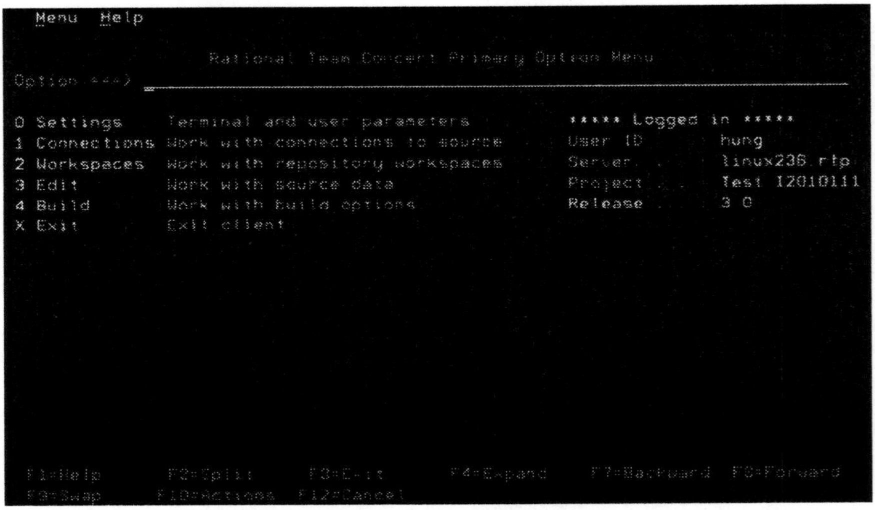

Figure 7.31 – Jazz Source Control and Build on z/OS

7.7 – Keeping it Real

Gaining leverage from contextually appropriate approaches to software development means the ability to rapidly reuse choices that are especially attuned to the type of domain and demand patterns for the endeavor. While templates capture such a starting point for teams and reflect high probability options for consideration, they are not absolute as software development is highly uncertain. Over time, if the same patterns show recurring success for various situations, usage statistics will indicate more likelihood that the templates are robust and stable. In Figure 7.32 below, common form factor templates are presented to teams during self organization alongside other enterprise specific templates and common industry methods. Each industry method template provides varying degrees of completeness. It could be said that where popularized industry methods are more general in nature, targeting as much of the mass market as possible, the form-factor based templates within *Advisor* are unique in the industry in that they offer highly specialized experience patterns that encompass not only the assembly of highly contextualized practices within a software delivery ecosystem, but also reflect the continual learning that the system achieves through correlation of experiential data.

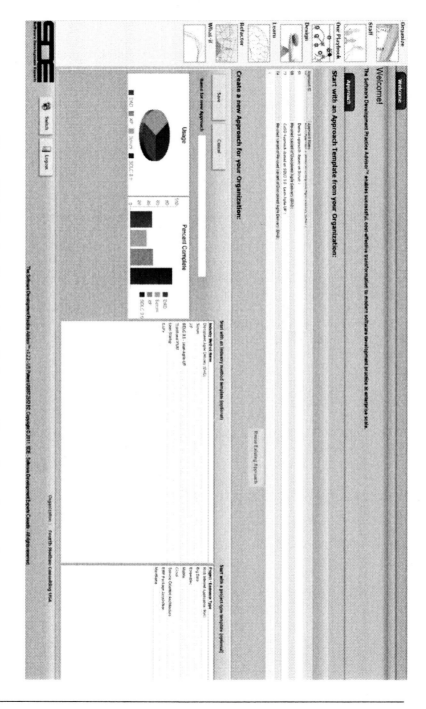

Figure 7.32 –Reusing Organization, Industry or Form-factor Approaches

Chapter 8: Lean Staffing

"Making good decisions is a crucial skill at every level."   Peter Drucker

Having vested seven chapters in devising smarter approaches to the development of software and the optimal configuration of the various contextual Value Streams within Enterprise IT, we now turn our attention to the supply side of the equation. Just as the demand pipeline strongly informs the needs of our software development endeavors in terms of practices, so too does this contextualization filter down to defining fit for realizing those practices in terms of staffing.

When we look at the aspect of intelligent supply chain management in software development, the term "Division of Labor" inevitably enters the debate. Software development endeavors are faced with choices related to the coupling of skill sets to individuals in the form of role definitions. Adam Smith articulated the advantages of Division of Labor for enhancing human productivity in his 1776 classic *The Wealth of Nations* [1]. Through specialization, allocation efficiencies are achieved by taking advantage of workers' differing skills and talents according to the principle of comparative advantage. Division of Labor is fundamental to the modern world economy which has seen huge increases in production volume and variety. Such specialization has resulted in a far higher standard of living than would be otherwise possible. Yet such a concept is not without opponents including sociologists, philosophers, artists and social activists [2]. They argue that Division of Labor and specialization results in increasing economic interdependence among larger and larger populations spread over larger and larger geographical areas. Instead of individuals or families producing all of what they will need, the individual specializes in producing only a few things and then acquires all other desired goods or services from the production of other specialists through some type of exchange mechanism. Of concern is the non-economic side-effects like more hierarchical class systems; less pride and emotional satisfaction in ones workmanship, difficulty in arriving at political and moral consensus due to the separation of concerns among societies specialist participants; and less sense of community and belongingness. Such critiques have been lodged by notable sociologists like Karl Marx [3] and Max Weber [4].

Organizations will manifest their overarching philosophy related to efficient and effective Division of Labor in close concert with their cultural values. Just as software development practices and tactics possess an affinity to each of the cultural quadrants of the *Competing Values Framework*, so to do the resultant roles that realize these practices. Alterations made to the degree of specialization will result in the most angst when it comes to change initiatives, as it is likely to rub up against status quo social network configurations, personality types, ideologies and organizational politics. Knowledge and skills acquisition takes time to assimilate, so alterations to role definitions also runs into lead time considerations. Enabling smarter staffing requires being cognitive of the risks associated with the pace of dynamism in domains and technologies and the difficulties in manually matching skills to these contextual drivers and the practices that will also be dynamically altered throughout the course of software projects. Effective staffing governance requires timely access to fitness-for-purpose data on all these dimensions such that risks related to the most important determinant of delivery success (the people) can be mitigated.

8.1 – Every Marine is a Basic Rifleman

The US Marine Corps (USMC) faces extremely difficult situational environments that are unpredictable and extremely fluid. Many parallels have been made between the nature of software development and the applicability of how USMC units are structured. One of the many "maxims" that are indoctrinated within this service is that of cross-training, most notably "every Marine is a basic rifleman" [5]. The intent of this provision and readiness requirement is to build robustness into the organization at the most basic level of their core mission - they are first and foremost *trigger pullers*. From that basic skill, members then branch out into their area of specialization. It means every Marine must qualify with his/her rifle at least once a year regardless of position so that any Marine could fulfill a post such as convoy escort, guard duty, etc. It also means that if a Marines position was overrun, they could stand and defend themselves. However, this maxim does not mean that it is their actual job or that they have received the required training to fulfill that role in a combat zone.

Within software development, if an Enterprise wishes to leverage the above maxim for the benefit of robustness, what skill should be interpreted as being equivalent to a "basic riflemen"? Clearly, the skill of pulling triggers is fairly static and doesn't change at the pace like that of software technology. Many within IT like to equate this advice to mean "basic programming". One could argue that the starting point should be basic programming skills regardless of the plethora of languages that come and go. Others may argue that it represents the core business concepts that are central to the Enterprise. It really comes down to where an enterprise should build "readiness" and obviously this means everyone being ready for the changing business conditions, not everyone being ready for all the changes in technology. Given this "Generalist" base, various specializations come and go with the changes in technology. The core business basics change less frequently, like the USMC core mission. Therefore, critical in the formulation of an organizations skill-sets are the "fundamentals".

The concept of a Generalist-first hiring strategy is sometimes referred to as looking for "T-Shaped" people [6], referring to candidates who first and foremost understand the "big picture" and have the lateral vision to know where to look to dig deeper. Unfortunately, many within IT take a decidedly introverted view of the Division of Labor for either ideological reasons, or for political and competitive reasons. On one end of the spectrum is the drive towards *Hyper-specialization* [7]. This is reflective of the overly prescriptive big planning up-front mindset and the neat compartmentalization of humans into micro-tasks. On the other end of the spectrum is a counter movement towards Generalization or *Hypo-specialization*. Here, a jack-of-all-trades perspective is prevalent with no differentiation in skill-sets or responsibilities. Figure 8.1 illustrates the spectrum of Division of Labor strategies as commonly referenced within software development methodology vocabulary:

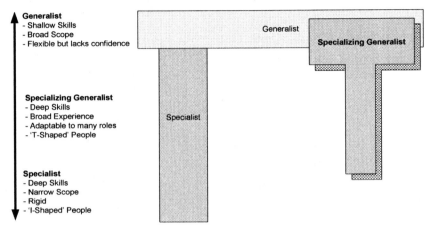

Generalist
- Shallow Skills
- Broad Scope
- Flexible but lacks confidence

Specializing Generalist
- Deep Skills
- Broad Experience
- Adaptable to many roles
- 'T-Shaped' People

Specialist
- Deep Skills
- Narrow Scope
- Rigid
- 'I-Shaped' People

Figure 8.1 – Specialization Spectrum

At one extreme end of the above figure, Hyper-specialization represents a new concept enabled by technology and globalization forces. The term was coined by Thomas Malone from MIT's Collective Intelligence Research Initiative [9]. Such a strategy suggests that enhancements in efficiency can be realized by focusing tasks to those who are best suited to perform them; similarly, by decomposing tasks in such a way by intermediaries so that competition ensues can drive production costs down. One such application of this strategy is IBM's "Liquid" strategy [10], whereby well defined outcomes are outsourced to competing service providers on a micro-demand basis. Risks cited with this extreme approach to Division of Labor includes the threat of "digital sweatshops" and labor market "arbitrage". Obviously, under threat of commoditization due to globalization and disparate costs of living between first and third world countries, professional software developers have a problem with this concept.

At the other extreme end of the spectrum, the Division of Labor philosophy espoused by the Scrum methodology is one of Hyper-generalization. Much of this ideology stems from the method's origins from eastern, specifically Japanese culture. The cultural norms within Japan are for employees to enjoy lifelong employment in which the management system is one in which all employees participate, from the top down and from the bottom up, and humanity is fully respected. Directional planning is through *Hoshin Kanri* "which leverages the collective thinking power of all employees to make their organization the best in its field". [11] With Scrum, very little differentiation is advocated, with only 3 roles - Scrum Master, Product Owner and Team Member. When one looks at the skill-sets required to be effective in these roles, it is no wonder that being effective using Scrum is hard. In the case of the Product Owner, being the "single wringable neck" requires both problem domain knowledge, solution domain knowledge in terms of constraints and boundary conditions, organization skills, diplomatic and conflict resolution skills and the like. It is definitely the anti-thesis of specialization, and a role which is under extreme time pressure due to being the single most important constraint that can cause Sprint timeboxes to be blown. In the case of the generalist Team Member role, social pressure is applied to every member of the team to learn skills not indigenous in their experience or schooling, and work on tasks regardless of title. Such a **"spread the jam thin"** strategy assumes that technologies are relatively stagnant, that cross-functional effectiveness is universal among participants, and synergies among the various disciplines of work in software development are non-existent. Under such conditions, the outcome is often "Social Loafing" [12], whereby team members rely on social hygiene rather than real contributions so as to leave the heavy lifting to a few individuals.

An overarching philosophy regarding specialization or lack thereof has implications on organizational structure and distribution, and vice versa. A mismatch between skill-set cohesion and organizational structure introduces risk in social terms as well as technical terms. As discussed in Chapter 5, this is related to the issue of flow. Technical practices can enable smaller, more efficient and effective teams but doing so requires a different Division of Labor choice than one of Hyper-specialization. Lean Work-cells as an organizational pattern implies the need for cross-functional skill-sets such that Responsible Autonomy exists. With this Lean Thinking approach, iterations are abandoned altogether and replaced with a focuses on micro-increments. Each micro-increment is a *Minimal-*

Marketable-Feature [13] and can be released independently of all other features. Instead of performing all of the delicate planning for a batch of features such that the coordinated sprints will result in a coherent output, features are assigned to *Feature-Crews* that can be planned out just-in-time in such a fashion to be decoupled from any of the other planning by other crews. Figure 8.2 illustrates the Lean Feature Crew organizational configuration and associated one-piece-flow aspect:

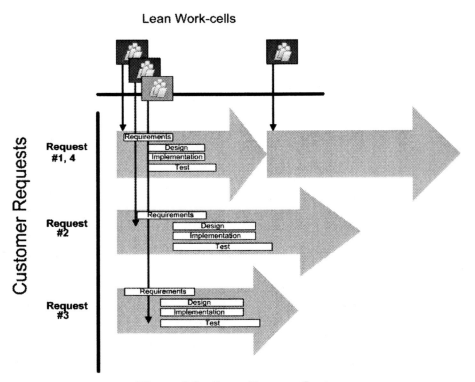

Figure 8.2 – Lean Feature Crews

These teams are cross-functional, with problem domain and solution domain representation. They act like a mini-business venture, responsible atomically for all aspects of meeting customer demand. Instead of being part of a larger and larger composite, they act similar to USMC units with autonomous authority. They are freed from temporally more sensitive fixed cadences, they can focus on the actual realization rather than coordination overhead. They also survive from product assignment to product assignment. This means that once the team has "normed" and is performing well, every attempt is made to maintain this emergent behavior. Teams evolve an understanding of the participants within their ranks, the personalities involved, the key strengths and weaknesses. Instead of ripping them apart immediately after they have gone through the team lifecycle, the team is preserved. This implies a matrix strategy at the **team level rather than the individual level,** a fundamental shift for most organizations. This is not to say that specialists are not needed in this configuration. Figure 8.3 illustrates this hybrid supply chain configuration relying on small cross-functional teams pulling from specialist teams as needed, just in time:

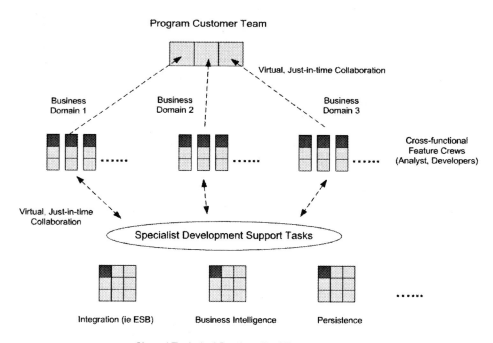

Figure 8.3 – Cross-functional / Specialist Team Hybrid

No team specialization occurs in the upper layers of this hybrid structure, and the developer-analyst pairs should be specialist-generalist in nature such that they can deliver the feature fully as a pair. Instead of component based decomposition based on specialization, the self organizing teams are small and self sufficient to be able to deliver the value independently. The definition of what is a shared service team and what is not should be made on the basis of maturity of the technology and cost of finding the scalable resource pool with this skill.

Such a strategy is consistent with "Post-Fordism" [14]. In contrast with the first half of the 20th century based on the production lines in Henry Ford's automotive factories performing repetitive specialized tasks, Post-Fordism is characterized by small batch production, economies of scope (gaining efficiencies through efficient product lines) rather than economies of scale, specialization of products, different types of customers, and a trend towards a white-collar, feminized workforce. Also prevalent with this trend is a skill-flexible core of workers and a time-flexible periphery. Post assembly line thinking has also been accompanied by changes in politics and prominent ideologies. Cultural changes includes the rise in individualist modes of thought and behavior and a culture of entrepreneurialism.

8.2 – Practice-driven Staffing

In all economic activity, the laws of microeconomics apply. The *Marshallian Cross* [15] of "supply and demand" governs decisions made in business. Software development is not immune to this principle. Microeconomics necessarily matches the fitness-for-purpose of the supply in concert with the demand within any project context. In markets where competition exists for labor, the aggregate of industry demand and industry supply determines the equilibrium prices. The software delivery market is always changing due to constantly evolving supply-side and simultaneously demand-side economics. However, at a single point in time, it is always the intersection of demand for IT services and the supply of people to fulfill various roles within software delivery determines the price or cost of staffing projects. Project staff represents the single largest cost in developing software and therefore has a first order effect on making the determination of *Return on Investment*. At the moment that staffing software endeavors occurs, the price paid for personnel P is illustrated below in Figure 8.4 and is a result of supply and demand curves:

Market Equilibrium

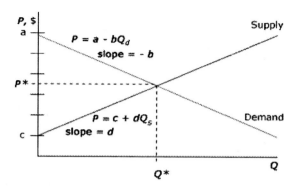

Figure 8.4 – Software Delivery Microeconomics

In the software development space, we know that demand is outstripping labor supply [16]. In terms of supply and demand curves, this represents a constantly shifting demand curve with a more slowly shifting supply curve to the right. We can view this in the above chart as a shifting of the demand curve to the right indicating a greater quantity of demand for software. Figure 8.5 illustrates the effect of rising demand and a relatively stagnant supply-side response:

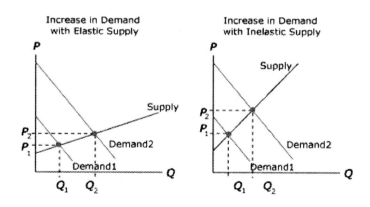

Figure 8.5 – Software Delivery Microeconomics

As time proceeds and the worlds' appetite for software continues to grow, the gap between quantity demanded and quantity supplied is widening.   Each major expansion in software development - automation (60s), productivity (80s), web development (90s), mobile (00s) - has been additive to the total stock of software in the world. This is because the old stuff doesn't go away. We're currently in the midst of another structural increase in the demand for software development labor, this time being driven by analytics and smart devices (the alleged "internet of things"), with the odd halo application (e.g., wearable tech) thrown in for good measure. Add to that technology demand shock from a 30% growth rate [17] in tablet and similar device computing and you can see why there is every indication that for the foreseeable future, demand for software developers will continue to increase at a rate faster than the supply of software developers available to develop it.   According to IDC 2012 [18], labor costs are increasing substantially, as illustrated in Figure 8.6:

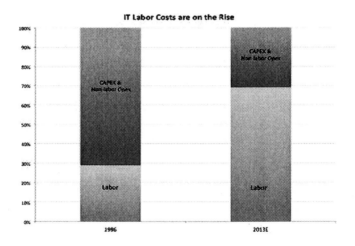

Figure 8.6 – IT Labor Costs [18]

With an effectively fixed supply curve, this is putting upwards pressure on the equilibrium price. Compounding this imbalance is the fact that the labor gap is widening at an accelerating pace because of tectonic shifts occurring in technology. Recent trends like Big Data, Mobile and Cognitive Computing are disrupting software development market economics in a discontinuous manner.   *Digital Disruption* as it is sometimes referred to is having a drastic effect on the demand curve. Rather than the oversimplified linear curves presented above, the curves are actually curved to reflect the non-linear nature of demand shifts. Significant determinants on the degree of curvature and include increasing technology complexity and the lack of time to respond to such shifts. A more realistic demand curve for software development is illustrated in Figure 8.7:

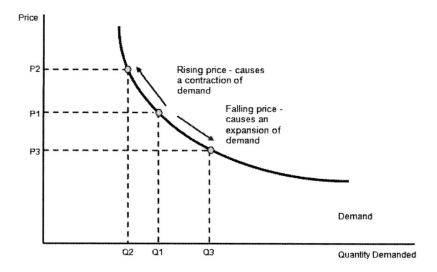

Figure 8.7 – Non-linear Demand due to Digital Disruption

To address this very real threat to business, Enterprises must innovate more efficient and effective staffing models. The low-lying fruit of throwing bodies at the problem is tapped out. Independent of the problems that Fordism and assembly-line thinking in knowledge intensive domains and the challenges this creates related to Offshore resourcing strategies, tapping into this resource base has run its course in terms of shifting the supply curve to the right. It has also run into the same non-linearities that are representative of true supply-side curves such as hiring friction, resulting in diminishing returns in the effectiveness of labor arbitrage. Figure 8.8 reflects the challenges of current supply-side tactics:

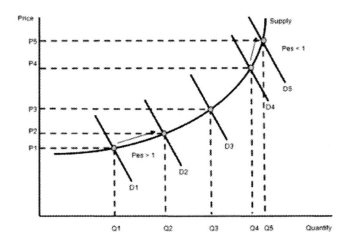

Figure 8.8 – Non-linear Supply Curve due to Friction

The non-linear nature of the software development supply curve illustrates the effects of price "elasticity". In the above case, the slope of the supply curve increases as one moves further to the right on the curve. An increasing slope in either the supply or demand curve reflects decreasing elasticity in either supply or demand. The impact on price means that as elasticity decreases, the effects on price are magnified. Figure 8.9 illustrates the general effect of inelastic supply on price pressures:

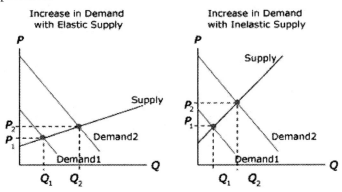

Figure 8.9 – Price Elasticity of the Supply Curve

To reduce the cost risks of the labor shortage requires thinking about how to alter the slope of the supply-side curve. It just so happens that batch size affects the elasticity of supply-side economics by altering and linearizing (flattening) of the supply curve slope. Through Lean Thinking and the organizational structure described in the previous section, supply needs to be matched to demand in a just-in-time manner.

The way of working for a team determines how a team will fulfill the demand. The combination of the fine-grained demand (aka the requirements) and the contextually appropriate way of working determines the needed staffing supply at any time of a software endeavor. Therefore, depending on the division of labor choices as reflected in the software practices employed, the requisite quantity of personnel and their respective skill-sets determines the supply side of the equation. When this matching is performed on a one piece-flow basis, we have the ability to better fit our limited supply with our increasing demand. By pulling staffing cycles in the context of smaller pieces of demand, we can optimize our staffing utilization. This happens in different ways depending on whether we are talking about the feature crews, which are long-lived domain intensive staffing profiles, or the specialist teams that support them.. In the former, we want to preserve the "team-ness" and the emergent behavior where team members have built the social structure and the trust bonds to be able to anticipate each others' moves, somewhat similar to a high performance sporting team. We also want to prevent the negative productivity impacts of "context switching" [19]. In the latter case, we can decouple the rapid pace of technology and the associated non-linear effects related to the supply curve such that more elasticity is created through just-in-time requisitions. Specialists can be pulled for the more in-demand and transient resourcing that must keep pace with the constantly changing technology landscape.

Through the selection of software development practices for a single increment of product, a pull signal is sent up the supply-chain. The software development practices, when made in a contextually appropriate manner, represent a fine-tuned signal of required skills to be pulled from the supply-side. These skills not only have a shelf life, but they need to be packaged with other skills that result from other cohesive practice selections. Practices are potentially leveraged for a short timeframe, perhaps only as long as a single iteration. This implies that skills matching is highly dynamic as opposed to the one-size-fits-all, fire-and-forget hiring practices of assigning "resources" to projects for the duration. JIT staffing provides laser focus on the staffing needs and represents the contextualization of the supply-chain all the way to the source. To achieve this, we need to facilitate rapid provisioning of fine-grained staffing requests by resolving the many-to-many relationships between methods (practice-sets), division-of-labor responsibilities (roles), and skill-sets - all performed just-in-time. Figure 8.10 illustrates the relationship between method selection and skill-sets:

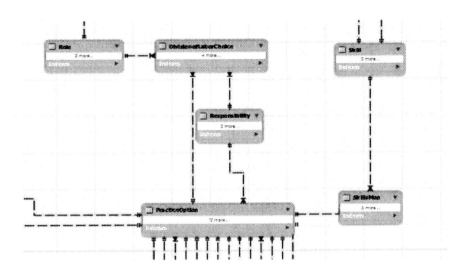

Figure 8.10 – Context-Practices-Skills-Roles Many-to-Many

From the just-in-time staffing requisitions a team generates, we now require a mechanism to understand the depth of experience required to be effective in execution of that aspect of the endeavor, and the level of experience that candidates possess at that moment of fulfilling the requisition. Experience is constantly being accrued, and availability is also highly dynamic, so the ability to make point-in-time assessments regarding the changing demand, changing roles and skillsets required, and changing supply is critical if we are to achieve the benefits of supply chain optimization.

8.3 – The Learning Curve

Just because we have staff that assert they have certain skills that are necessary to execute a team's playbook doesn't necessarily mean they are "fit-for-purpose". Such fitness requires that they have domain expertise to realize the demand, they have some degree of capability related to the emerging technologies being selected and leveraged, and the practice fundamentals reflective of their human capacity. Experience plays a big role in determining how productive they will be in discharging their responsibilities. To truly match supply with demand and therefore control costs and maximize value requires an assessment of this additional dimension of fit. Various approaches exist in making determinations of skills capability. Not surprisingly these skills acquisition models are essentially the same but differing in their origins and communities where they find affinity.

The first model that articulates "the learning curve" is also the oldest and originates from the Martial Arts of Aikido, Jujitsu, Judo and Karate in Japan. *Shu-ha-ri* [20] articulates the essence of the stages that one goes through towards mastery of an art. It is similar in philosophical nature to other European traditions related to artisanry originating from medieval times. The software development world, most notably the Agile community, has latched onto this interpretation and associated cultural and philosophical nuances. Obviously, Lean Thinking has a close affinity to Shu-ha-ri as well. Figure 8.11 illustrates the kanji representations and their associated English translations:

守 Shu - to learn from tradition

破 Ha - to break the chains of tradition

離 Ri - to go beyond all knowledge

Figure 8.11 – Shu-Ha-Ri

In the Shu stage, the student works endlessly to copy what the Sensei does and tells him/her to do without modification through repetition via *Katas* (the form). The pupil is not to attempt to understand why they are doing what they are attempting to perfect. In these traditions, it is the teacher who decides when the pupil is ready and can move to the Ha stage. In the Ha stage, the student can question the skills that have been learned and why they have been practicing the mechanics in such a manner. After lengthy reflection and having effectively broken the chains of current tradition in performing the art, they are ready to follow their own path forward and transcend the current body of knowledge. This marks the beginning of the Ri stage. It represents the birth and coming of age of the individual, and the transcendence in the art to pioneer new knowledge. At this stage, the pupil exceeds their master.

One cultural observation that is obvious from this mentoring is the constraints of social protocol and order. There is a clear "rank and file" within the learning process for an apprentice, and this reflects broader Japanese society. This can be seen to be similar to other traditions such as where one sits in a room and who should be furthest or closest to the door based on social status and rank. Western competitiveness and the notion of "climbing the corporate ladder" as it is commonly practiced in corporate America is non-existent within Japanese culture where avoiding conflict and maintaining peace and tranquility is paramount. This clearly indicates a cultural affinity of this approach to skills acquisition to those organizations who have a propensity towards eastern philosophy and ideology, likely exhibited in firms within the "Clan" quadrant of the Competing Values Framework. Loyalty and devotion by a student to their master is non-negotiable and unconditional. Also implicit with the Shu-ha-ri sequential progression is that it favors a Specialization view of Division of Labor. Shu-level students are not to attempt any "mixing of schools" of thought in the art as it is not seen as efficient.

Western culture has studied the issue of skills acquisition, most famously the Dreyfus model by Stewart and Hubert Dreyfus from the University of California at Berkeley in 1980 as commissioned by the United States Air Force [21]. In this work, they theorized that as the student becomes skilled, he depends less on abstract principles and more on concrete experience. Five stages of knowledge acquisition were articulated which characterized skill level on the basis of the mental functions of Recollection, Recognition, Decisions, and Awareness. *Novice* learners exhibit rigid adherence to taught rules or plans and these students cannot exercise "discretionary judgment". *Advanced Beginners* have limited situational perception, and treat all aspects of work independently and with equal importance. Becoming *Competent* means coping with the "crowdedness" of multiple simultaneous activities and the volume of accumulated information to enable some perception of actions in relation to goals deliberate planning formulates routines. *Proficiency* means that a holistic view of situations is enabled such that deviations from normal pattern of skill applications can be perceived. At this state, maxims are employed to adapt to situations at hand. Finally, the *Expert* stage allows the learner to transcend reliance on rules, guidelines, and maxims armed with an "intuitive grasp of situations based on deep, tacit understanding" and has "vision of what is possible". This stage of skill acquisition has the learner using "analytical approaches" in new situations or in case of problems.

Clearly western organizations have historically approached the skills-transfer process and the learning curve quite differently than eastern tradition. While the Dreyfus model may look similar to the stages of Shu-ha-ri, the progression and nature of instruction reflects the relatively low-context nature of cultural norms. Look no further than the plethora of training offerings and IT industry certifications, with software development being no exception. The business reality (some may say impatience of western corporations) has typically shown up as a limited appetite for lengthy internships under such close mentorship as exhibited under the martial arts model.

A refinement of the Dreyfus model emerged specifically for software development through the work of Meilir Page-Jones [22]. The "Seven Stages of Software Engineering Expertise" elaborates on the phenomenon of "the J-curve" which eludes to the fact that until individuals fulfill the rite of passage by actually *living* the new skill(s) under the stresses of a real project, they are at high risk of reverting to old practice. Access to level 5/6 mentors or coaches is critical to prevent this back sliding. The model is also useful in that it pragmatically relates productivity to stage of expertise, something we wish to optimize in IT Enterprises. Figure 8.12 illustrates the 7-Stages of Expertise model, which was also mentioned in Chapter 6:

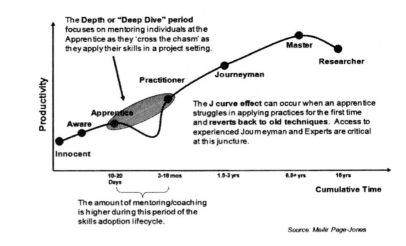

Skills Levels
1: Innocent
2: Aware
3: Apprentice
4: Practitioner
5: Journeyman
6: Expert
7: Researcher

Figure 8.12 – Seven Stages of Software Engineering Expertise [22]

The model is very insightful to the level of experience necessary to be effective in software development, but its formation was made popular by a metaphor of hunting as follows [22]:

Stage 1: Innocent

A Stage-1 person has never seen or heard of bears. It would not occur to a Stage-1, if he encountered a bear, that the bear could be hunted. Neither would he realize that a bear is a potential source of danger.

Stage 2: Aware

A Stage-2 person has seen an occasional bear and has read articles in airline magazines suggesting that bears may be hunted. Moreover, a Stage-2 probably has friends that have hunted bears and has learned some desultory but intriguing facts about bears and their habits. He is motivated to learn more.

Stage 3: Apprentice

A Stage-3 has attended a 5-day seminar on bear hunting. During this seminar, the participants form into teams of three or four and practice hunting very small bears under the ever-watchful eye of the instructor. After a few interim setbacks, by Friday afternoon all the teams have successfully hunted their bears. They fill out evaluation forms attesting that "bear hunting is very useful and relevant to my job." However, they are barely prepared for the world of real bears.

Stage 4: Practitioner

The Stage-4, having completed formal bear-hunting education, is full of confidence. He's ready to transcend the minuscule bears of the 5-day workshop and go out for real bears, larger bears, fierce bears. He's ready for Ursa Major. His manager is also keen to send him out with the latest bear-hunting techniques because the users want fur and they want it yesterday. Unfortunately, in the resulting scramble the budding bear hunter may be sent out without a map and with the wrong calibre arrow in his longbow. In the heat of ursine confrontation, the Stage-4 may also forget or misinterpret his classroom instruction and precipitate disaster. It's typical that some Stage-4s get *some* bears; but it's also typical that some bears get some Stage-4s.

Stage 5: Journeyman

The Stage-5 has survived the traumas of Stage-4 and has bear hunting down cold. The Stage-5 uses modern bear-hunting techniques naturally and automatically; in fact, he can't imagine how he ever got along without them. He is accurate and productive: The Steering Committee merely points out the bear and he hunts it within both budget and deadline. The Stage-5 is the exemplary modern hunter that salespeople of bear-hunting seminars refer to in their brochures.

Stage 6: Master

Stage-6 bear hunters have internalised not only the mechanics of bear hunting but also the principles underlying the techniques. Stage-6s know more than rules: They know why the rules exist and even when it's permissible to break them. For example, a Stage-3 or 4 may stand upwind of a bear accidentally and scare off the bear. However, a Stage-6 may know that by wearing Yogi-Spray Deodorant he can stand upwind without being detected and can thus surprise the bear from an unexpected quarter. Because of their deep knowledge, Stage-6s are very capable of training others in hunting techniques.

Stage 7: Researcher

Stage-7s are asked to write books and give talks at bear-hunting user groups. They are also engaged in extending and generalizing bear-hunting techniques to solve new problems. For example, a Stage-7 may extend bear hunting to work also on Big Foot or he may even develop the ultimate Yeti-Oriented Hunting Methodology.

The Seven Stages of Expertise model provides a simple relative and anecdotal scale by which to assess where team members are on the "learning curve" for any particular skill. Given this framework, different approaches can be leveraged to perform assessments on individuals in a relevant and useful manner to determine fitness for purpose of potential staff members. One approach that is very popular in Human Resources circles is to perform "self assessments", also known as *Introspectives* [23]. Introspection refers to a higher level mental function in which individuals reflect on themselves through meta-cognition. Obviously, such assessments can be highly biased, so to provide a more accurate picture of an individual's capabilities in a skill area, a practice known as *360-Degree* reviews is also common [24]. Having both sets of data related to skill level related to project requisitions enables the identification of gaps in perception. Such gaps may represent very real risks to the software investment, with narcissistic tendencies becoming obvious. Although such reviews can be misused and result in poor behavior when tied to financial compensation and job security, performing these reviews at the outset of an improvement initiative serves as valuable input for a baseline of capability. It should be noted that such peer reviews often depend heavily on social bonds and length of relationships in determining capability assessments. Therefore, only through empirical observation as to the patterns that result related to investment outcomes can we determine the accuracy of these assessments.

Once we establish a baseline of skill proficiency, we can understand which individuals we have available across the enterprise to staff software endeavors. We can track progress against the learning curve as assignments are made over time, and collect metrics that relate to their application of skills and the outcomes that ensued. In this way, we can use the heuristics of stage progression to forecast when an individual will achieve the various stages in a skill. This affords targeted investment to increase skill-sets based on anticipated demand and strategy.

8.4 – Keeping it Real

Due to the large number of practices that can be brought to bear on software projects to contextually match a way-of-working to the demand pipeline, with each practice requiring many skills for their efficient and effective execution, the staffing process is ripe for improvement in most enterprises. Typically, when faced with this complexity, organizations settle for simple and more coarse-grained matching of individuals to projects, even if they are thinking situationally in terms of ways of working. Add to this, the dynamism related to the ever changing portfolio of projects, sometimes on the order of several hundred, and you have a recipe for Human Resources mediocrity. *Advisor* addresses this challenge head-on by providing the ERP (Enterprise Resource Planning) capability sadly lacking in IT Enterprise. Now with the confluence of contexualization of the software development portfolio, smarter practice-based hybrid ways of working, organizational structures and Division-of-Labor optimized for flow, and fine-grained skills mapping to the resultant demand requirements, cost efficiencies are now possible in the IT supply chain. Staffing elasticity requires reducing the complexity of the increasingly supply-demand environment dynamism.

The first step enterprises take in optimizing the supply chain is to establish a baseline of human resources capability through the Staff component in *Advisor*. Individuals once added to the roster for an organization are asked to perform self-assessments whereby they register the skills they possess, and their feelings about how capable they are in these skills. This is cross-correlated with the broader peer perspective of the same set of skills for an individual to quickly arrive at the starting profile for all who are available for assignment to software development endeavors. Visually, these assessments will be leveraged initially for assignment. Later this same assessment information is accessible in the Delivery Intelligence aspect of the Learn component such that exploratory analysis can be waged related to staffing risks when results are not as expected during in-flight endeavors.

Figure 8.13 illustrates *Advisor's* Skills Assessment tab within the Staff component. It shows a listing of all individuals known to the system within the organization, and in the interests of "openness and transparency", all skills profiles are visible by default. This allows members to reflect on their peers' stated abilities when they attempt to assess how well they match up.

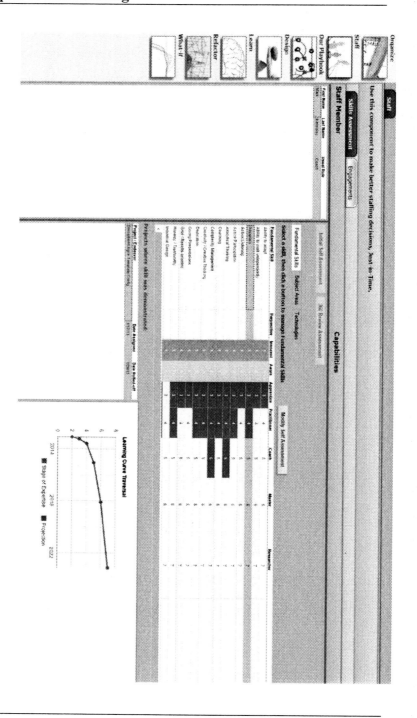

Figure 8.13 – Skills Baseline Assessments

With a capability baseline assessment performed across the enterprise, teams leverage the Self-organization capabilities of *Advisor*. Subsequent to declaring their way-of-working, the next step is to fully assign staff members to the endeavor. The leadership of the team or their management structure can now begin the process of staffing in an intelligent manner. Their first task is to generate the staffing requisitions for the project or endeavor. *Advisor* uses the practice, role and skillset mappings to create the needed slots to serve as a starting point for optimum staffing. Armed with a high fidelity view of the needs matched with the nature of the demand, minor adjustments can be made by manually adding additional headcount for a specific role requisition, or can remove requisitions as he/she sees fit. Similarly, fine-grained adjustments can be made to skillset requirements by adding or dropping line-items for each overall requisition. Figure 8.14 illustrates the Requisition aspect fo the Staff component.

Once we have completed the profiling of our supply-side, and profiling our demand-side, we are ready to match supply and demand. Performing assignments is made on a fit-for-purpose basis, with the likely best fit being the highest scoring candidate that is currently available and on the "organizational bench", and has the best percentage of skill matching. A staffing manager can review the matching scores and drill deeper to understand the skills that are missing or are currently indicating that the candidate is under qualified. They can choose to accept the risks posed with assigning that individual to the project in question, or can perform mitigation by leveraging just-in-time training or coaching to elevate the standing. If the manager decides to accept a candidate and also accept the risk, they can later revisit the decision when looking at poor results to determine if the risk has materialized. Finally, if the staffing manager does not like the profiles they are seeing as being currently available, they can turn their attention to talent acquisition and look externally for candidates that fit using one of *Advisor's* supply-chain staffing partners. Figure 8.15 that follows illustrates the Assignment aspect of the Staffing Component.

Once an assignment is completed, which may be short-lived or for the entire duration of a project, a staffing manager facilitates a debrief and roll-off of the engagement. Such a process accounts for the experience, both in terms of duration and intensity. This accounting is fed-forward such that accurate future assessments of fit-gap are available for future endeavor assignments.

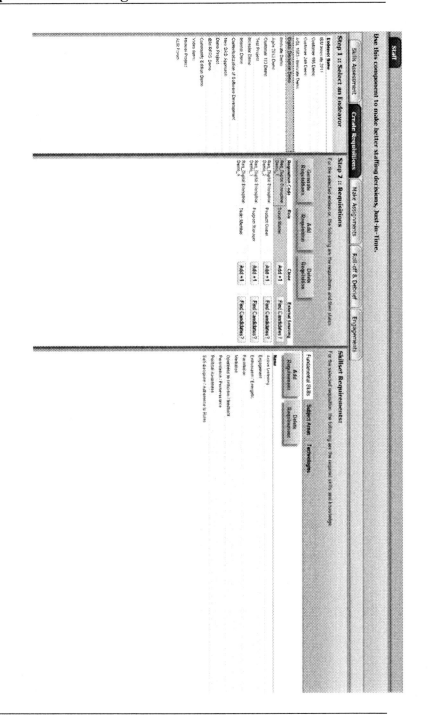

Figure 8.14 – Requisition Generation from Playbook

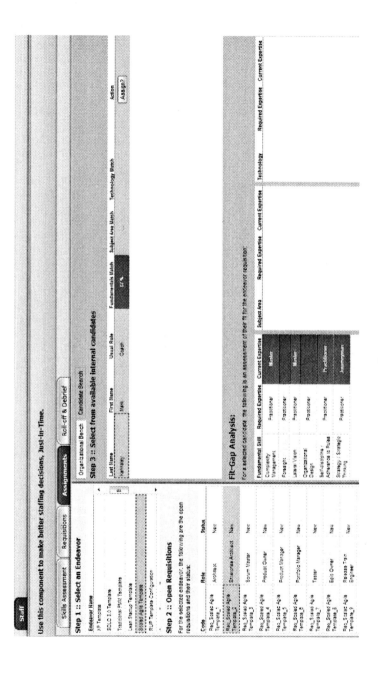

Figure 8.15 – Skills Gap Assessment

Chapter 9: Decision-centric Capability Improvement

"People don't resist change. They resist being changed!" – Peter Senge

It seems that everyone these days is touting a silver bullet approach to change or "transformation" Often it is unclear what exactly an organization is buying other than a bunch of billable hours, as there are varying degrees of snake-oil being peddled out there. Most often, a change management approach or strategy is nothing more than a *12-step Program*. All that is provided is a loosely described process with some interesting but non-practical insights into organizational psychology. It is almost as if a new shiny object is discovered in a consultants' travels, and an entirely new service offering is built around just that epiphany. The branching and differentiation in this space has followed much the same hyper-competitive pattern that software delivery methods have experienced. Such change "meta-methods" seem to becoming more and more prevalent in consulting rhetoric, likely because of their profitability and the volume of prospects now tackling this issue, sometimes for the second or third time. With modern methods having now gone mainstream and only *Laggards* [1] remaining, prospects when it comes to transformation of modern practice encompasses the more profitable volume of the *Early and Late Majority*. Table 9.1 is a compendium of change management "methods" of every make and persuasion, courtesy of a business-centric transformation consulting firm who similarly believes in integrating the essential and valuable practices within each of these approaches into a coherent, non-myopic strategy within many Fortune 500 Enterprises. In similar fashion to *Advisor*, they have the vision of concretely realizing their ideas in pragmatic fashion with their *Change Accelerator* system and their Emergent *Accelerating Change and Transformation (ACT)* method: [2]

Change Method	
Being First	*Change Leader's Roadmap* [3]
Boston Consulting Group	*Change Delta* [4]
Bridges	*Transition Model* [5]
Change First	*People Centered Implementation (PCI) Model* [6]
General Electric	*Change Acceleration Process (CAP)* [7]
Implementation Management Associates	*Accelerated Implementation Methodology (AIM)* [8]
John Kotter	*8-Step Process for Leading Change* [9]
Kubler-Ross	*The Change Curve* [10]
LaMarsh	*Managed Change Approach & Methodology* [11]
Kurt Lewin	*Three Stages of Change* [12]
PRITCHETT's	**Change Management Model** [13]
Prosci	**ADKAR** [14]

Table 9.1 – Change Management Methods

Needless to say, singular and out of context strategies that do not holistically account for the wide breadth of what has been learned in the field of organizational and social psychology do not have a very good track record. Even with all of these approaches to change, wave after wave of transformation have failed. Any form of strategic change, of which transformation of an enterprise's software delivery ecosystems is one instance, has historically only achieved an average success rate of 30%. We are not improving when it comes to how we approach major change, and as shown in Figure 9.1 illustrates, this flat trend:

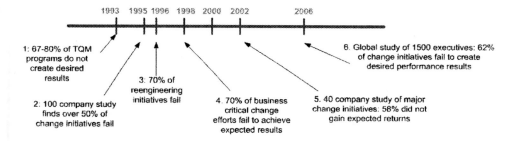

1. Stephen E. Brigham, "TQM: Lessons We Can Learn from Industry, *Change* May-June 1993

2. John P. Kotter, "Leading Change: Why Transformation Efforts Fail", *Harvard Business Review* February, 2000

3. Daryl R. Conner, "Leading at the Edge of Chaos", *NY John Wiley*, 2004.

4. David Miller, "Successful Change Leader", *Journal of Change Management*, vol. 2, no 4, pp 352-368.

5. J. A. Clair and R. P. Rao, "Helping Employees Embrace Change", *McKinsey Quarterly*, no 4 2002.

6. Organizing for Successful Change Management: *A McKinsey Global Survey*", June 2006.

Figure 9.1 – Change Management Success Rates

Clearly something has been missing from the equation in all the aforementioned recipes if the success rate trends remain flat. The question naturally is - what is the missing ingredient that has eluded organizations since the early 1990's?

9.1 – Coal Miners had it Right

Connecting the dots related to the puzzle and unsolved mystery of successful change strategy starts in the 1950's in a seemingly unrelated area - British coal mining. In the late 1940's and early 1950's, members of the Tavistock Institute of Human Relations [15] were chartered to study why a new approach to coal getting immediately following World War II was achieving low productivity despite improved equipment. Even with advances in technology and machinery, specialization and predictive scheduling, the results inexplicably were poor with the Longwall Method of Coal Getting [16]. This mass-production, batch oriented "innovation" was resulting in high attrition rates even with higher wages and better amenities. Severe morale challenges included despair and indignation, poor recruitment impetus, lasting psychological effects, disruptive conflict between shifts, and pay grievances. Given this poor state of affairs, grass-roots innovations in work structure related to segmentation into "room-and-pillar" schemes, along with attention to social-shortcomings and improvements in "group-relatedness" had remarkable effects in remediating the negative effects that went far beyond the advancements with various technologies.

To explore the phenomenon, Kenneth Bamforth and Eric Trist immediately focused in on the social aspects of the workers. What they discovered was that the coal-mining context amounted to "bad conditions and bad work" including hot, wet, dusty and dangerous conditions that were highly variable. This explained the need for a specific social structure similar to the prior "Hand Got" approaches. In this approach to coal mining, small autonomous yet responsible pair-groups were deployed who could function equally effective in a variety of engineering layouts. The effectiveness of these small groups could be attributed to the total significance and feeling of closure of their work and associated accountability. Each group had the complete set of coal face skills, and had craft pride and artisan independence, similar to the concept of cross-functional teams in today's software development approaches. Group members selected each other based on longstanding knowledge of each other, with full knowledge that a long term relationship would result. In circumstances of injury or death, it was not uncommon to see mates caring for the family of the fallen. These teams were highly adaptable to variable conditions and were left to work to their ability level. Importantly, the psychological effects of "dangers in the darkness" and isolated nature of the work necessitated the small autonomous work units and social "closeness".

The Hand Got approaches were not without difficulty however, as *tribal* competition was a common local optimization phenomenon related to lobbying for the best coal seams, sometimes through bribes. Yet these tribal conflicts "contained the bad so as to not destroy the good" aspects of the approach.

Through technological advances, coal mining became mechanized and thereby changed the organizational structures that were entrenched. Nationalization drove change such that a degree of **scale** was introduced and therefore a level of intermediaries. The first introduction of the Longwall method divided work into three 7 ½ hour shifts of workers, each performing a single specific function on the coal extraction "face" running a continuous front of 200 yards over a 24 hour period yielding somewhere around 200 tons per cycle. The idea was to create larger batches or "long" wall extraction increments to maximize productivity. Each face unit at scale was broken down into the first shift of 10 cutters who would drill holes for the "fires" to be shot to break apart the coal with explosives; a second shift of 10 rippers who would break the coal apart; and a third shift of 20 "fillers" would extract the coal. The schedule was fixed and ignored the reality of highly variable conditions, with no robustness or slack built into the sequential shift schedule.

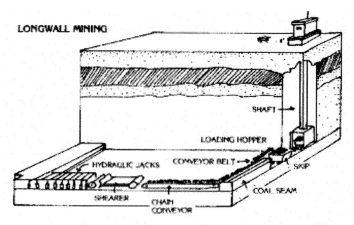

Figure 9.2 – Longwall Coal Mining [16]

Under this large scale work structure, several difficulties appeared almost immediately upon introduction. The unstable nature of chaining the shifts and tying them to specialized functions led to cascading failures and social tensions among the second and third shifts. The result was a lack of social integration of the whole unit of which coherence was necessary to be able to being the next face segment. As a result, management would assert that they were not receiving the necessary support from the men in taking broader responsibility beyond their narrowly defined tasks, and the workers complained that they were being tricked by "stick men" who intermittently interfered with the hard work at the coal face. It would be left to angry and suspicious bargaining when extra "bye work" was necessary to recover from missed filler shifts. This led to all manner of psychological defenses due to the stress from the full magnitude of the instability of the work system. Observations included high incidents of psycho-somatic and neurotic disorders with men "sitting in silence and attacking the coal face in towering rage or leaving in the face of panic". The overwhelming retreat was to blame the system in a form of co-dependency.

Based on this seminal work, the ongoing mandate of Tavistock was to apply the learning to better design work environments and understand the interconnectedness of management systems, technology and humans. Notable influences and collaborations included famous organizational psychologist Kurt Lewin and founder of social psychology, group dynamics and organizational development [17]. What followed was the articulation of "Socio-technical Systems" [18]. This field and discipline approach the design to complex organizational work through recognition of the interaction between people and technology in workplaces. This was the obvious finding of the Longwall Coal Mining study which exposed the interplay between technology enablers and the impact on social groups, and vice versa. Such systems were found to be complex due to the inherent complexity of the "figure" (social dimension) and the "ground" (contextual environment). To be successful in any work environment, a joint optimization must be sought. The core principles of Socio-technical Systems Theory [18] are:

1. Responsible Autonomy – teams versus individuals

2. Adaptability – simple organizations doing complex tasks

3. Whole Tasks - minimum critical specification

4. Meaningful Tasks – total significance and closure

Figure 9.3 illustrates the scope of Socio-technical System study:

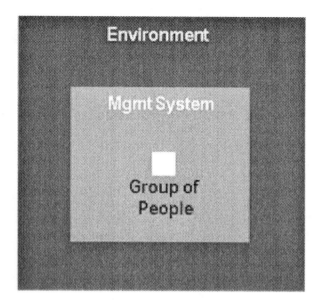

Figure 9.3 – Socio-Technical Systems [18]

Obviously, one can recognize the similarity of this body of knowledge and the Universal Kernel described in Chapter 5. At the heart of both illustrations is humans that have both social and psychological needs. It is imperative that management systems start to look at the whole and business enterprises must give first-order attention to the human aspects of what drives individuals towards *Operational Excellence*.

9.2 – Bring your Own Method

Applying the lessons of Socio-Technical Systems and driving towards a credible strategy for successful change requires looking at the relevant theories of what motivates people. One such model is Frederick Herzberg's "2-Factor Theory" [19], which suggests that you can only de-motivate people when it comes to the various extrinsic options like rewards or financial incentives, pressure tactics and the like (the so called "carrots and sticks"). He referred to these as "basic hygene factors", and when they are out of line with the minimum expectations of organizational members, they cause a negative motivational effect. Other than that, they are insufficient in unlocking the potential of the organization and motivating individuals to perform at their highest levels. Rather, intrinsic motivators, those that involve the design and nature of the work itself are the ones that can actually motivate us human beings. Figure 9.4 illustrates Herzberg's 2-Factor Theory:

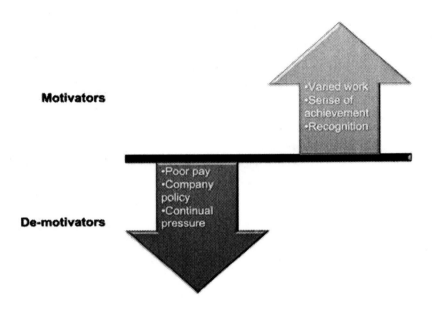

Figure 9.4 – Herzberg's 2 Factor Theory

It should be obvious that this is aligned with the findings of Tavistock and the study described in the previous section related to Socio-Technical Systems. This is also consistent with recent research studies covered in books such as Dan Pink's *Drive: The Surprising Things that Motivate Us* [20], and others on the subject. In the latter case, three key attributes are raised related to motivation - **Autonomy, Mastery and Purpose**. In fact, this is a subset of the *16 basic desires* [21] that motivate all humans.   Table 9.2 describes these basic desires that can be leveraged as intrinsic motivators:

Basic Desire	Explanation
Acceptance	The need for approval
Curiosity	The need to think, master things
Eating	The need for food
Family	The need to care for others
Honor	Being loyal to a group
Idealism	The need for purpose
Independence	Being an individual
Order	The need for stability, stable environments
Physical Activity	The need for health, exercise
Power	The need for influence of will
Romance	The need for love and sex
Saving	The need to collect
Social Contact	The need for friends
Status	The need for social standing
Tranquility	The need to be safe
Vengeance	The need to strike back

Table 9.2 – 16 Basic Human Desires

With motivational theory in mind, we can easily explain the lack of success with change management to date. Up until now, we have been pushing various schemes and ways of working on teams and individuals, basically robbing them of some of their most fundamental desires. The industry has been **pushing** change rather than **pulling** change through the foisting of wave after wave of methodology on people. The net result is all this process "Shelf-ware" is mediocrity at best with a continuance of software development train wrecks.

Worse than this, "methods" have been demotivating an entire industry. Instead of whomever saying "lets adopt Agile Method X" or "we are going to rollout Agile Scaling Thingy Y", we must instead change our calculus to be empowering teams to achieve their basic intrinsic motivators, especially the ones that relate to self determination. The process of self organization specifically addresses these basic desires. Instead of the current strategy to accommodate some degree of variability within an enterprise by pushing different "options" on teams but making them work within the confines of these popularized methods, to be effective with change, organizations must instead embrace the notion that there is only one method in the land of methodology - "Our Method". Such a method for each team is a hybrid of whatever will get the job done. Let your people tell you how they want to deliver to the objectives they are to realize. Govern based on the investment business case for the piece of software to be built, not the way of working and the stuff produced by it. Issue "command intent" for what you will need to make informed business decisions, but be honest about the value of that request in how you will manage in a knowledge worker environment of large uncertainty. In other words, discharge fiduciary and due diligence (the Responsible part) by managing to the interface, not the implementation, in investment centric terms. Empower your teams by giving them guidance and choice, and most of all self-determination for the results that are expected of them (the Autonomy part).

Such a paradigm of method brand **agnosticism** represents a huge learning opportunity for the enterprise with all the empirical data that will be available for optimizing outcomes. Obviously this requires an efficient environment where the organization can capture the learnings of what practice works and what practice doesn't work from a rather large base of possibilities and experiences. It also requires steering teams around the potholes of prior lessons learned so mistakes of the past are not repeated - proactively. This is the complexity part of socio-technical systems, and must be mitigated or else anarchy will ensue. Mitigation of this complexity requires situational awareness (in our industry we call this contextualization), and the support of a new emergent trend in the IT industry - cognitive systems. This new trend is being forged at a rapid pace, as is evident by the 2014 announcement by IBM with the $1B investment in the Watson Business Unit [22], along with their associated Cognitive Systems Initiative [23]. The concrete realization for this level of delivery intelligence and organizational learning is already manifested within the *Advisor* expert system technology.

9.3 – Cognitive Bias

Humans are fallible. We are prone to some strange behavior and poor or irrational decisions due to the intrinsic flaws in our brains. These flaws are called "Cognitive Bias". Two systems are related to the cognitive ability of people [24]. The first is the Automatic System, which refers to that part of the brain that is the oldest and is responsible for rapid uncontrolled reaction that is unconscious and effortless. The Reflexive System is what produces what we would refer to as thinking, the controlled deliberate and effortful processing of information and stimulus and the deductive decision making process. The challenge in today's environment of *Digital Disruption* and the accelerating pace of business is that people within Enterprise IT do not always have the luxury to take the slow route to arrive at the countless decisions that must be made during the knowledge intensive software development effort. With increasing complexity and the sheer number of decision to be made comes decision fatigue and poorer decisions. Therefore, there is always the temptation to rely on the Automatic System far more than we should. As pressure is placed on teams using techniques like Time-boxing, the effects of decision fatigue affect our ability to compromise and formulate tradeoffs. The problem is that while the Automatic System is rapid and effortless, it is far more subject to all forms of bias. While the Automatic System is also experiential, it is often difficult to tell whether decisions are being made by genuine experience, or by default through biased processing. If left unmitigated, these biased decisions lead to poor outcomes.

The root cause of the various forms of bias in our thinking boils down to some basic things that affect humans and their decisions: the Automatic System taking shortcuts through the use of heuristics; mental noise; limitations in the processing capability of humans; emotional or moral motivations; or social influence. Bias can be categorized as stemming from either decisions related to social interactions within the Socio-technical System, or through engagement with the technical environment of the software endeavor. Specifically, all the cognitive biases below in Tables 9.3 and 9.4 commonly occur with teams making decisions related to the execution of their software projects:

Cognitive Bias	Explanation
Actor Observer Bias	The tendency for explanations of other individuals' behaviors to overemphasize the influence of their personality and underemphasize the influence of their situation
Backfire Effect	When people react to disconfirming evidence by strengthening their beliefs.
Bandwagon Effect/ Herd Instinct	The tendency to do (or believe) things because many other people do (or believe) the same.
False Consensus Bias	when fatigued, see consensus where it's not there
Dunning Kruger Effect / Superiority Bias	An effect in which incompetent people fail to realize they are incompetent because they lack the skill to distinguish between competence and incompetence
In-group Bias	The biased belief that the characteristics of an individual group member are reflective of the group as a whole or the tendency to assume that group decision outcomes reflect the preferences of group members, even when information is available that clearly suggests otherwise.
Cheerleader Effect	The tendency for people to appear more attractive in a group than in isolation
Out-group Homogeneity Bias	Individuals see members of their own group as being relatively more varied than members of other groups
Self-serving Bias	The tendency to claim more responsibility for successes than failures
Stereotyping	Expecting a member of a group to have certain characteristics without having actual information about the individual.
Status Quo Bias	Tendency for people to like things to stay relatively the same
Subjective Validation / Belief Bias	Perception that something is true if a person's beliefs demand it to be true

Table 9.3 – Social Cognitive Bias

Cognitive Bias	Explanation
Ambiguity Effect	The tendency to avoid options for which missing information makes the probability seem "unknown."
Anchoring Bias	The tendency to rely too heavily, or "anchor," on one trait or piece of information when making decisions (usually the first piece of information that we acquire on that subject)
Availability Effect	The tendency to overestimate the likelihood of events with greater "availability" in memory
Confirmatory Bias	The tendency to search for, interpret, focus on and remember information in a way that confirms one's preconceptions
Distinction Bias	The tendency to view two options as more dissimilar when evaluating them simultaneously than when evaluating them separately
Hindsight Bias	the tendency to see past events as being predictable
Framing Effect	Drawing different conclusions from the same information, depending on how or by whom that information is presented.
Optimism Bias	Tendency to be overoptimistic about the outcome of planned activities
Recency Effect / Peek-end Rule	Tendency to weight recent events more than earlier events

Table 9.4 –Technical Cognitive Bias

How can we trust humans to make unbiased decisions if enterprises are to bestow Responsible Autonomy upon teams to self-organize? How can executives reap the change management motivational benefits that such a strategy affords to drive successful and lasting transformation to modern practice? The answer lies in our ability to guide and constrain teams in a *Libertarian Paternalism* sense, and nudge teams and individuals away from poor, biased choices. The *Advisor* expert system choice architecture delivers such a capability, and mitigates the effects of bias but still provides an environment of empowerment and pragmatic exploration. Nudges of various forms can help guide people to avoid making poor decisions due to the normal temptations to rely on fast thinking, absent of any safety net.

9.4 – Emergence or Patterns?

Mitigating potentially risky choices resulting from the empowerment of a strategy is only one aspect of the due diligence required by enterprise management. Avoiding risky choices altogether represents another means to address the cognitive bias problem. Reuse of prior experience in the form of **Patterns** enables teams to reference classes of project experience that have proven to be contextually appropriate. Patterns are defined as *solutions to recurring problems in context*. Patterns at a fine-grained level are synonymous with practices in terms of ways-of-working. At a coarse grained level, patterns are representative of practice-set templates, potentially representing whole methods. Such reuse at a large scale relates to capturing broad and statistically significant empirical data such that confidence in application of these patterns is generated. Usage of patterns-of-success through either entire sets or sub-sets of practices also accelerates the decision making process so that engagement in the actual work can proceed sooner. *Decision-centric Capability Improvement* (DCCI) represents a strategy that leverages to the fullest extent *a priori* experience through the facilitation of the pattern recognition and assimilation.

Figure 9.5 illustrates the overall model of Decision-centric Capability Improvement:

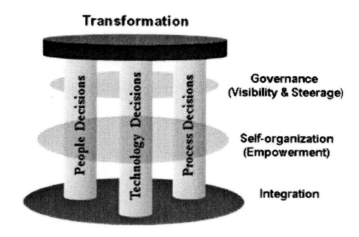

Transformation

Governance
(Visibility & Steerage)

Self-organization
(Empowerment)

Integration

Figure 9.5 – Decision-centric Capability Improvement

With DCCI, pattern experience is made available due to the enablement of the holistic reductionism that is reflected in the Universal System's Thinking kernel. The integration of all prior software development practice knowledge is required to empower self-organization that is critical to motivational theory. The breadth of practice coverage from methods and bodies of knowledge available to be mined comes from over 50 years of albeit fragmented industry knowledge. This integration must be subject to data supporting the efficacy of this experience and grounded by management science and a robust underpinning model. With this approach, organizations must be supported to deal with the essential complexity of the domain through automation while simultaneously avoiding the accidental complexity that has occurred to date resulting from silo'd consideration of container methods. Without the ability to enable the rapid assembly of practice experience in the context of a holistic Value Stream, teams would still exhibit various forms of Cognitive Bias and deliver sub-optimal outcomes.

Self-organization capability at the scale of the enterprise builds upon the integration capability. To enable sound decisions in a timely fashion, the people in your organization with the most up-to-date information about efficient and effective tactics for software delivery must be empowered to make choices. At scale, this is a manifestation of the *Theory Y* philosophy of management and provides the critical motivational missing link. Instead of static process-ware sitting on a shelf telling a team how to work, teams must be able to efficiently and effectively declare how they will work based on their understanding of the context of the endeavor. Enabling these decision rights not only mitigates   the   issues   of   division   that   challenge   large-scale transformations, the decision patterns themselves serve as knowledge to be used for organizational learning.

Without the visibility into the choices being made, steerage is impossible. You cannot influence in a positive manner what you do not know is wrong. Without visibility into the decision making process and the levers to influence the choices made, the ability to discharge a fiduciary level of duty and govern effectively such that risk is efficiently mitigated would be superficial at best. This influence or steerage is informed not only by the current snapshot of decisions (both practice and supply-chain decisions for an endeavor) but also the patterns that emerge related to the effectiveness of the self-organization process itself. Steerage of the enterprise as a whole towards improved capability requires the holistic attention to the three major types of decision that are subject to human error - approach or process decisions, people decisions related to staffing the endeavor based on the approach to be taken, and the high-order solution decisions. Transformation of capability only occurs in true, material form when all potential sources of risk are mitigated.

In contrast to this decision-pattern orientation strategy is the strategy of relying on *emergence* as seen in the Kanban Method [25]. Often misunderstood as a software delivery "method", it is actually an evolutionary change management approach. This strategy makes heavy use of Eliyahu Goldratt's mesmerizing "Theory of Constraints" (ToC) and his Five Focusing Steps [26]. While the approach manifests the mechanism of the *kanban* pull-system and the principle of maximizing flow through the implementation of WIP Limits, it is limited to exploitation of constraints and does not address elevation of constraints in true ToC doctrine. The issue with the Kanban Method is that it relies too heavily on faith that an optimal delivery ecosystem will emerge in a timely fashion such that outcomes are improved. Teams are given too much "libertarian" autonomy at the expense of the "paternalistic" responsible part. While this may be attractive from a consulting perspective requiring expensive *Sensei* level expertise to be effective, the avoidance of reuse in the form of the universe of practices amounts to reinventing the wheel for each and every endeavor. Internal knowledge of how to be effective in the small set of practices is left to organic and viral propagation. Moreover, the Kanban Method purports to allow teams to simply leverage the methods they currently utilize, yet the management science and the pull-system mechanism is in conflict with the differing value stream network configurations, and assumes simple serialized I-Plant processes. Figure 9.6 illustrates the various process configurations that are possible, with the I-plant clearly being the simplest, and unlike what really happens on software development projects:

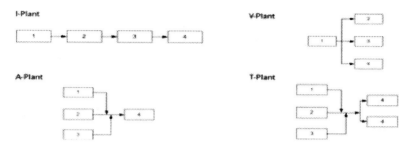

Figure 9.6 – Process Configurations

Finally, while the collection of data that enables feed-forward parameterization and reuse of successful kanban board designs is theoretically possible, socially the practice of leveraging physical forms of kanban is by far the most prevalent. Even if organizations try electronic or digital kanban environments, the implementations do not capture the decisions and learning related to the evolutionary improvement process. The physical mechanism of the pull-system is automated, but the metadata related to how the parameterization in terms of WIP Limits and buffers correlated to contextual demand is absent.

Fundamentally, Decision-centric Capability Improvement represents a departure and decoupling of the management science related to modern practice from the populism, marketing and rhetoric of the industry to realize a paradigm of purposeful organizational design. This reflects the philosophy of pragmatism as opposed to faith-based reasoning. Instead of reliance on hope for optimal delivery ecosystems to emerge and make a difference on outcomes, DCCI drives the System's Thinking based design and makes heavy use of pattern reuse and risk mitigation to lower the costs of transformation to modern practice and empower a new level of due diligence.

9.5 – Better Decisions mean Better Outcomes

Better decisions mean better outcomes. It is reasonable that if teams make better decisions regarding technologies and their way of working, if IT executives are empowered to make better decisions about their in-flight portfolio, and if HR Departments are armed with better requisitions regarding the necessary skill-sets needed to achieve successful endeavors, better business outcomes will occur. The risk of Anchoring, Bandwagon Effect, Deformation Professionnelle, Dunning-Kruger Effect, Confirmatory Bias or Hindsight Bias are highly probable based on the current state of the IT methodology. To enable sound decisions free of bias that can otherwise lead to less than optimal software delivery outcomes, risky approach choices need to be identified and mitigated. To achieve this, choices must not be myopic but rather consider experience in the form of practices wherever such practice experience may be found and verified as effective. The trust vested in the teams to organize in such a way that is likely to yield optimal outcomes must exist within the realities of efficient and effective governance. The enablement of true self-organizing teams at scale within the constraints of the enterprise's management structure and associated fiduciary vesting requires automation to provide the data which can yield the same goal of openness and transparency espoused at the team level. Investors and the management they entrust must have visibility at portfolio scale to make the right investment decisions regarding real options and be afforded "predictive analytics". This is the "New Deal" between management and professional software delivery personnel.

Better decisions only occur when both errors and bias are mitigated, and that such mitigation is performed in a timely manner. Late decisions can be as risky as bad decisions due to our inability to exercise the option we have selected, or due to the destabilizing effects on dynamics as a result of the delay incurred. Inventory and backlog of decisions can also lead to decision fatigue and can overwhelm downstream segments of the value stream. Figure 9.7 illustrates the balancing that decision makers must achieve, which represents a balance between risk of delay and risk of error. Ultimately, this requires identification of the optimal strategy for determining how much evidence and Reflexive thinking should occur based on an organization's risk tolerance.

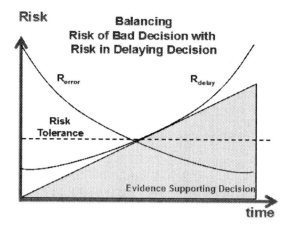

Figure 9.7 – Bad versus Timely Decisions

To ensure that overall flow of decision making proceeds smoothly for an endeavor, the self organization process must not be subjected to delay or stalling. Lengthy startup delays incurred by teams exploring ways of working and staffing fitness can be as detrimental to the overall delivery ecosystem as poor decision flow related to arriving at the software solution. Automation ensures that guidance is provided for the overall process of self-organization in a timely manner and that decision progress performance is easily discerned. The typical scenario without such capability is to simply say that a team is "using Method X", which obfuscates the essential complexity of contextualizing their endeavor and determining fitness-for purpose. Figure 9.8 illustrates the robust Self Organization process as manifested within *Advisor*.

Figure 9.8 – Self Organization @Scale

Once a team has reflected on the context of their software project or product delivery endeavor, they also assess the culture of the broader organization in which their team must coexist. Subsequent to such contextual observation, the team exercises their discretion regarding their way-of-working through practice choices. With these inputs, risks associated with such choices are identified such that accompanying advice can be given to teams in a timely manner. This expert knowledge delivery occurs in leau of reliance on a human coach for all but the more thorny issues that may arise. True to the nature of self determination and the associated motivational benefits, risks that are identified can be acknowledged by the team and the associated refactoring advice taken. If however the team feels otherwise, they can reject the advice and retain the choices they have made. Ultimately the only method that matters is "their way-of-working", not some method that has been foisted on the team by an overzealous consultant or a Theory X manager. The team can get on with it so to speak and learn from their experiences using their method as quickly as possible.

Once experiences are accrued and feedback cycles have occurred, the team may discover opportunities for improvement in either their way of working or their staffing profile. Such observation is valuable to the enterprise and should be captured within a system so that other teams across the enterprise can benefit from their lessons learned. Performing retrospectives through automation provides the organizational reach that is absent with Post-it Notes. Figure 9.9 illustrates the Inspect and Adapt process as manifested in *Advisor*.

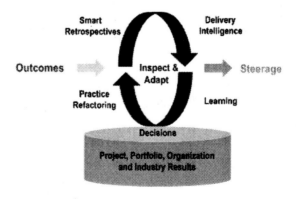

Figure 9.9 – Inspect and Adapt @Scale

Effectively, governance means steerage, and performing higher-frequency inspection and adaptation within endeavors rather than after the fact leads to more optimal trajectories for software projects. Instead of waiting for problems to mount with an initially exercised decision related to either approach or staffing, the openness and transparency across the portfolio empowers everyone to recognize bad conditions and do something about them. The empirical data informs managers or other leadership of current operational status, and provides such intelligence free of blind spots and bias. Correlation of delivery intelligence and the current operational progress of the endeavor can be correlated to the current risk profile of the ecosystem such that refactoring can be pinpointed and timely. Sometimes though, teams will not have enough experience to determine causality. This could be due to an unprecedented situation that either the team or the organization at large has not observed before and codified in rules. Or, it could be due to fatigue setting in resulting in the inability to understand the current state beyond the mere symptoms. In either case, refactoring support is sometimes needed. Leveraging 5-whys [27] and Cause and Effect Analysis [28] analysis are useful techniques from Lean Thinking, the former of which is extremely powerful if complemented with machine learning. If, through many instances of causal analysis, certain patterns become more prevalent within a particular organization, those "neural pathways" become etched into the 5-why's process, and refactoring advice can become sharper and more targeted.

The net result of Decision-centric Capability Improvement as a strategy is that change is continuous and avoids the 18-month reset button cycle that is so common and wasteful in the IT industry. Figure 9.10 illustrates the new pattern that emerges, which prevents the back-sliding and false starts that plague change management success rates.

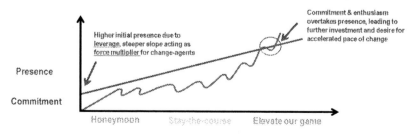

Figure 9.10 – Continuous Change versus False-starts

Instead of hitting the wall and having the third 6 month period in the 18-month cycle be "wrap it up", renewal and enlightenment replace the false starts and frustrating change pattern. With visibility into real progress with the transformation, executives are likely to want more of what is working and move from "stay the course" to *Let's Elevate our Game.* Change visionaries, sponsors and their guiding coalition are able to continually monitor and "touch" the change.   Transformation is always **top of mind.** This contrasts the change anti-pattern described in Chapter 1. Executives will have moved on mentally at this point, assuming nothing is wrong with their investment until it is too late to make course corrections. At that point, many other concerns have risen to the top of their attention vying list, so prior failing investments become the first to get chopped.

Such a successful change pattern is referred to as "Sticky" [29]. Sticky changes are ones in which are simple, unexpected, concrete, credible, emotional, and story based. With Decision-centric Capability Improvement, a simple focus on decisions means IT change leaders are aligned with how the business thinks about investment. Such a novel approach is unexpected, as the industry tires from wave after wave of prescription being pushed on teams. A transformation platform makes the change environment concrete, especially one that is built using the credibility of System's Thinking. Celebrating patterns of success tends to instill a sense of empowerment and euphoria when following DCCI, as the gorilla is off everyone's back and people can go about their work. Sharing stories of success in an open and transparent manner means everyone feels safe about the change, not threatened or at risk.

9.6 – Decision-centric Software Architecture

The third leg of the Decision-centric Capability Improvement strategy involves decisions related to software architecture. How decisions are made related to the solution of a business problem materially affects the outcome of the IT investment. Such "high-stakes decisions" are tightly interrelated to the approach or process for waging them, and the people performing software architecture. Historically, the definition of software architecture has been highly variable and poorly understood. Emphasis within the IT community has been related to Viewpoints, Views, and Perspectives [30]. However, recent observations in industry suggest that software architecture is more about mitigating the risks surrounding significant IT investment decisions than with the approach to communicate and capture the knowledge within a solution. A software architecture can be viewed as a *solution decision-set*. The architectural reasoning process can be viewed as analogous to Investment Portfolio Management with the Architect being more like an Investment Manager. A system's software architecture evolves as and is synonymous to a set of significant design decisions that address stakeholder concerns about the Qualities-of-Service of a solution. Figure 9.11 illustrates the spiral nature of the decision-making process:

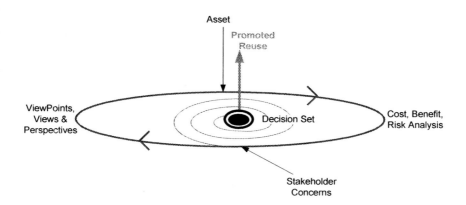

Figure 9.11 – Decision-centric Architecture

Decision-centric reasoning techniques address a multivariate problem because the architecting process must deal with multiple concurrent concerns. A decision-centric approach is an evolution from the viewpoint-centric approaches that have emphasized visual modeling and blueprinting to describe design decisions. However, architecting is much more than the techniques used to reduce complexity and communicate precisely. Architecting is about balancing competing interests from multiple communities of stakeholders, and about being able to support those decisions on the basis of cost, benefit and risk – the overall "goodness" of the solution in concrete terms.

Many similar terms relate to the IEEE 1471 (Recommended Practice for Software Architecture Description) [31] concept of *Stakeholder Concerns*. Some of these come from other bodies of knowledge including Quality Attributes (SEI) [32], Qualities of Service (real-time space), Non-functional/Supplemental/Supporting (RUP, OpenUP), and "URPS+" or "ilities" (Booch). It is this type of requirement/statement of need that serves as the architectural drivers for a solution. An architectural driver (also known as a Sensitivity Point) is a force that shapes the ultimate solution tactics and decisions. Although a broad array of solutions may "work", there exists an optimum solution that achieves balance among competing stakeholders. It is architectural drivers that assist the architect in arriving at the optimum solution in the most efficient manner, and it is architectural drivers, that if ignored, lead to spectacular failures.

Reasoning about the trade space of stakeholder concerns is performed both visually through blueprints, and through the use of well known decision tools. Applying the pair-wise comparison technique within the Analytical Hierarchy Process (AHP) [34] enables the unbiased and efficient ranking of stakeholder perspectives. Figure 9.12 shows the basic linear algebraic form of AHP. In modified forms of this approach, application of the first-level of analysis only occurs as specified within the AHP process in a facilitated group forum to achieve group consensus as to the matrix cell scoring. Techniques implicit within the method identify bias and assist the Architect in facilitating negotiations related to priority.

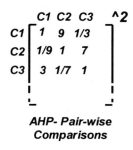

**AHP- Pair-wise
Comparisons**

Figure 9.12 – Analytical Hierarchy Process-AHP [34]

From the prioritized stakeholder concerns, groupings that correlate to common "Quality Attributes" can be arranged into a Utility Tree, with the cumulative rankings per Quality node arising from the related concerns. The resultant Utility Tree in Figure 9.13 represents the Architectural Utility as viewed and negotiated with and between stakeholders, which is leveraged within the alternatives and tradeoff reasoning process.

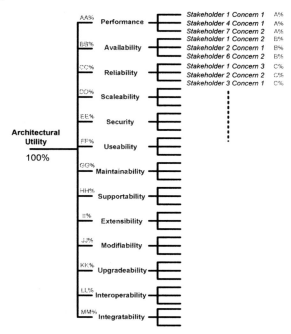

Figure 9.13 – Multi-attribute Utility Tree (MAUT) [34]

Quality Attributes of concern represent various *Aspects* of quality of the software architecture. Therefore, defining which concrete functionality is to achieve various qualities (or scales of service quality in the case of degraded service modes) is essential to ensure that the quality investment in the solution is focused and optimized. Identification of the functional context for reasoning about the highest ranked Quality Attribute/Concern is achieved by selecting the indicative Use Case scenario realizations (also known as architecturally significant Use Cases). Each Stakeholder Concern should leverage one Use Case scenario for further exploration. Such Use Case realizations also form the basis of defining associated Quality Scenarios (a.k.a. Quality Test Cases), which are required to facilitate exercising the evolving executable architecture to provide concrete evidence of solution merit to architectural governance bodies and interested stakeholder communities. Figure 9.14 illustrates the use of extension Use Cases as Aspects [35] to frame Quality Scenarios in the proper context.

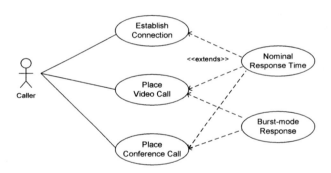

Figure 9.14 – Using Aspects as context for Qualities-of-Service

During the process of architecting a solution, the above "test harness" will serve as a quantitative basis for reasoning about the overall solution. A reference catalog of proven patterns/tactics that have been leveraged within specific prior efforts is consulted. Synonymous with the term tactic, a pattern is a solution to a problem within a context. This level of reuse is logical (sometimes referred to as "derivative" reuse) but guides the architect towards physical implementations and aids awareness and identification of various sources of manifestation of the tactic. Figure 9.15 illustrates the relationship between a quality attribute and the various tactics that can be taken.

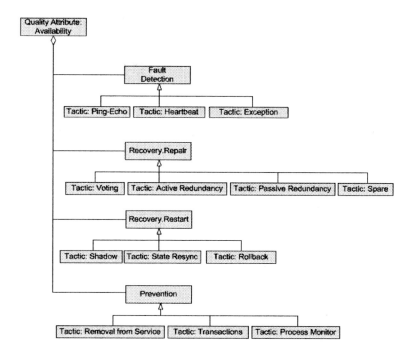

Figure 9.15 – Quality Attributes and Tactics/Patterns [36]

The objective of recognizing a reusable pattern is to "seed" a necessary decision related to addressing a concern by leveraging a candidate approach. These proven tactics represent prior successful decisions, typically showing repeated successful deployment on at least 3 prior developments. Such tactics serve only as candidate decisions, because reasoning is required to determine applicability with the project's context. Reasoning about a candidate decision occurs in two ways. The first is the historically common approach – visualization. For the Use Case Realizations selected to reason about Quality Attribute implications and possible tactics, relevant Viewpoints and Views are prepared for the comparison of alternatives, and later to communicate choices. This elaboration includes structural elements from either logical and/or physical views. Figure 9.16 illustrates the nature of Viewpoints and Views as articulated in IEEE 1471.

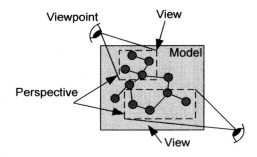

Figure 9.16 – Viewpoints and Views

Perspectives and their related collection of views are leveraged to perform the same function for cross-cutting concerns. Visual Modeling supports the decision reasoning process in that it reduces complexity. It is just one tool leveraged by the Architect to understand the various aspects of the required solution, and serves the additional purpose of communicating such reasoning in an un-ambiguous and precise way.

Concrete assets that can be leveraged in realizing the structural elements required by the realized scenarios become apparent through the visualization.   Typically these are known as mechanisms, or more generically building blocks, and imply a scale of physical implementations ranging from design class clusters -> frameworks -> components/services -> packages.   Acquisition of tangible assets, rather than custom development yields lower risk for fulfillment. The quickest way to accelerate development and reduce uncertainty about outcomes is to "build less stuff". The challenge with acquisition-orientation as a strategy for development is getting visibility into the degree of fitness-for-purpose of the building block(s). Visual Models from prior efforts can facilitate gap analysis; this is because visual models help us understand, and we need to understand the element of reuse under consideration. Use Case Scenario realizations enable an efficient and unambiguous approach to gap analysis.   Scenarios represent stimulus by which Quality attributes can be exercised (a.k.a Quality Scenarios).

The second tool available for reasoning about the fitness for purpose mentioned above is through investment analysis. Bringing a decision "all-to-dollars" [37] through the quantification of benefits, costs and risks of the fulfillment decision enables an actionable way to successively add more decision elements to the set. Portfolio analysis as the decision set grows and tradeoffs are identified enables "what-if" reasoning to occur. Thinking of an architecture as a decision-set is akin to treating it like an investment portfolio – like a stock portfolio. Performing similar analytics on the decision-set portfolio enables identification of the optimum decision-set, such that the latest incremental candidate decisions can be recommended to the stakeholders of the architecture. Inevitably, various tradeoff points exist between concerns and their associated quality attributes. Such tradeoffs require the negotiation and facilitation skills of the architect to stress the overall goodness of the holistic solution. Key to successful ratification of candidate decisions is to mitigate the tendency by stakeholders to locally optimize individual concerns. Rather a focus on the overall mission of the system should be emphasized.

With each successive decision taken on how to address each ranked stakeholder concern, the goal is to converge the potential solutions available, such that each successive analysis of alternatives and respective tradeoff space becomes smaller. This is enabled through the weighting of the concerns at the onset of architectural reasoning, and because the concerns are elaborated and negotiated on a weighted order, the probability of converging in an efficient and stable manner is high.

Finally, after it is determined that a solution (entire decision-set, aka architectural stack), or portion of the solution (individual decisions) is value-add, such decisions need to be identified as candidates for other projects to reuse. Central enterprise repositories typically facilitate architectural Asset Management and can facilitate visibility into opportunities that exist to future project architects. Such mechanisms are part of a broader knowledge management effort relating to IT delivery lessons learned.

9.7 – Keeping it Real

If we can all agree that we can always do better, then the simple question of "how are we doing" is not too much to ask. Answering this question can take two different forms, depending on whether you are looking at it from a financial opportunity standpoint or from a risk management standpoint. In the former case, the most popularized framework for answering this question is the Capability Maturity Model Integrated (CMMI) model from the Software Engineering Institute at Carnegie Mellon University [38], now a separate for-profit organization [39]. This framework not only provides a structure of key practices that over time have supporting data to suggest certain financial benefits related to software delivery, it also provides an assessment approach, certification scheme and qualification training program for assessors. Determination of a maturity level is made by performing a Standard CMMI Appraisal Method for Process Improvement (SCAMPI) [40] assessment of differing degrees of formality. These assessments are typically ad hoc, and can take some time to perform, sometimes due to less than expected results from teams and therefore under less than amicable circumstances. From the risk management standpoint, controls are imposed on teams so that risks related to software delivery in theory can be prevented. Compliance mandates and requirements suggest higher levels of discipline through more formal practices. Often these higher levels of formality are assumed due to bias and overdone rather than actually being required. The most common controls framework from a compliance perspective is the Control Objectives for IT (COBIT) [41] framework. This framework is a rigorous set of practice guidance and accompanying standards of care that are mandated across the full breadth of the value stream. COBIT (currently at version 5) is driven out of the Accounting and Audit community and maintained by the Information Systems Audit and Compliance Association (ISACA).

In the case of these "litmus test" frameworks, each represents a practice set view of the Universal Kernel presented in Chapter 5. Simply put, they are Views without the accompanying model. With the Systems Thinking kernel, not only can gaps be quickly presented to teams or management in a just-in-time fashion, the relative magnitude of gaps in terms of ecosystem performance, stability or risk exposure can be determined. These frameworks simply represent one of many views of the underlying model of how software development endeavors actually function. Figures 9.17 and 9.18 illustrate CMMI and COBIT real-time assessments based on a team's current practice choices:

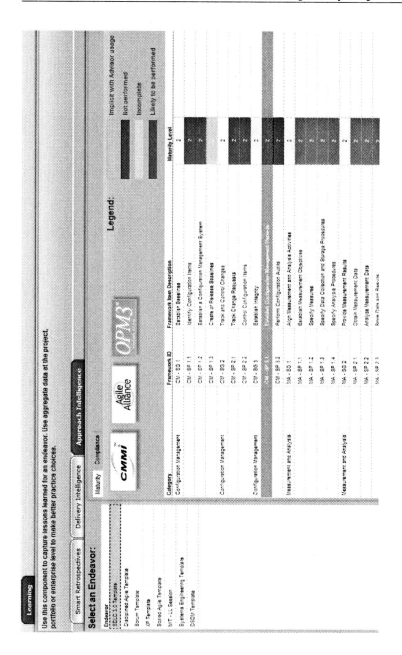

Figure 9.17 – JIT Maturity Assessments

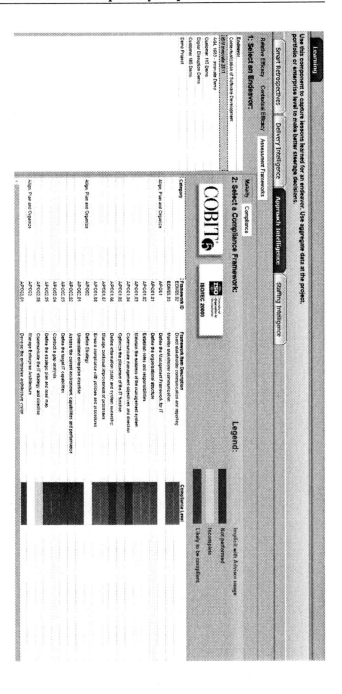

Figure 9.18 – JIT Compliance Assessments

Instilling the spirit and intent of Kaizen means continuously evolving baselines of experience in terms of ways of working and associated staffing profiles. Codifying *Standard Work* can be done either by prescription or through rules of thumb and policies. The dynamic nature of software development as knowledge work and the rapid pace of technology churn demands that the latter approach be taken by organizations. To implement this practice and realize Decision-centric Capability Improvement, an enterprise can start with a set of generally accepted practices and rules based on their contextual and cultural efficacy, and based on their adoptability. Over time, distinctly unique patterns will emerge for the specific competitive pressures and realities of each organization separately. It is the job of management, with unique visibility into overarching corporate strategy and direction, to implement guidance in the form of policies. Such policies can be in the form of "nudges", or can be stronger in the form of mandates and governance requirements. Having a platform that can dynamically evolve to provide a custom, context-specific rule-base is essential to exercising pragmatic, non-intrusive governance. Without it, the quality of controls and the quality of compliance evidence is highly variable.

Advisor provides an out-of-the-box rule base that evolves as more is learned industry wide about practice efficacy and cultural affinity. The COTS rule base can be over-ridden if an enterprise deems their context to be entirely unique. Alternatively, reuse of the rule base can be leveraged along with custom extensibility as more is learned on their organizational improvement journey. Configurability in terms of triggering rules, contextual thresholds, risk identification and refactoring practice advice are all options for tailoring the system. Figure 9.19 illustrates configuration of the expert system rule-base:

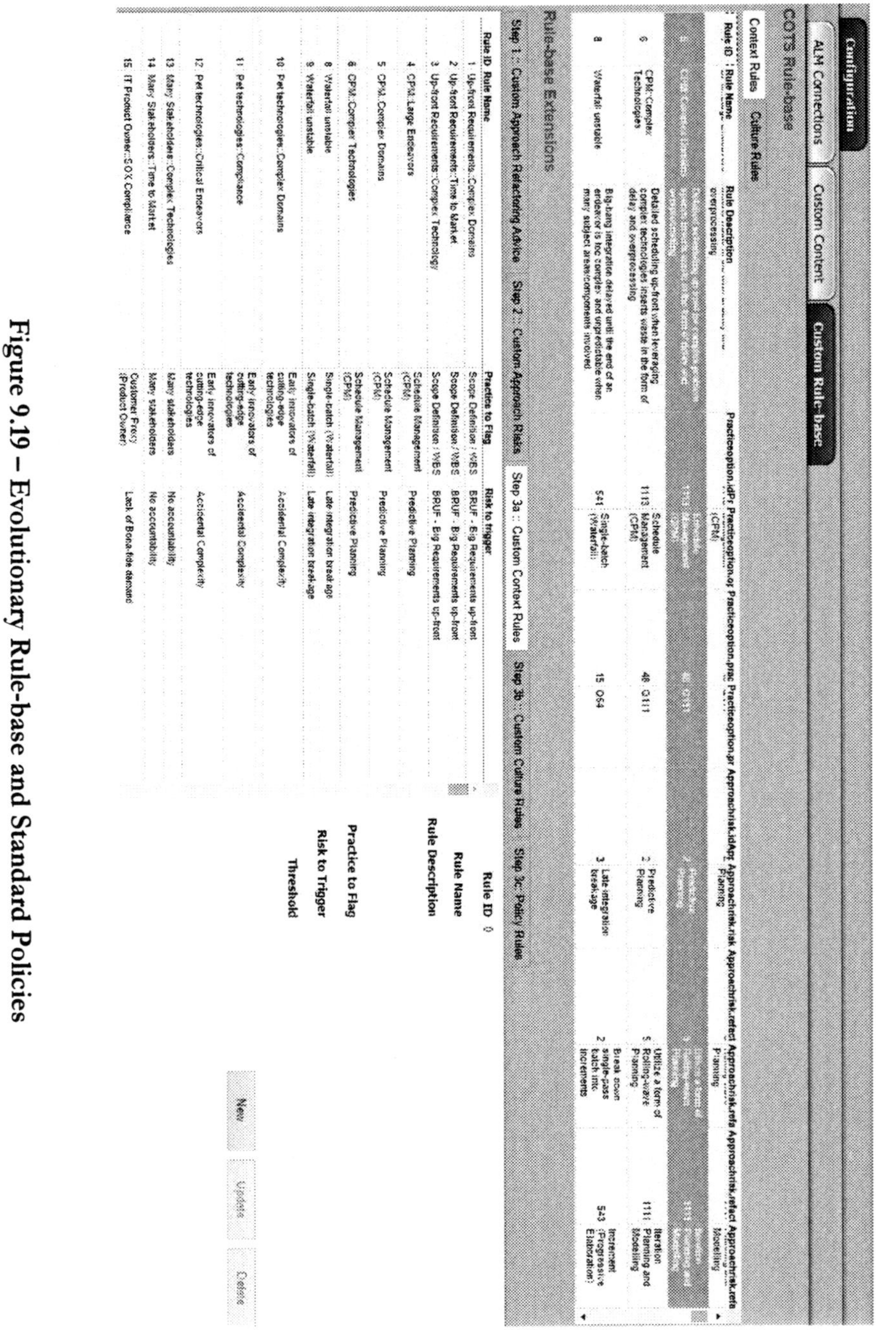

Figure 9.19 – Evolutionary Rule-base and Standard Policies

McKinsey has very recently come out with change management advice, advocating *Platforms for Change* as opposed to *Programs for Change* [42]. A "Platform for Change" is defined as a social technology that makes large scale collaboration and experimentation easy, transparent and effective. Such a platform encourages participation and engagement beyond one's immediate constituency, facilitates root cause analysis, fosters experimentation of many contextually relevant solutions for improvement and provides the responsible autonomy to spur innovation.

According to McKinsey, three shifts in approach are necessary:

- From top-down to activist-out. To make real and pervasive change across the enterprise, responsibility for initiating change needs to be syndicated.

- From sold to invited because transformational change is only sustained through commitment by empowering everyone in the enterprise with the "how".

- From managed to organic, which means placing less emphasis on a centralized organization to control change but rather building self-organizing teams that identify opportunities for improvement and are compelled to experiment with their hypotheses.

The *Advisor* Transformation Platform realizes these strategy elements at the reach of the enterprise through its cloud-based architecture. The platform facilitates the type of openness and transparency required to stimulate true and sustainable change such that everyone is vested and engaged in the transformation. The fundamental *mindset* shift required to evolve organizational culture and the management system is catalyzed through Advisors inherent empirical system's thinking and stimulates the spirit of curiosity and experimentation. Without such a concrete capability, dealing with the increasing pace of environmental disruption and value stream complexity is not possible.

Chapter 10: Empiricism at Scale

"If you can't measure it, you can't improve it" - Peter Drucker

Empiricism means data. Yet the current rhetoric within the Agile community is heavily biased towards *Socially Distributed Cognition* [1] and reliance on tribal knowledge, akin to stories being passed down from generation to generation regarding practice, staffing and technology efficacy. Apparently, the strategy of relying on "The Borg" for persistence of empirical observations is favored over databases and analytics. Agilists will in one breath espouse the virtues of empiricism, but in the next socially convenient breath, attack all technology forms of retrospective learning. This means total reliance on yellow Post-it notes and emphasis on *Swarming* [2] around whiteboards is the only popular and socially acceptable "true agile". Interestingly, little is ever discussed about how one might engage in *distributed swarming*, or how to capture the event data that reflects the dynamic changes of state that are always occurring, even with physical forms of the workflow entity state machines or kanban boards. It also never appears to be socially convenient in a "high trust environment" to discuss how such a broad stroke tactic would aggregate result data even if it were captured across the breadth of the portfolio. This example of the *Scotsman Fallacy* [3] goes directly to the issue of *Epistimology*, which is theory of what constitutes knowledge. Philosophically, such rhetoric implies an ideology of faith as opposed to reason, and the rationalistic-contrarian viewpoint of *Fideism* which holds that beliefs may be held without evidence or reason, even if in conflict with evidence and reason [4].

At the scale of the enterprise, observations regarding the efficacy of software delivery decisions pragmatically requires going beyond the rhetoric that low tech is always better. The aggregation of retrospectives and lessons learned data can only happen if supported by technology with the reach to cover the diversity of how modern IT organizations are distributed. To be fair, Agilists are correct in their grievance towards tool vendors. While correlation of results data which corroborates assessments of performance and progress to the various high stakes decisions requires technology as a practical matter, at scale, data is likely to exist within different vendor stacks for different teams and associated endeavors. Wave after wave of attempts to "normalize" software delivery infrastructure components into a homogeneous, single vendor solution have invariably failed for enterprises of any significant scale and contextual diversity. Similar to the continual "election cycle" for software delivery methods, so too are the seasonal cycles of tool birth and death related to planning, requirements management, quality management and configuration management infrastructure.

The challenge for enterprises is to find a balance which empowers delivery intelligence at scale without the de-motivation risk of big infrastructure being pushed on teams. Enactment of the diverse ways-of-working across the enterprise using various workflow tools and technologies (and even the socially acceptable low tech mechanisms) must be decoupled from the practice of empiricism, thereby freeing governance to be independent and segregated from tool details and vendor churn. Put another way, the software delivery portfolio *interface* should be separate and apart from its *implementation* such that the impact of change in the underlying projects are isolated and hidden from view for the stakeholders and investors in the Value Stream.

10.1 – The Learning Organization

A *Learning Organization* [5] is an enterprise which maintains a continual pace of innovation to remain competitive, and develops an adaptive capacity to respond to threats while embracing a changing marketplace. Famously articulated by Peter Senge at MIT, such an organization is connected to their customers and focuses on all aspects of quality. There exists a commitment to experimentation and curiosity whereby its personnel feel safe enough to explore and take measured risks. It is hard to argue against these attributes regardless of ideology or the current negative state of IT industry rhetoric. The elements that define this type of corporate mindset includes systems thinking, personal mastery, mental models, a shared vision, and team learning. Establishing a software delivery environment that leverages *System's Thinking* empowers people to study their business as a bounded object and learn about its performance through measurement of the whole <u>and</u> its various parts. Encouraging *Personal Mastery* goes directly to the heart of motivational theory, and entails a focused effort and commitment on the part of the individuals and the support from the organization. Learning in such an environment involves challenging the *Mental Models*, existing organizational memory, norms, customs or traditions and current theories-in-use in a non-confrontational manner. Additionally, such an environment promotes inquiry and trust. Additional motivation and alignment in the form of a *Shared Vision* is cultivated across the organization at all levels to energize and focus the ongoing learning. Finally, Learning Organizations emphasize *Team Learning* to enhance boundary crossing and encourage openness and sharing. All of these elements require robust knowledge management infrastructure to enable persistence, dissemination and improvement of organizational learning. By definition, Learning Organizations are synonymous with an empirical mindset. Therein lies the power of such a concept to sway undecided constituents towards a middle ground and away from the extremes within enterprises. While affording the portfolio visibility and transparency to management of the operational status, so too will the ideals of such a workplace resonate with staff members.

The deepest form of learning at either the individual or organizational level is referred to as "Double-loop Learning" [6], as illustrated in Figure 10.1:

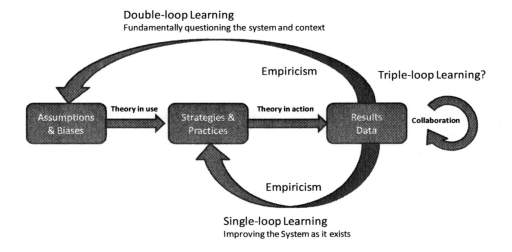

Figure 10.1 – Double-Loop Learning [6]

This model of organizational learning from notable business experts Chris Argyris, a Harvard professor [7], and Donald Schön, an MIT professor [8], complements the strategy of the Learning Organization. As articulated in *Organizational Learning: A Theory of Action Perspective*, [9] designing work environments to achieve intended consequences only, maximizing personal winning through unilateral or dictatorial leadership, and commonly invoking defensive reasoning leads to limited collaboration and therefore weak learning. Notable learning side-effects include strong ownership of tasks by individuals who take a defensive posture, ask for limited help, and provide limited help to others. In contrast, when work environments are designed that empower free and informed choice and joint task control, the results are minimally defensive interpersonal relationships and group dynamics. This latter design reflects so called Double-loop Learning, the deeper and more long lasting organizational learning. It is therefore important to create a learning environment with an open culture that promotes inquiry and trust.

With Double-loop learning, the inherently human assumptions that we possess and the plethora of Cognitive Biases are constantly challenged related to our strategies and practices. While the inner feedback loop is leveraged continuously to steer our actions and optimize outcomes, the outer loop provides feedback as to whether we should be performing the actions we currently are undertaking at all. In effect, we leverage empirical observations to "step outside of ourselves" and reflect on why we are even instantiating the business system in its current form and in its current context. Perhaps if we are to move the goal post, the current strategies and tactics we are leveraging for our software delivery ecosystem become irrelevant and moot.

Arguably, the definition in Theory of Action above implies a third loop of learning, the controversial and ambiguously defined *Triple-loop Learning* concept [10]. In fact, when one looks at the model from an interdisciplinary perspective using the power of a Feedback Control Theory model, the inner loop immediately surrounding individuals and representing their collaboration is what is described most notably by Argyris's environmental factors. Therefore, if you agree with this observation, such an environment mirrors at a high level the model of the *Universal Kernel* for software delivery ecosystems presented in Chapter 5 and a way-of-working freedom of choice environment.

10.2 – Inspect and Adapt

In the early to mid 1990's, Victor Basili from the University of Maryland articulated a strategy that reflects at a conceptual level that of *Advisor* and the spirit of reuse and empiricism. What was different in this early vision was a focus on artifacts rather than decisions as with Decision-centric Capability Improvement, and the lack of expert system technology to facilitate the guidance to projects and a platform for risk mitigation. Nevertheless, the feedback process of learning from data resulting from process execution and the feeding forward of this packaged knowledge in some form to future project teams was clearly articulated. It should be noted that this was not some vague conception, but reflected many years of purposeful reuse tactics at NASA. In the *Experience Factory* strategy [11] it is suggested that the core of an improvement strategy is the need for reusable experience, and that each development cycle yielded a better understanding of the software business. In effect it represented a "corporate learning event". Figure 10.2 illustrates this strategy:

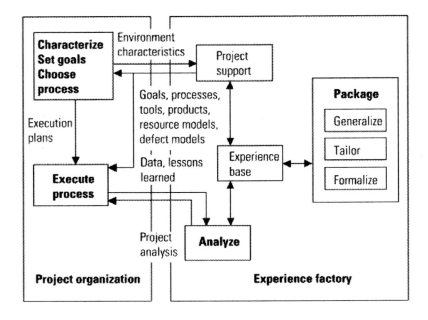

Figure 10.2 – The Experience Factory [11]

The benefits cited through application of the Experience Factory strategy to organizations were the following::

- Establishing a software improvement process substantiated and controlled by quantitative data.

- Producing a repository of software data and models that are empirically based on everyday practice.

- Developing an internal support organization that limits overhead and provides substantial cost and quality performance benefits.

- Providing a mechanism for identifying, assessing, and incorporating into the process new technologies that have proven valuable in similar contexts.

- Incorporating and supporting reuse in the software development process.

It is likely that adherents to a faith-based philosophy will object to such rigor and may in fact invoke the adage "correlation does not imply causation". While this is true, it is equally true that correlation does not necessarily rule out causation either. Correlation can be used as powerful evidence for a cause-and-effect relationship between a treatment and benefit, a risk factor and a disease, or a social or economic factor and various outcomes. Care must be taken to prevent abuse because it is easy and even tempting to come to premature conclusions based upon the preliminary appearance of a correlation. This is why enterprises need to systematically apply the principle of *Inspect and Adapt* such that statistical credibility can be earned from the insights that such data collection affords. When aggregated industry-wide, such *Big Data* [12] has the potential to enable *Predictive Analytics* [13] in the sense that outcomes can be anticipated and forecasted within the constraints of stochastic systems. Getting the data means that power laws will emerge over time as to the meaningful discretizations of context factors, the meaningful risk thresholds used by triggering rules and inference related to Estimated Time to Arrival (ETA) projections. Getting the data also means that an improving understanding of the context of various practices and their influence on the overall ecosystem will emerge.

10.3 – Normalized Velocity & Cycle-time

What to empirically observe and what measures to collect needs to be informed by the model of how software delivery works - the Universal System's Thinking Kernel. From this mindset, we know that we want to understand progress made against the tracking variable for the system, probed at the output of the system. This tracking variable is the reference signal for the endeavor, the time-varying logical scope which represents the fine grained demand and captured statements of need. To compare the input signal of the ecosystem with the output of the ecosystem to inform steerage and exert influence requires the same unit of measure. If we characterize the intake of a software product or project as *Desired Outcomes* [14], we have a much better understanding of the contributions of those demand elements towards the value proposition of the software. This prevents us from "boiling the ocean" and measuring all sorts of meaningless things within the ecosystem. When approaching empiricism and measurement, it is always pragmatic to understand the goals of the system in question. Such an approach generally has existed for quite some time in the form of *Goal-Question-Metric (GQM)* [15].

From Chapter 6, if we are interested in optimizing productivity, we care about both efficiency and effectiveness, again requiring like and meaningful units of scope for their assessment. If the expected number of outcomes delivered per unit of time yield no gap with the reference signal, then the project ecosystem has achieved maximum productivity approaching efficiency alone. Unfortunately, there is always some "loss" or error in the signal processing, and therefore we are interested in understanding the time-varying effectiveness and the trends. If we see drift downwards in our effectiveness, we are incurring technical debt which is affecting our overall productivity over time. This is where the metaphoric term "velocity" comes in, and it is not without controversy and increasingly negative rhetoric. Once Agilists realized that they would be subject to scrutiny related to this measure (which was advocated instead of measurement of task deadlines), they balked at it and likened comparisons made for this metric between teams to be akin to desiring a sweatshop. Nevertheless, velocity was an Agile invention and it just so happens it is the right instrumentation from a System's Thinking perspective. To be able to forecast an Estimated Time of Arrival (ETA) for the software endeavor, we need to understand the moving average of the speed over ground so to speak, the velocity. Note that this measure represents a vector, not a scalar, as it is directional in nature focused on progress towards a goal.

In the interests of establishing a *Learning Organization* and fostering an environment of *Triple-loop Learning*, a significant challenge arises when we wish to collaborate on learning about cause and effect related to our tracking variable and therefore comparing velocity across the enterprise. Much of the rhetoric related to dropping the velocity metric [16] within the Agile Movement stems from the differences among teams and the differing approaches they use to implement the sizing of scope elements and the associated accounting for measuring progress. The latter associated with the *Definition-of-Done* related objection is the easier of the two to remedy, which should be guided by the fact that only realized scope that can serve as input to the project system "comparator" in System's Thinking terms should be valid progress. In other words, only when a few cycles of the feedback loop have been fully traversed can units of scope be counted in determining current "velocity". It is the former objection with the use of velocity that is more of a challenge. To understand how to rectify this and still yield a meaningful indicator for learning and steerage reasons, we must first understand that the practice of leveraging the amount of scope delivered or burned per unit time relies on *relative sizing*. This means that teams are free to use different units of measure in their estimation of the size of the demand they are working against per cycle. If we were talking about sailing, we might be talking about the difference between nautical miles, statutory miles or kilometers. The software development analog related to the use of velocity as a Relative Sizing [17] metric would be discretization using Fibonacci sequences, T-shirt sizes, or the use of analytical approaches related to various forms of requirements technique like Function Points, Object Points, Feature Points or Use Case Points [18, 19, 20, 21]. The difficulty lies in being able to identify when a team is in distress, or could learn from other teams that are achieving optimum delivery results and humming right along. This implies the need for some form of "normalization" and the use of *Normalized Velocity* as opposed to the raw form of the metric. To normalize the amount of scope delivered by a team per unit of time, we must first start with the following assumption:

Two teams functioning within roughly the same contextual environment should more or less be covering approximately the same amount of ground as each other.

Consider two similar sailboats attempting the same crossing from West Palm Beach to Bimini. Each are similar contexts and have the same goal - they both want to arrive in Bimini, which is 100% of their goal. In other words, they are similar "classes" of "project" or endeavor. What can vary is the tactics that are leveraged - the heading they will take to "crab" across the gulf stream, the quality of seamanship of the vessels, the quality of the crew, etc.. Both need to attain 100% of the goal. Each tack is an iteration where more is learned about their project ecosystem, and they cover a percentage of their journey each cycle. If one crew is covering 10% of the goal each cycle and another is only achieving 1% of the goal, we might be inclined to pull the thread and inquire further what is going on and whether it is an illusion as to whether the former crew is outperforming the latter. Figure 10.3 illustrates this metaphoric scenario:

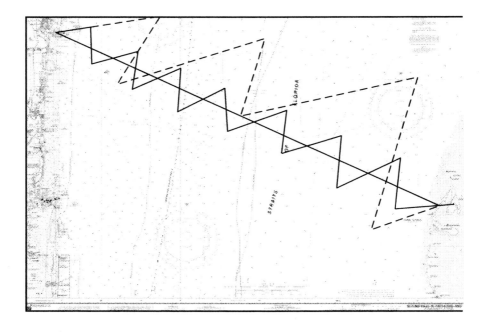

Figure 10.3 – Normalized Velocity Metaphor

It could be that the amount of time between tacking is 10 times as long in the latter case which would mean that when normalizing the raw metric of percent of "scope" covered per iteration, they are the same. However, what is important is to watch this normalized velocity metric and how many nautical miles are being covered per cycle over time. It is likely that in the latter case, the crew is being set down in the Gulf Stream in a different fashion than the tighter loop crew who is following a tactic more akin to "crabbing" across the stream. While on its own this might not appear so meaningful, upon further analysis one can understand that if looking at the entire contextual envelope of the voyage, including the "point of sail" and the wind direction, being set down more is disadvantageous from the physics of the sail which will approach a "close hauled" state and eventually "in-irons" after some time. This would be analogous to technical debt in the software development world. Even though one might measure the first crossing using statutory miles, and the second crossing using nautical miles (over ground that is), the universal measure that we can normalize to is the percentage of the crossing (the scope) per cycle. Such a metric is only a *relative index* of performance similar to the Richter scale, or Relative Humidity as opposed to an *absolute* measure [22]. It is meaningless on its own without context and historical learning.

Organizations can leverage such an approach to governing their portfolio for inquiry purposes. Applying filters that relate to the various context factors for the different endeavors within an organization enables the quick identification of anomalies that may or may not warrant further exploration and explanation. We can further normalize the raw percentage of scope per iteration to account for team size, complexity or iteration duration. Once this leveling occurs, teams can look for outliers that suggest that learning is possible one way or the other. Even though two projects may be fundamentally different in scope (like one sailboat is going to Bimini, the other is going to Freeport), highlighting their relative percentage of scope per cycle will illuminate tactical differences due to the nature of their respective voyages. Beyond the comparative analysis among teams and their endeavors across the enterprise (which is not intended to be used to punish but rather be used in the spirit of driving mastery as part of a Learning Organization) the moving average of normalized velocity is used for determining Estimated Time of Arrival. This ETA is subject to all the dynamism that is happening on the project like the changing scope or reference signal as a function of time, the changing performance and accrual of error or technical debt and the like. Looking at a range of moving averages is necessary to reduce the uncertainty due to the stochastic nature of knowledge work and forecast "the date", which isn't a single date but rather an ever changing range of dates.

The corollary to velocity is cycle time - that is the amount of time to realize a single unit of scope. In similar fashion, this measure, which is closely related to throughput and the amount of work in progress, must be normalized. Saying that it takes 14 days to deliver a single User Story for one team, and takes 30 days in the case of another team is meaningless unto itself. Cycle time must be normalized again to the percentage of total scope to be meaningful, and tracked over time for any delivery intelligence to be accrued. Enterprises should be mindful of silver bullet rhetoric related to cycle-time versus normalized velocity, as each has the same issue of inferring the equivalence of scope size. Agile tactics to exert massive amounts of effort "grooming" product backlogs through such hacks as story splitting runs the risk of degrading into "big requirements up-front" if taken to perfect normalization. Approaching such granularity is likely necessary to be effective for addressing this issue and runs the risk of inserting delays and a significant bottleneck in the single Product Owner.

For software delivery the following table captures the relative measures and efficiency index related to normalized velocity:

Step	Explanation	Formulae
Normalize scope progress per cycle to percentages	How much "ground" is being covered per cycle. Percentage of total scope is the common unit of measure. Analogous to comparing every regatta sailboat to nautical miles and speed over ground.	**Normalized Velocity (Raw) = Points burned / Total Points**
Quantile Normalize for context factors	Adjustments for different delivery vehicle types and environmental complexities. Context factors represent Log-Normal distributions. Analogous to accounting for different sailing conditions, vessel types, waypoint durations and crew size.	**Normalized Velocity (Cycle-length) = Normalized Raw / Days** **Normalized Velocity (Size) = Normalized Raw / Size** **Normalized Velocity (Domain) = Normalized Raw / D-Complexity** **Normalized Velocity (Tech) = Normalized Raw / T-Complexity**
Relate Velocity to cash burn rate	Indicator of cost-efficiency for achieving contextually normalized velocity. Analogous to fuel efficiency if motoring.	**Relative Velocity Efficiency Index = Contextually Normalized Velocity X (Cash burn / Total Budget)**

Table 10.1 – Normalized Velocity Calculations

10.4 – Value Stream Infrastructure

Value Stream infrastructure is known in the IT industry under the buzzword "Application Lifecycle Management – ALM" [23]. Built from a foundation of Process-centric Configuration Management [24], workflow-centric tooling provides the ability to define the practices or processes to be leveraged first, then match the tooling second. This is important because binding the outputs of work (and their storage within configuration management infrastructure) to workflow dynamics with timestamps enables a Lean Thinking perspective and collection of cycle-time metrics. Architecting a strategy for ALM usage that is driven first and foremost from a reflection on the Value Stream starts with articulation of multiple views that facilitate the reasoning about significant decisions to be made related to vendor offerings. Given the common value stream activities that were articulated within Chapter 6, we can start by elaborating a logical view independent of any physical tool choices or vendor offerings.

We can apply the same techniques that we apply to engineer a system-of-systems for typical business domains when architecting the workflow systems support for the Value Stream. We start with articulating a logical structural view of the software delivery enterprise. There are three types of abstractions in this structural view when leveraging "Object-oriented Business Engineering" techniques [25]. These are *Business Workers, Business Entities and Business Systems.* The tools that make up the value stream infrastructure are Business Systems.

IT enterprises typically consist of a structural decomposition based on division-of-labor choices and skill-sets. Most publicly traded enterprises require a formal segregation of these discipline-centric organizations due to compliance mandates and CapEx/OpEx accounting rules. This has caused controversy within the Agile community, but shouldn't necessarily be seen as bad practice, or ceremony for the sake of ceremony. The segregation of duties that are commonly required within SOX and other compliance standards make reasonable sense. The problems start occurring due to root cause issues related to automation. When automation is insufficient or lacking (also becoming a standard of care within compliance norms), agility suffers due to manual and error prone practices. Figure 10.4 shows six segregated support organizations – *Development Services, Software Configuration Management Services, Build & Release Management Services, Independent Quality Assurance Services, Asset Management Services, and Operations.*

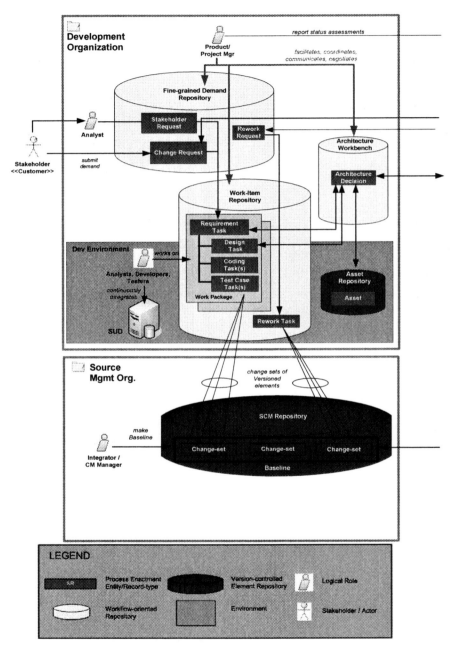

Figure 10.4 –Value Stream Infrastructure - Logical View

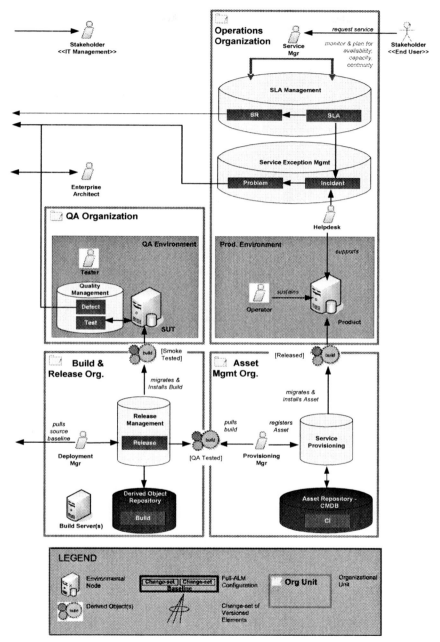

Figure 10.4 – Value Stream Infrastructure - Logical View

The discussion that follows represents an experienced based example of the abstractions and workflow involved in modern software development. The context boundary of the IT organization is defined by what is outside – namely the Business Actors. For IT enterprises, the actors are stakeholders typically referred to as *Customers*, and *End Users*. Business stakeholders acting in the role of a Customer submit demand to the IT organization, whereas End Users are the Business Workers who leverage systems once they are deployed. Demand for the implementation of software systems is captured through a queuing system. Such systems are generically called *Request Tracking Systems*, and represent the entry point for IT Demand. Note that the demand for IT system's development can be new or can be the result of existing system operation, and as such represents change requests for existing systems. Changes to existing systems identified by End Users can be fed from other IT infrastructure systems closer to operations like that from Service Management [26] infrastructure (Problem or Incident Management, Capacity Management, Performance Management, Availability Management and the like). To facilitate efficient prioritization of IT demand for service, the multiple entry points for Product Requests should be managed in a single Request Tracking System. All demand for a single Product represents the Product Backlog, and lives beyond projects during the Product's potentially multi-generational lifecycle.

Various specialized roles (also Business Workers) within the IT enterprise serve as the supply chain required to realize the demand. Analysts serve the useful role of helping to clarify the IT demand in such a way as to help Customers understand when demand has been fulfilled, or to help articulate demand in such a manner that solution domain realization is efficient and effective. As such they serve to facilitate the extraction of tacit knowledge in what are typically "Requirements". The first amplification of the demand as worded from the Customer starts the Request workflow. High-level characterization of the Request sets the stage for evaluation by a representative cross-section of the stakeholder community. This ensures that system impacts are assessed and that the demand is prioritized in relation to its relative importance with other IT system demand.

Once demand is prioritized, it remains in queue and potentially subject to changes in prioritization. The elements of demand will have been shaped to resemble either User Stories, Scenarios or Features if they are well formed and actionable. The Analyst helps to ensure that either of these are minimal and will result in valuable capability upon completion and leave the system in a stable state. With iterative development, an entire project team will tackle a batch of approved demand from this queue. With Lean, only small batches of demand (also known as micro-increments) are addressed per realization team. Depending upon the organizational configuration, similar amounts of demand may be worked on simultaneously as that of teams leveraging timeboxed iterations and their batch of demand. Limits enforced on the work in progress per team implements the practice of Digital Kanban.

For a Request that is changed from the *Approved* state to the *In-Progress* state, the first thing to be done by a self organizing team is to define the work breakdown for the Request. This task planning occurs just-in-time, and only for a single Request. This avoids the waste of performing predictive planning for an entire project or future iteration. Also, the true measure of progress comes from comparing the burn-down of the Product Backlog over time. Task progress information is used by the self organizing team to aid in managing the risk to delivery and to identify and reason about work improvement.

If the demand captured at a high level and leveraged for characterization and prioritization is not actionable for the team to fulfill the Request, one of the Tasks will leverage the specialized skills of the Analyst. Analysts are tasked with elaborating demand into a form that is actionable by developers. This knowledge extraction of the problem domain does not necessarily mean documents. Requirements can be persisted within the process enactment infrastructure in the form of database records such that documentation can be printed in the form of a report or view at any time. This form of Requirements storage is more valuable, as other interesting attributes (also known as Requirements Attributes) can be coupled with the textual description of the demand such that separate traceability, prioritization or effort attribution is not necessary. With only a small lead time to elaborate requirements, Analysts immediately switch to developing tests acting in the role of "Test Designer". Some self organizing teams like to elaborate requirements into such a form as to equate to acceptance tests instead, such that two differing work products are combined into one. Developers then begin the work to realize the Request with the necessary source code and builds. Developers within these self organizing teams possess both design and implementation skill-sets, similar to the multi-hat wearing of the Analysts. Each role whether it be Analyst or Developer works in the context of Tasks, with one Request containing multiple realization Tasks. Tasks represent not only the work breakdown, but serve as the linkage with configuration management infrastructure. The output from a Task is one or more Work Products. Work Product versions are collected in what are known as "change sets". All the versions of files for whatever configuration item types are being created are collected in the Task change-set. When all work is complete for a Task, the entire change set is "delivered" or merged into the shared or integration branch. During this stage of a Task's workflow, any parallel development merge conflicts are resolved due to the fact that many workers may be changing the same configuration artifact (source code unit, document, etc.) at the same time. Once all the versions of files within the change set are delivered to the integration branch, these versions are then visible to the rest of the teams for the product. Typically, a policy requires a re-sync by team members on a periodic basis to ensure that merge conflicts do not occur too frequently. The action of delivering a developer change-set should trigger a build of the Product through the application of the continuous integration practice. This build and execution of unit tests is on a near-continuous basis for large scale Products. Continuous frequency builds can occur depending on the branching structure leveraged as well.

When all Tasks for a Request are complete, the Request can be transitioned to the *Complete* state. This enables the inclusion of the Request in a Release. Depending on the Release frequency this can occur immediately, or can be batched to coincide with a useful and sustainable Release window. When included in a Release workflow, it is labeled or "baselined" together with other Requests and signaled as ready for independent testing. The Build and Release organization oversees the independent and re-creatable build of the Product from source code. Following a successful build, this organization is also responsible for deployment of the build to the segregated QA environment once it is ready to receive the new target of test. In mature organizations, this typically initiates full automatic regression test suite execution. Results are evaluated by a Tester or Test Manager, typically with signoffs associated for later use in determining production readiness of the Release baseline. If quality is within established risk tolerances, the baseline becomes a valuable asset. This asset is ready to be secured in a Definitive Media Library and a Configuration Management Database (CMDB) [27].

The final stage of the overall workflow for a Request occurs when approvals are collected by the various stakeholders for the change event. Not only must the Business organization signify readiness to accept the change, but the Operations organization must acknowledge their ability to support the Release deployment and the operational support after the change is made. This includes the Service Operations activities of Helpdesk, service monitoring and system administration.

From the discussion above, it can be seen that there are many moving parts that more or less are reasonable things that must occur for software to be released into an organization of any reasonable complexity, scale or risk tolerance. To achieve business agility and sustain efficiency and effectiveness, all of the systems involved must be seamlessly integrated into an overall value stream. This requires that the systems that are leveraged for each stage of this complex workflow to work together. Figure 10.5 describes the dynamic view of the scenario described above.

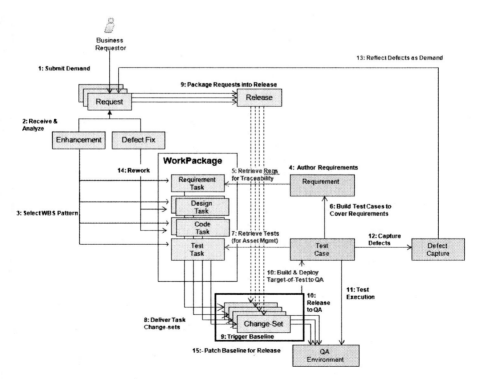

Figure 10.5 – Request-to-Release Scenario

10.5 – Hybrid ALM

One of the root causes related to the opposition to the usage of tools in software development within the Agile community stems from the common strategy employed by vendors. Typically, tool vendors strive for selling <u>all</u> the tools that make up SDLC infrastructure. They attempt to win all the business even if they are not in the best position to fulfill the need. As such they drive a homogeneous *best-of-brand* message. This sales strategy typically stems from the "Microsoft Office" pattern. Microsoft pioneered the notion of a suite of products that are sold as a set to yield attractive savings over the purchase of individual products incrementally. The tool vendors have leveraged this pattern for the most part and continue to strive for full lifecycle penetration to this day. To enable bundled solutions to be sold, most vendors are forced to acquire emerging or competing products to fill gaps in their offering. This in no way means that the best product or technology is acquired. It just means that they have to have an offering without which they cannot compete. This leads to the same kinds of system-of-systems integration problems that occur within enterprises, but when left to the vendors, it results in vendor lock-in.

The typical scenario is where a tool vendor gets a meeting at one or more levels of the organization and attempt to make a case for their assets. They usually claim to have "all the bases covered" and can offer capability in all the various disciplines that realize software product delivery. They deliver somewhat of a magic show in terms of razzle-dazzle demonstrations of their products from *their* view of the software engineering world. After these initial conversations and meetings conclude, either one of two things occurs. The purchasing organization is so confused that they buy the pitch - lock stock and barrel. The tools are purchased en-masse so as to get the biggest discount and it is left to the purchasing organization to figure out what to do with the new acquisition. The more pragmatic course of action would be to force a detailed gap analysis, treating the tool vendors like any other COTS and focus on deferring decisions until enough information is present to make the least risky choices. This usually involves "bake-offs" or "conference room pilots", something the tool vendors typically try to avoid as it leads to a lengthy sales cycle. While the tool vendor company executives would like to see fitness-for-purpose for their offerings and would like to "do the right thing" because of the likely downstream erosion of good-will, other levels of their organizations feel the pressures of Wall Street related to making their number.

The challenge with modern SDLC infrastructure is that vendors are in competition with each other, and this usually leads to a fundamental lack of collaboration. While API's of various forms are professed by each vendor, creating integrations among the various parts is no trivial matter. Some vendors subscribe to the OSLC (Open Services for Lifecycle Collaboration) [28] standard, basically an IBM driven standard emerging out of the Eclipse Mylin project [29]. Other vendors adhere to the OData standard [30], a Microsoft driven standard. Niche vendors like Tasktop [31] and OpsHub [32] have capitalized on these standards, and largely control their evolution. Acting as *plumbing* between the various ALM components, the challenge is to find coverage for all the tools that are currently existing within an enterprise. Even if one of these "enterprise service bus" vendors achieves 100% coverage, instantiating these tools is not a trivial undertaking. Due to the highly diverse schemas that usually emerge in most IT shops, extensive mappings that are brittle and prone to breakage are required. Akin to large scale ETL (Extract-Transfer-Load), regardless if the integration is performed on an event by event basis, cost of maintenance is high. Even with all of this, such integration hubs do not aggregate data in such a way to facilitate analytics. To facilitate this, a data warehouse is required, as is developing and sustaining the ETL Jobs, the Operational Data Store (ODS) and Data Marts. Obviously, this too is no trivial matter.

Another challenge with heavyweight ALM is that it is never done. It is akin to continual construction of a freeway like the Interstate 405 in Los Angeles California [33]. While it is comforting to envision the normalization of all ALM infrastructure into a fully integrated, *best-of-breed* form, it never happens. Meanwhile, portfolios cannot wait for the latest and greatest Requirements Management tool to be ripped out and replaced. It seems that Agile Planning tools change in popularity like the seasons. Clearly, another strategy is required to enable **lightweight** and non-disruptive portfolio visibility. Decoupling the toolset chaos from governance needs is the first step in embarking on a pragmatic Hybrid ALM strategy. Driving reporting needs and the chosen empirical metrics should first and foremost be based on what an enterprise's business philosophy is and how stakeholders want to govern their investments. Once such an interface to the software delivery ecosystem is defined, special attention must be given to the adoptability so as to ensure that de-motivation does not occur. Figure 10.6 illustrates the various physical vendor components and competitive choices that make up the value stream segments:

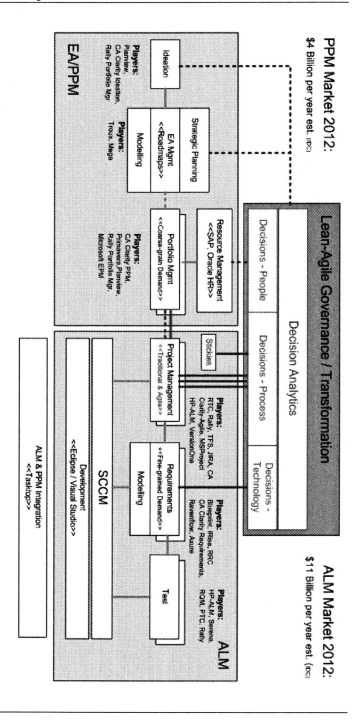

Figure 10.6 – Decoupling Value Stream Infrastructure

In the previous figure, driven from a *Decision-centric Capability Improvement* strategy, we can see the decoupling of the components and data subject areas leveraged for governance and change management from the operational support systems that make up the Value Stream infrastructure. This serves as the **interface** to management and governance functions that is stable and provides the coherent set of indicators to steer the portfolio effectively. Realization of the various component **implementations** in a Lean and lightweight fashion that meets the objectives is what remains. Given a component architecture as illustrated that accounts contextually for the various vendor offerings, we can make apple to apple comparisons for what is best-of-breed at a point in time. Industry analysts constantly assess the evolution of the vendor offerings and strategies [169, 170] and can be referenced when making choices for the various service realizations described in this section.

To achieve *Lightweight ETL*, we reduce the cadence of data extraction to that of our retrospective rhythm. Such a reasonable frequency for "Inspect and Adapt" is all that is necessary to achieve effective steerage of the portfolio. Anything more, like with some vendors professing the virtues of "real-time" analytics is extremely wasteful. The volume of data and the sheer number of subject areas in such data warehouse components like IBM Rational Insight (a Cognos based solution) [34] requires that nightly processing occur to ease load on operational OLTP systems. Even if the load was not an issue for large-scale enterprises, it is highly unlikely that executives will give this level of analytics detail that much attention. What executives need is the ability to manage by exception when dealing with the scale of most Fortune 500 enterprises, and this pragmatic governance strategy only requires simple metrics, the most important is rate of change related to simple productivity measures for efficiency and effectiveness. Empowered to correlate this *Operational Excellence* data to the important decisions that determine favorable outcomes, true and meaningful governance of the current state of the portfolio and its trajectory is afforded to executives.

10.6 – Keeping it Real

Decoupling tool vendor shenanigans, never ending "under-construction" ALM, and the toolset bias that exists within organizational silos establishes the conditions for effective, pragmatic governance. The *Advisor* platform achieves this by simplifying the extraction of outcome oriented metrics for correlation to decisions. This is a new capability within the software delivery industry. Such an environment creates the kind of openness and transparency required for organizational learning to occur at scale, and realizes "The New Deal" between management and staff. The endless game of cat and mouse, gaming of reports, status obfuscation and social loafing can be replaced by the ideals of giving discretion to innovators, and giving back to the enterprise that provides economic opportunities to people.

Advisor is the first capability that facilitates **Smart Retrospectives** at enterprise scale. All other ALM technologies simply provide a freeform text field to capture such reflection, and do so without any correlation to event data. When a team zigs and then zags from iteration to iteration, no intelligence is gathered as to changes in ecosystem response as a result of the changes that were made. Due to a lack of contextualization of practices within the ecosystem, these systems merely collect historical footnotes. What is required however is collection of metrics related to the time-sensitive observations and mood of the team while in-flight. Knowing the perspective of the "boots-on-the-ground" at the point in time they are making these observations is statistically significant when enough enterprise data is aggregated. Similarly, it is highly significant when industry-wide trends are aggregated with respect to tuning the parameterization of the Universal Kernel for simulation purposes. This coupled with lightweight baseline snapshots of the current position (i.e. burndown state), crossing coordinates (total cumulative scope), how much we are being "set down" (rework and defects), how much fuel we have (budget) and how much fuel we have burned (cash burn rate per iteration) all enables us to infer cause and effect over time. For such operational data, we can mine the core records in simple fashion to support the auditability of the assertions. Such a **lightweight data warehousing** strategy is feasible due to the fact that it is the first derivative of the "track" of our endeavor that matters most. Radical shifts in the slope of our burndown will become immediately obvious and serves as a pragmatic yet extremely effective transparency mechanism. Figure 10.7 illustrates Smart Retrospectives:

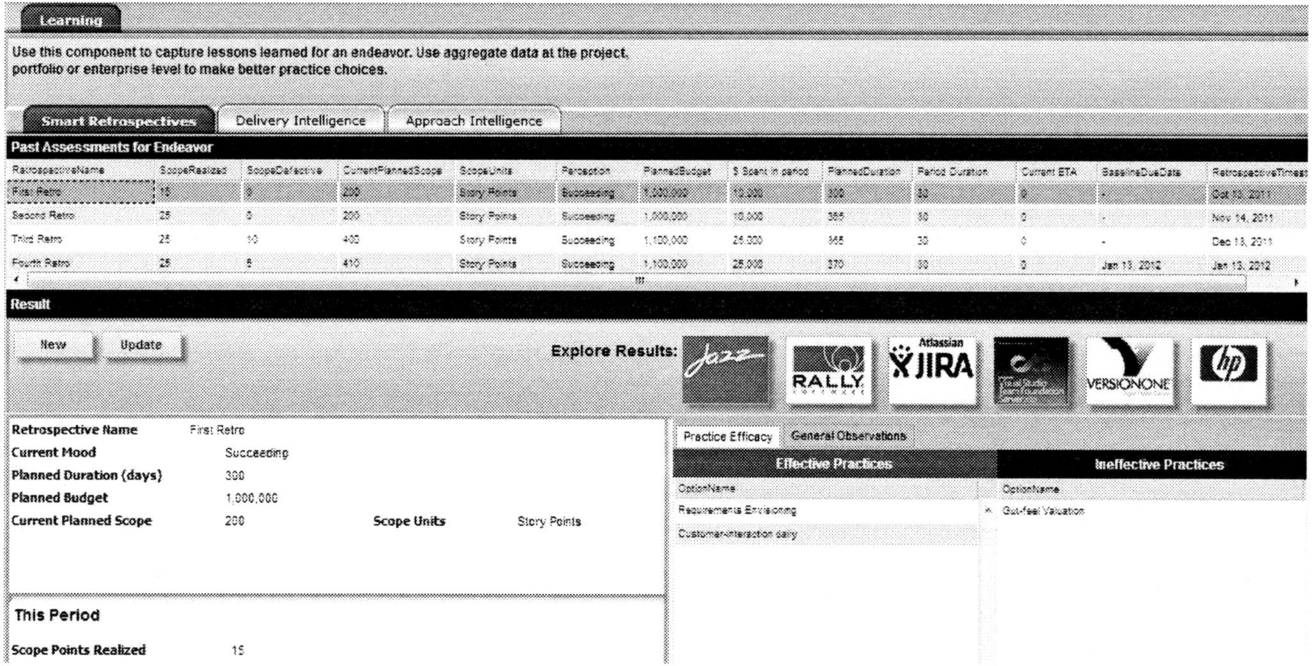

Figure 10.7 – Advisors' Inspect Component with Smart Retrospectives and ALM Data Mining

The lightweight data warehousing capability of *Advisor* leverages various service-oriented integrations with common ALM vendor stacks. Data mining is provided to query workitems and provide selectable result sets along with dynamic filtering through the OSLC or vendor proprietary REST interfaces. The team can use such filters, typically related to state, in relation to their definition of done. Selection of one or more records is accounted for in the retrospective being completed by the team, and double counting is prevented. Accumulation of scope burn is provided automatically, but can be accompanied by adjustments. The selected dataset is pulled and stored in lightweight form in *Advisor* to support future audits.

The most common form of an operational management system in use within either the Lean or Agile communities of practice is the physical taskboard. While Heavyweight ALM is constantly pushed on teams, the majority are small and co-located, and such attempts only serves to de-motivate and frustrate them. Instead of continually forcing the will of a tools-group on these teams, collecting simple reporting metrics at the retrospective cadence provides an effective management reporting interface that removes the huge blind spots in the portfolio. The constant complaint from executives is the difficulty in getting meaningful status unless they attend product demonstrations. The ability to aggregate portfolio health is severely hampered. The answer that is consistent with the sociology and organizational psychology of the situation is to embrace teams diversity and the power of self determination. Just as teams are free to self-organize around their way of working, such self determination should extend to the toolset enactment of their methods, even if low-tech.

Empowered by real, non-gamed data, portfolio managers and executives with a Fiduciary Duty over large sums of money (typically on the order of $1B in Fortune 100 companies) can now quickly identify opportunities for engagement with teams. Simple Earned Value (scope-based) indices, ETA, and % complete instrumentation across the entire portfolio is provided. Usage of honest Earned Value is important as it represents common ground between Agilists and Traditionalists when a meaningful WBS is integrated. Side-by-side burndown trajectories can show the respective date forecasts for various sections of the portfolio. Figure 10.8 illustrates **Delivery Intelligence** within *Advisor*.

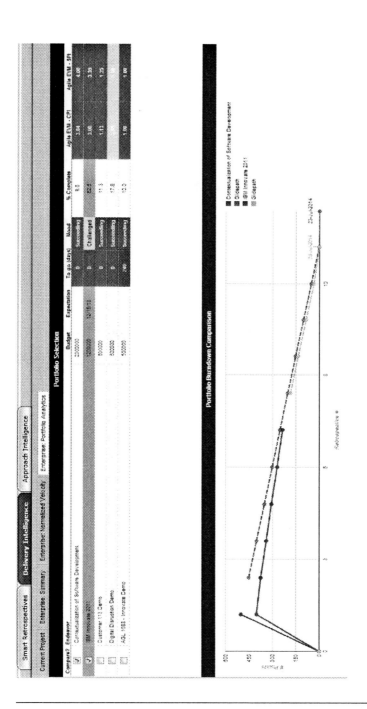

Figure 10.8 – Lightweight Portfolio Analytics based on System's Thinking

When a Portfolio Manager observes trends that look to be problematic or sub-optimal, what is important in the discharge of effective governance is being provided the levers to do something about it. Instrumentation is only part of the steerage tools, and influence needs to be focused on the teams that are struggling in a timely manner due to the high degree of dynamism in software development. Once risk is sensed in one part of the portfolio through the easy to attain comparative analysis, drill-through capability focuses attention on a single burndown trajectory. Pulling the thread further, management can assess the risks that were accepted by the team when they self-organized. With their current *Playbook* risks, management can suggest practice refactorings that were part of the original advice given by the expert system. With their current staffing profile where personnel were low in proficiency on specific skills, management can provide targeted training or coaching to those who need it. Figure 10.9 illustrates the risk analysis capabilities that extend governance beyond simple operational data:

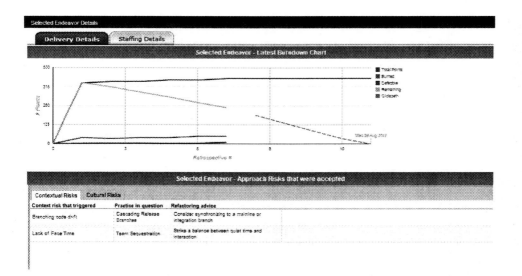

Figure 10.9 –Endeavor Risk Analysis

Sometimes it is difficult to pinpoint where help is needed from the burndown curves presented at either the portfolio comparison level or the individual project level. Taking the first derivative of these curves yields velocity trends. At a single team level, these can be correlated to the practice refactoring that has occurred at each retrospective boundary. When comparing across the portfolio, this requires normalization for any meaningful intelligence to be gained. Again, it is important to avoid the stereotype that management is abusing the velocity metric for oppressive means. Instead it needs to be re-asserted that comparing Normalized Velocity across teams is solely for the purpose of identifying where knowledge transfer investment should be focused in a timely manner. Making more effective use of the coaching dollars also ensures that teams who actually need the cycles get them. Figure 10.10 illustrates the application of Normalized Velocity within the *Advisor* platform.

Even with such robust and pragmatic instrumentation and risk mitigation capabilities discussed so far, sometimes the team or management can't quite pinpoint the root cause of their problems. This reflects the fact that within the context of any single endeavor only so much experience exists. While senior team members and managers have seen much more software development scenarios and anti-patterns than junior members, nothing compares to the ability to leverage the collective knowledge and experience of the broader enterprise or the entire industry. *Advisor* provides a negative-inference 5-why's based **Refactoring** component to assist teams with causal analysis beyond the symptoms they are observing. Obviously this is what experienced coaches provide, but leveraging an expert system isn't impacted by the bias that humans possess. Similarly, through machine learning, advice given as a result of traversing the 5-why inference graph improves over time by etching the most common pathways for a specific enterprise and nudging teams towards the more likely pathway of successful refactoring. While coaches may be able to provide deeper causal analysis and learning, such a facility addresses the majority of symptoms, the low lying fruit so to speak, so that coaches can focus their attention on the thorniest of problems. Figure 10.11 illustrates the 5-whys component for implementing "Adapt".

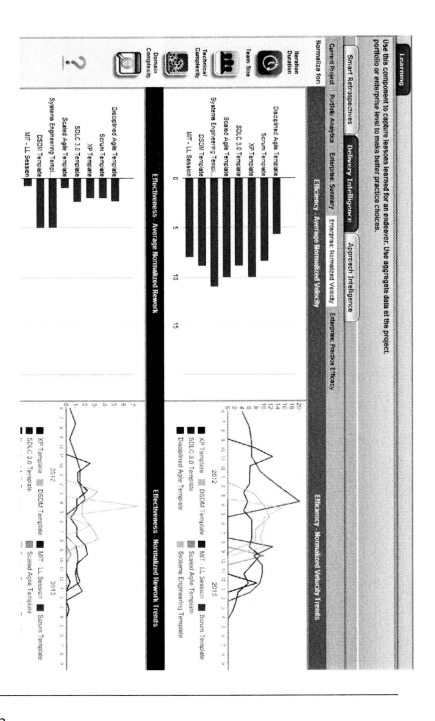

Figure 10.10 – Advisor Organizational Learning Component

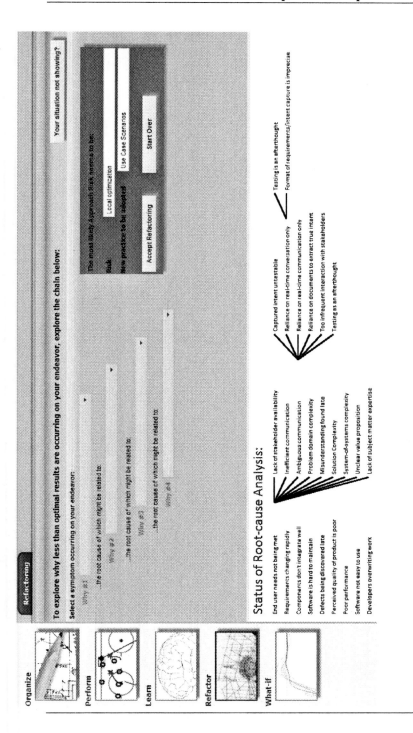

Figure 10.11 – Advisor 5-Why's based Approach Refactoring Component

Chapter 11: Hyper Agility

"Innovation distinguishes between a leader and a follower" - Steve Jobs

Now that we have explored all the necessary pieces for contextually configuring the software delivery value stream, we are free to explore innovative and valuable ways of working that fit the situations an enterprise may find itself in. Such represents an application of *Triple-loop Learning*. The industry is always changing, including technologies, practices and skill-sets. Similarly, enterprises are faced with significant threats and challenges requiring our software delivery ecosystems to continually evolve and improve. It has become a business imperative for organizations to improve outcomes and emphasize a results-oriented culture. No longer can businesses afford the luxury of ignoring very real competitive pressures in favor of sequestering their people and taking an inward looking focus.

Unfortunately, advances in the software delivery approaches, while slowly making progress, are being far outpaced by the degree of agility required in today's marketplace. The collective industry suffers from a high degree of stagnation and myopathy related to effective practice. If you ask 10 folks on the street what Agile equates to they will all likely say Scrum + XP. It is hard to believe that after almost 20 years these incumbents are still viewed as a silver bullet. This meme and accompanying community reinforcement is the biggest single product marketing stroke of genius our industry has seen in a long time.

Based on such trends as Mobile ubiquity, the Internet of Everything, Big Data and Predictive Analytics, we see the pace of *Digital Disruption* increasing, not decreasing. Added to that, the pressures of natural selection are alive and well in what has been termed *The Age of the Customer* [1], where demands for insanely rich customer software experience trumps all. Clearly we are falling behind in our ability to keep pace with the demand for business software and the requisite innovation to enable enterprises to compete. While ideas related to treating established enterprises like startups (Lean Startup) is a noble attempt to think outside the box in solving this problem, it is likely still too conventional an approach and suffers from the unenviable statistic that 75% of startups still fail [2]. *Emergent Vision* and trial and error [3] can only take us so far. Clearly a fundamental and discontinuous shift in how we structure software endeavors is necessary. We must question everything and confront the myriad of bias that exists within our thought processes.

Questioning everything and leaving our bias at the door raises some interesting propositions to consider: why do we allow technologists the large degrees of freedom within our enterprises, effectively succumbing to all the commercial pressures and market differentiation that introduces so much complexity into our software projects; why do we leverage the poorest forms of communication and collaboration for the most critical aspect of software endeavors - that of arriving at a "meeting of the minds"; why do we consistently allow teams to select methods by default based on industry popularity rather than fitness-for-purpose; and finally, why do we continue to entertain negligence in "Waterfall" management systems contrary to mountains of management science that refutes populist sentiment.

As discussed in Chapter 8, enterprises also have to address the issue of labor shortages and the fact that IT demand is outstripping supply. Labor arbitrage has already been tapped out, so new innovative ways of optimizing supply utilization needs to be considered in concert with any attempt to accelerate the pace of value delivery. Simply throwing more bodies and horsepower at the problem is a non-starter due to *Brookes Law* [4], and for the simple fact that those fictitious resources are non-existent. The problem needs to be addressed by a fundamental shift in Value Stream thinking.

To explore these questions further, we will focus on the RIA and Mobile software development archetypes as discussed in Chapter 7, which are important because according to Gartner, the 30% per year growth in Tablet sales as of 2014 [5] implies the need for **Hyper Agility**. The remainder of this chapter will present an application of the teachings of this book and extend the systems thinking principles to their extreme to address the mission critical business need to materially improve our software game and accelerate value delivery.

11.1 – Disintermediation

If one's goal is to deliver the maximum value to the investors that pay for software, then attention to the Value Stream seems natural. If we cast aside all the bias and assumptions that are deeply ingrained in popular methods, we are free to attempt to think outside the box. Considering the totality of the issues discussed earlier in this text, we are free to design ways of working that are contextually appropriate and culturally digestible. One trend related to the Value Stream that has emerged as business enterprises attempt to maximize shareholder value is *Disintermediation* [6].

Within business strategy and economics, disintermediation is focused on "cutting out the middlemen" or the removal of intermediaries in a supply chain. Instead of traditional distribution channels, business models are structured to connect directly with customers. Such a business model underpins the competitive strategy of large big-box retailers like Walmart, Costco and Lowe's Home Improvement which attempt to reduce costs by reducing the number of intermediaries between supplier and buyer. Within Information Technology, notable examples of disintermediation includes Dell and Apple, which sell many of their systems direct to the consumer—thus bypassing traditional retail chains. The key enabler of these value stream configurations was having succeeded in creating brands well recognized by customers, profitable and with continuous growth. With the internet, disintermediation has accelerated with retailers further cutting costs through a virtual presence in addition to their physical presence in a strategy known as "bricks and clicks". Cloud computing has now emerged to further this trend beyond inter-supply chain B2C and B2B opportunities to now target B-within-B (BnB). The Cloud disintermediates users from the underlying technology through OpenSource and Cloud-based API's such that internal supply chains that realize the existing and shifting external supply chains are now getting attention. Disruption is occurring on both the supply and demand side: the value chain is shifting, and new business models are emerging resulting in value creation and removal of inefficiencies.

Parallels can be drawn between the electrical industry and the IT industry, as described in *The Big Switch* [7]. In the early days of the power generation industry, enterprises generated their own on-premise electricity using internal experts and support staff. As power generation systems matured, businesses began to adopt a more efficient and cost-effective approach whereby centralized power systems fed a distribution network with metered access that allowed businesses to access services where and when needed. Companies receiving electrical service through a distribution network no longer required a dedicated staff of internal experts. In recent years with IaaS (Infrastructure as a Service) and PaaS (Platform as a Service), there has been a similar trend within IT [8]. Note however, that the next step in Power Generation was a return to private micro generation as technology matured and advances in management and simplicity emerged. While the aggregation and operation of the large-order capital investments have remained centralized, other aspects of the power generation equation have disintermediated at different points in the value stream enabled by technology. In a similar fashion, we are seeing a similar pattern emerge within IT. The ability to generate IT value in the form of software is distributing to more decentralized business side idea incubators, with the "grid" being maintained by the "central utility". In this way IT is becoming commoditized. Enterprise IT is beginning to experience the outer bands of a great storm of disintermediation which is fueled by self-reinforcing market efficiency that is sure to transform the IT landscape. Over time free markets have a powerful and often abrupt way of discarding people, process and technology which are weak links in a value chain. According to Gartner this paradigm shift started in early 2012. By 2017 marketing departments will be spending more on new IT systems than CIOs [9].

One attempt to tighten the value stream and better integrate the delivery of software can be found in the DevOps movement. However, this represents a sustaining innovation, which only attempts to reduce second order inefficiencies and dysfunctions of a legacy approach to software development. Far more disruptive and generative in terms of implications for the overall value stream is the notion of "BizOps". Empowering Marketing and Product Strategy departments to implement software is required due to the need for the tightest of feedback loops necessary to converge on and test speculative hypothesis of new product revenue streams. The tight integration with Ops is required to ensure that when "customers look behind the curtain", a sustainable product operation is present. It must be robust and performant, serviceable and maintainable if the incubated software is to be more than a flash in the pan. **BizOps** as a disintermediation concept implies that the IT department is fundamentally transformed to support rather than be lodged within the critical path. Instead, marketers and business strategists innovating new products are the mainline, with IT on the sidelines coaching and preparing for the sustainment of the latter evolutions of established products.

11.2 – Business-centric Development

What would happen to all we hold dear in software methodology land if those that hold the knowledge for what to build were able to easily express their thoughts and ideas in concrete software form. As in what if the SMEs (Subject Matter Experts) built at least the main flows of the application and were driving the bus, with technology specialists in the passenger seat keeping them out of the rhubarb and keeping them from going off the rails? How much more efficiency and effectiveness would such a strategy yield? We know that success heavily depends on extracting that which is deeply hidden within the SME consciousness - so called "Requirements Engineering". Even with all the team building, organizational design and self help guides conceived of to date, we also know that relationships between humans has a rather poor track record. Perhaps our focus has been entirely in the wrong place. Continually trying to fix the dysfunction between Business and IT, or management and the workers hasn't put a dent in the project train wreck statistics. What if we have been trying to force a solution to a systemic problem of humans getting along? Acting as *marriage counselor* or *diplomat* has a pretty poor track record in our broader society as is evident through divorce rates, general intolerance of various forms, and even wars.

Two types of knowledge exist – explicit knowledge (also known as "focal awareness" in Cognitive Sciences), and tacit knowledge ("subsidiary awareness") [10]. With tacit knowledge, people are not often aware of the knowledge they possess or how it can be valuable to others. An iceberg metaphor is typically used to describe the distribution of the two types of knowledge within people related to a specific area. As shown in Figure 11.1, explicit knowledge is the part above the waterline that we see; tacit knowledge is the part below the waterline and much broader and deeper.

Figure 11.1 – Tacit Knowledge Metaphor

One aspect of tacit knowledge is that trust is required for its extraction and therefore transfer to another individual. All current methodologies are reliant on a conveyance of knowledge about a business problem so that it can be enacted in software. All require the painstaking process of separating the knowledge from the SME before incarnation into software. To do this effectively requires trust to be built, which also takes time which is often not granted or long lived as project teams go their separate ways after the endeavor is over. Much of the practices within the field of Software Engineering assume a segregated IT and the need for intermediaries.

Methods have therefore focused attention on improving the trust-bonds within teams of people, with documents and other approaches attempting to facilitate the transmission and various forms of persistence of this tacit knowledge. All these assume that SME's are not capable of "developing" software, or at the very least would not wish to do so.

With the explosion of the internet and social networks, recent research has focused on the notion of *Collective Intelligence*, sometimes less formally referred to as "The Wisdom of Crowds" [11]. Software Development methodologists have tapped into this and the various forms of multi-agent systems that are often categorized as *Complex Adaptive Systems* and popularized by the "new science" of Complexity Theory [12]. The application of these threads of inquiry seem to represent a form of Confirmatory Bias, almost as if there is some affinity with various forms of social agenda and a desire for collectivism. It also shows a heavy bias to one school of thought related to Organizational Knowledge Management, that being the teachings of Takeuchi and Nonaka and their belief that Japanese culture and ideals trump anything western thinking can yield. Their models of innovation and organizational learning lean heavily on collectivism and minimally on individualism, as obviously reflective of Japanese culture in general [13].

Little in the way of practical application ever emerges with talk of ant hills or bird flocking when IT consultants profess their brilliance. However, contrasting such network configurations for software development teams and that of a single human brain is useful insofar as assessing the relative communication performance between neurons within a SMEs brain versus attempting to deliver the same results with the (hope of) emergent intelligence from networked brains. It should be obvious though that we as humans do not have the same mechanisms that are now being studied in insects and birds related to electromagnetic signaling that allow such complex behaviors to exist [14]. Agility is clearly related to either a group's reaction time or an individual's reaction time. If we are seeking to maximize agility, if one looks at the simple Reaction Time Test as illustrated in Figure 11.2 below, it is reasonable to assert that a single brain as a Complex Adaptive System is capable of much higher communication performance internally and therefore Reaction Time performance than the poor cousin - mere Complicated Systems that we construct to staff software development projects through networked individuals.

Figure 11.2 – Reaction Time Performance

In addition to the inherent latency in thinking performance with interpersonal relationships, other inhibitors to the transfer of knowledge between individuals exist [15], again heavily related to tacit knowledge. Specifically, the following factors impact the transmission of ideas and knowledge between individuals:

> **Causal Ambiguity** - the undefinable portion of knowledge is embodied in highly tacit human skills;

> **Unprovenness** - knowledge with a proven record of past usefulness is less difficult to transfer;

> **Lack of motivation** - reluctance to share crucial knowledge for fear of losing ownership, a position of privilege, or superiority; on the opposite end of the transfer, this represents the reluctance to accept knowledge due to 'not invented here' syndrome;

> **Not perceived as reliable** - a trustworthy source is more likely than others to influence the behavior of a recipient;

> **Lack of absorptive capacity** - largely a function of their preexisting stock of knowledge;

> **Lack of retentive capacity** - initial difficulties during the integration of received knowledge may become an excuse for discontinuing its use and reverting to the previous status quo;

> **Arduous relationship** - the success of such exchanges depends to some extent on the ease of communication and on the 'intimacy' of the overall relationship between the source unit and the recipient unit;

These difficulties also reflect the fact that much of the communication channel between humans is what is referred to as "high-context" communication, relaying subtle cultural nuances that must accompany the knowledge transfer for inherent stickiness of the content. Table 6.1 below illustrates the percentage of communication that is achieved through the various mediums.

Table 11.1 – Statistics regarding communication effectiveness [16]

Communication Component	Percentage
Words	7%
Voice (pitch, speed, volume, tone)	38%
Visual (eye contact, body language)	55%

From this, we can surmise the nature of the losses that are incurred with common software development methods. Each attack this problem at various segments of the knowledge transfer chain, but none address the root causality of the knowledge attenuation. Figure 11.3 illustrates the typical social network topology for developing software when requiring extraction of SME knowledge and transference to an intermediary:

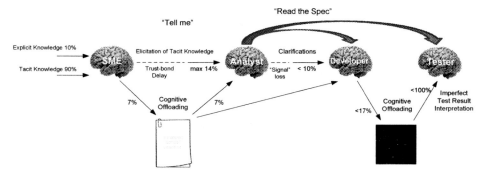

Figure 11.3 – "Complicated Adaptive System" of brains

From the above, we can see that most knowledge is tacit, with mediocre results to date in improving the trust-bonds required for efficient and effective extraction. We also can identify with the challenges of such a serial knowledge transfer chain, and note the order of magnitude in bandwidth improvements that could be achieved through internal communication pathways versus externalized communication pathways through intermediaries. Each of these suggests that our simplistic notion of improving performance through typical knowledge extraction practices, or by scaling teams to larger and larger sizes is exactly the wrong thing to do. Rather, it is knowledge and the extraction thereof that is the core constraint if we are taking a Theory of Constraints [17] view of the problem, rather than the various intermediaries and schemes we have concocted to apply band-aids over this core problem. We must **elevate** this constraint by changing the core function of the SME from knowledge mining to direct expression of their knowledge into software.

To architect a new Hyper Agility way of working we start with a seed crystal, and that seed crystal is the SME-developer. The concept is not entirely new, as *End-user Programming* has been explored in research circles since the mid-2000's [18]. Realizing the notion described previously as BizOps, we purposefully structure the Value Stream around what is usually seen as a bad thing - *Shadow Apps*. We leverage the various IT specializations in a satellite configuration around our core Business "performer". This individual or individuals are those who hold the deep understanding and often inexpressible thoughts and ideas of what needs to be built. In the mind of the business expert, much of this knowledge is tacit. Figure 11.4 reflects the change in socially distributed cognition with this new network configuration:

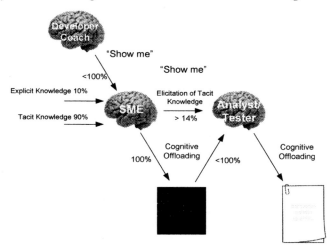

**Figure 11.4 – Star constellation around single
"Complex Adaptive System - CAS" SME Brain**

Such a strategy folds the typical social network configuration within all methods to date "inside-out". This is contrary to the assumption that a serialized process (an I-Plant, the slowest process configuration possible) and *exploitation* of constraints is the way to go.   This coincidentally is the focus in Kanban as the optimum configuration for the software supply chain. Instead, we arrive at a more complex and highly concurrent process configuration (an A-Plant).   Figure 11.5 illustrates the elevation of this core constraint through a servant leadership constellation surrounding the SME as opposed to the traditional overly specialized workflow. With this configuration, what once was viewed in Lean Thinking terms as Type I Muda (waste) now becomes Type II Muda and can be eliminated:

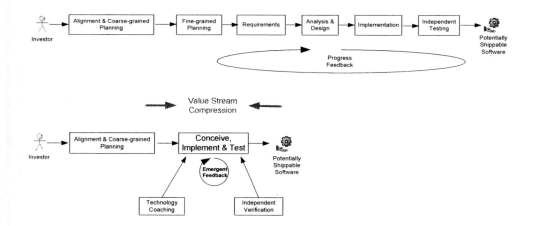

Figure 11.5 – Value-network Configuration for Hyper Agility

Exploring the ramifications of this re-configuration in more detail, and the opportunities that can be exploited, along with the challenges to the deeply ingrained bias that exists related to popular ways of working, consider the following practices and tactics:

11.2.1 - Specifications and the use of Interpreters (Analysts)

To date, all methods and practices have focused on the conveyance of intent between at least two humans. Look no further than social media to see how difficult this really is. Example practices include real-time conversation, with mere placeholders used to prioritize and capture confirmation (and purposefully transient as in the case of XP or other Agile approaches with User Stories), or through use of a full-time interpreter like a Systems/Business Analyst using techniques of various formalities and degrees of persistence like Use Cases or Traditional SRS specifications. In each case, the basic assumption is that this knowledge must first jump out of the SME's brain and into someone else's brain for any software to be developed. Regardless of format, formality or efficacy, a "meeting-of-the minds" is required. But why can't that conveyance of knowledge be through a more concrete, less variable form by actually having the SME realize their ideas directly in a simple medium that results in the actual system. If IDE's and solution stacks simplify, as they are now with Platform as a Service (PaaS) IDE's like IBM BlueMix [19] or various Visual AJAX environments [20], all of a sudden the tables are turned. Details about REST [21] or SOAP [22] service invocations can be coached through pairing by specialized developer expertise. Relational database normalization can occur outside the critical path by DBA expertise. Reuse API's such as those from Google Code [23] or Cloud Foundry [24] can be brought to the attention of the SME developing the emergent system, perhaps with technologists taking over periodically to produce a "walking skeleton" [25] of the API usage. Needless to say, a huge hole is opened up with current dogmatic interpretation and espoused orthodoxy of today's popular methods.

11.2.2 - UX Designers, Information Architecture, Personas and Wireframes

Because the actual Persona that cares about all elements of design is actually designing the system, if they don't like the end product, they have no one to blame but themselves for misunderstanding their inner desires. Wireframes become moot because of the low cost and rapid incarnation in the actual endpoint technologies. What if they do not speak for all SME's or end user constituencies? Even though a single nominated representative of a SME/end user constituency builds the interface of the system, coaching in areas like Information Architecture and Industrial Design is still needed to enable a broader meeting-of-the-minds. However this can be done in-line with the software development and in real-time, not serialized. Stakeholder mediation and rapid feedback to prospective customers is still required to arrive at a consensus of the target market or constituencies. However, at least it is the domain expert that is the one speculating on the function AND the form, not one step removed to developers or other serialized specialists. Again, coaches can steer these developments towards more likely desirable outcomes, leveraging Validated Learning in a much tighter feedback loop.

11.2.3 - Architectural Blueprints and their Draftsmen (Architects)

Design views and blueprints no longer become a critical path tactic for guiding the creative process, but rather serve as a tool by the SME to understand the complexity of their ideas or domain concepts. Design documentation adds value but as the persistence of knowledge, a long lasting artifact of the resultant solution at an abstraction level that enables understanding. However, these are not *models for the sake of models*. A strategy that relies on too low an abstraction level for documentation in the code optimizes the life of the solution domain technologist, but is inefficient when others need to rapidly come up to speed on the decisions that were made in realizing the software.

11.2.4 - Planning, Coordination and Status Reporting Ceremonies

Two revered ceremonies in Scrum are the Sprint Planning ceremony and the Sprint Demo. If we consider the Product Owner is dynamically prioritizing their personal backlog in some form all the time as part of the emergence process, what need is there to build a time-box full of tasks? Why attempt to predict these team tasks, which in the case of Hyper Agility, emerge in real-time and result in something akin to service requests when the practice or technical coaching need arises during the creation of the increment. The Sprint demo is happening to the Product Owner all the time within the very tight conceive / build / test cycle. Broader demonstrations occur through an observer pattern. Coordination only becomes relevant through things like the Daily Standup ceremony when multiple Product Owners are building software in parallel streams, leveraging parallel development branching mechanisms. Obviously, the notion of a Sprint time-box starts to become moot in favor of one-piece flow, and broader coordination with parallel value streams becomes a release cadence, decoupled from these *innovation emergence engines*. Finally, when it comes to the "Scrum Master", servant leadership becomes focused on primary artifact concerns (the product and its technology) - ironically not the "rules of the Scrum process"; don't forget it was always supposed to be *Individuals and Interactions over Processes and Tools*.

11.2.5 - Contracts and Stakeholder Management

The mantra related to *Customer Collaboration over Contract Negotiations* obviously becomes moot, because the "contract", which manifests a formal "meeting of the minds" is between the SME and the investors. Seeing as they are both on the "business side", collaboration between them is likely and contracts or formal commitments unnecessary. This means that the line between the Business and IT implicitly blurs, which was the original intent of the Manifesto value statement above. The only agreements that must be managed are the service levels between the SME's developing the system and the technologist and specialist coaches that are providing service. This always occurs between the mentor and mentee implicitly and always requires a trust-bond to be established, which is ill-served by low trust mechanisms like contracts. This trust bond is likely to be successful if long lived coach relationships emerge; otherwise, coaches will be replaced after only a short time, and risks that could affect the software development outcome are implicitly mitigated.

****

Figure 11.6 – Stage Performer Metaphor

The stage performer metaphor (Figure 11.6) has been around for awhile in the software development space [26]. The notion that it is the actor that makes a production successful fits especially well with Business-centric Development. The actor must dig deep into their consciousness to express the intent of the production, along with all the subtle nuances such that the deeply human emotional experience is born. It is the actors and actresses that are front and center. The Producers, Directors, Cameramen, Grips, Extras, Production Managers and Coordinators, Special Effects, and Set Designers are all on the sidelines in servant leadership of the live, highly dynamic performance. These supporting roles and cast members cannot manufacture the connection felt between the stage performer and the audience. So too is the nature of software development, as it is the connection between the business need (analogous to the theatric emotional need) and the implementer that must be made. Having the subject matter expert play the part of the "actor" only makes sense when framed in this way.

The division of labor strategy implicit within Hyper Agility and Business-centric Development provides a significant and overlooked opportunity related to untapped labor pools of knowledge workers. Through the wiring in of SME expertise, knowledge extraction barriers can be overcome and cognitive offloading can occur with less loss, thereby accelerating the emergence of software. Figure 11.7 illustrates the implications of technologies which enable direct cognitive expression and translation into a technology medium, with a notable and upcoming example being Gesture Computing [27] :

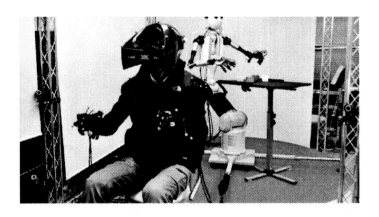

Figure 11.7 – Cognitive Offloading

Such a strategy directly addresses the biggest cost center in software development. Through technology innovation and disintermediation, "developer" resources can be tapped further up the supply chain, closer to the point of demand. Whereby a limit is being hit with respect to the exploitation of offshore labor, the new frontier of onshore, business savvy capability remains largely untouched. With the diminishing returns from offshore models as per *Brookes Law*, a SME-centric approach to enhancing the supply side serves as a high leverage, acceleratory and discontinuous jump in capacity. This is due to the more efficient utilization of specialist technologist resources in a non-critical path manner. Technologists will trend towards commoditization within the arbitraged labor pool. Incentive will materialize for employees to gain domain expertise and to expand responsibility into the SME developer role. Investors will realize large savings in terms of reduction of sunk costs and the obvious likelihood of better endeavor results. Such a strategy affects the supply-side elasticity by flattening out the supply side curve and changing its slope due to reduction in batch sizes through JIT. Leveraging Post-Fordism [28] thinking we have already seen a trend towards smaller batches and more cross-functional skill-sets to enable better outcomes. We can further extend this Lean Thinking towards just-in-time acquisition of talent and staffing on software endeavors., thereby improving the so-called "fungability" of enterprise personnel.

11.3 - Business-centric Development at Scale

With modern technologies emerging, a single SME individual can run circles around the so-called 7+-2 team heuristic. In fact, such an individual can run circles around larger teams. Ironically, the *Individual has Interactions* happening inside their own head at a much faster pace than any mere "complicated" system dynamic. As in each SME's brain is a Complex Adaptive System (CAS) and all the attempts to instantiate CAS through networks of individuals are a poor approximation (more often than not, such a configuration does not yield the desirable emergent properties, like that electricity you likely have felt on a high performance team - fun, joy, euphoria). Given the mainline effort emerging from a SME with the support of a few specialist individuals, hyper productivity ensues and all the dysfunctions and silver-bullet techniques attempting to improve those dynamics go away. Team size gets smaller, not bigger. This puts a huge wrench in the newest shiny object on the scene - The Scaled Agile Framework (SAFe) [29] , which really only adds a big requirements taxonomy and a big meeting facilitation approach with a more coarser-grained release cadence (*Agile Release Train*). In effect, it represents a Scrum-of-Scrums that occurs less frequently than the daily scrum, as that pattern has been shown to be quite problematic. Probing further into this assertion, assume we isolate the streams within a program structured around an investment theme, and create silo'd and parallel streams of activity for each application effort in the overall initiative. Figure 11.8 illustrates the effective revision to the Scrum-of-Scrums as advocated by SAFe:

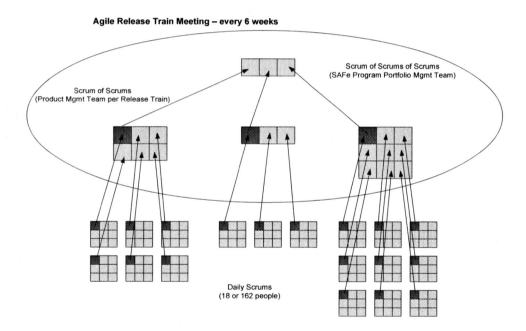

Figure 11.8 – SAFe modifications of Scrum-of-Scrums

As you can see from the above illustration, what SAFe brings to the table is a couple of layers of management for coordination, and a big Release Planning Meeting. This inserts planning directly in line on the critical path. While it decouples the cadence of development from the release of PSI's, it likely suffers from destabilization when one of the trains in the coordinated Release Train breaks down. It is not uncommon to blow a sprint, so equally likely to blow a coordinated release every 6 weeks. The mechanism of timeboxing is still leveraged to limit WIP and achieve flow, but this duration is arbitrary and likely drifts away from Critical-WIP (see section 6.1) once Release Train meetings run into difficulty. Figure 11.9 illustrates the overhead that impacts the timebox more and more as scale is increased:

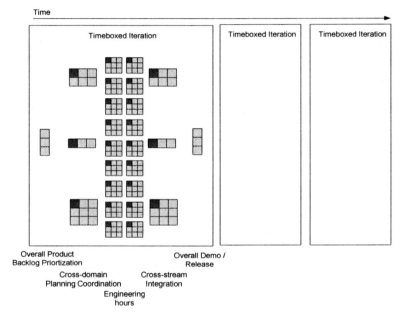

Figure 11.9 – Time-box compression

The Scaled Agile Framework also assumes the ease of forecasting release payload reliant on reasonably complete and high-fidelity backlogs and therefore high fidelity knowledge extraction from subject matter experts. This assumption for scale means that *big requirements up front* effectively occurs to enable smooth operation downstream in the delivery chain. Even if the "requirement types" have been labeled are under a different "Agile" name rather than Traditionalist terminology, the requirements taxonomy still assumes the ease of extraction of tacit knowledge from SMEs, and couples this knowledge extraction to a weak form of enterprise architecture activity (architectural epics and features) in front of Scrum team build-out on the release trains.

We know from SDLC 3.0 that the linear approach to scaling is to leverage Feature Crews in a small-batch cadence which is neither coupled to planning nor dependent upon up-front centralized alignment activities.

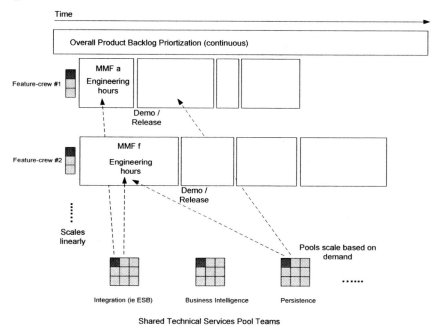

Figure 11.10 – Mitigating the non-linearity of Team size

One of the key differences in the above approach is the degree of isolation of independent, self organizing teams. These teams are cross-functional, with problem domain and solution domain representation. They act like a mini-business venture, responsible atomically for all aspects of meeting customer demand. Instead of being part of a larger and larger composite, they act similar to USMC units with autonomous authority. Due to the fact that they are freed from temporally sensitive fixed cadences, they can focus on the actual realization rather than coordination overhead. They also survive from product assignment to product assignment. This means that once the team has "normed" and is performing well, every attempt is made to maintain this emergent behavior. Teams evolve an understanding of the participants within their ranks, the personalities involved, the key strengths and weaknesses. Instead of ripping them apart immediately after they have gone through the team lifecycle, the team is preserved. This implies a matrixing strategy at the team level as opposed to the individual level, a fundamental shift for most organizations.

Establishing independent value streams in parallel also has a linearizing effect on the typical scaling curve. The reason it scales better is due to the impact of communication non-linearity as team size grows. If instead of growing a single team we add more granular teams, the scaling effect becomes more linear. Figure 11.11 presents the formulae that govern the effort related to cooperative problem solving and often associated with Brooks Law:

$$TeamEffort = \sum Effort_{person} + \left(\# Pairs \times Effort_{pair}\right)$$

where

$$\# Pairs = \frac{N^2 - N}{2}$$

and

$$N = number\ of\ team\ members$$

Figure 11.11 – Mitigating the non-linearity of Team size

What is obvious from this relation is that as team size grows, the potential number of communication links grows exponentially (non-linearly). This tells us that it is desirable to encapsulate communications within small teams so as to reduce the amount of communication overhead. If we keep teams small and have external communication links kept to a constant number which is also small, the resulting effort expenditure profile related to the effects of communication and collaboration becomes linear. A linear relation is far more likely to scale to the kinds of projects that Agile has shown to have difficulty accommodating. Figure 11.12 shows the difference on scaling:

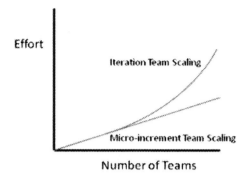

Figure 11.12 – Mitigating the non-linearity of Team size

With Business-centric Development, an inversion takes place related to the central coordination of the program, effectively placing this at the end of the cycle rather than up-front. If one were to view the Scaled Agile metaphor as being a central train scheduling approach, with Agile Release Trains being booked and then cleared for departure on a regular cadence, a SME-centric approach would not put such a central planning constraint in-line in the value stream. Instead, an agricultural metaphor akin to thought or "Idea Farming" in Figure 11.13 illustrates such an inversion to achieve scale. In this approach to scaling the value stream and the alignment period of time, feature crews (**idea farms**) are tended to by farmers (SMEs) to grow their software in a knowledge emergent fashion (grow their crops). They attempt to make the best land economics decisions and are afforded their ration of seed to emerge crop value (business domain budget). The central agricultural boards forecast the prices and crop yield, and establish harvest infrastructure and schedules accordingly (cadence of release trains and composition). They coordinate aggregation of the harvest (integration) and work alongside rail and trucking infrastructure to enable economies of scale for the industry (enterprise architecture capability and infrastructure planning). Specialists of various types provide service, either on-demand from central pools (ESB, DB, BI support) or embedded on the farm in the form of equipment maintenance and training (developer coaches and technologists). Agricultural inspection occurs from time to time to ensure the quality of the crop and mitigate effects of disease for the enterprise (Analyst/Tester).

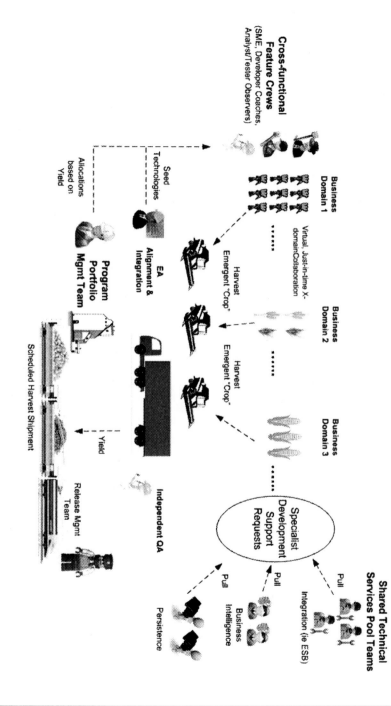

Figure 11.13 – Scale Inversion through Idea Farming

11.4 – Technology Enablers to New Ways of Working

Every era of development methodology has resulted from a paradigm shift in the underlying technologies. Early on, the business was reliant on "IT Departments" which were specialized to deal with the severe constraints and costs of computing on enormous Mainframe resources. The processes reflected the requisite cycle times for getting access to computing resources. It is no wonder that the Waterfall ensued, with nobody complaining due to the long lead times and dead time that had to be filled by such things as analysis paralysis or Big Design Up-Front due to the very high costs of failure. However, while such a way of working has long overstayed its welcome, new paradigms eventually shifted the methodology landscape. The degree of complexity in development and sustainment of applications tracks (albeit at a slower and discontinuous pace) to *Moore's Law* [30] which states that processing power doubles every 2 years. With client-server computing, new development environments emerged that took advantage of the 2-tier architecture, and simplification took hold in 4th generation applications (Clipper, dBase, Foxpro, Oracle Forms etc.) [31]. These development environments were still too complex for anyone but a technology specialist to be productive. As continued frustration on the part of the business mounted due to the turnaround time for incubating applications, vendors were incentivized to reduce complexity further within the paradigm such that the business themselves could implement software directly without the IT Department bottleneck. This solved part of the problem, yet resulted in a sea of "shadow apps", built without any coherent strategy in differing platforms like Microsoft Access or Sybase PowerBuilder [32], [33]. Maintenance required the eventual participation by IT specialists to care and feed for what was on the surface simple and seemed like a good idea at the time but due to their now mission critical nature required such services as Help Desks and Incident Management as well as Problem Resolution and Service Restoration. What was the missing piece in these early business-centric attempts to increase agility and facilitate more effective knowledge extraction was the holistic total-cost-of-ownership perspective which requires early and often collaboration between the business and IT operations.

Ironically, it is tools that enable the needed Hyper Agility for today's enterprises. Not exactly consistent with the Agile Manifesto's first value "Individuals and Interactions over Processes and Tools".

The emergence and maturing of cloud computing and Platform-as-a Service (PaaS) now represents the single most acceleratory tactic for achieving software development agility. Similarly, cloud-based IDEs remove the barrier to entry for those who wish to develop software, removing the haze and the noise that a hyper-competitive landscape and vibrant "standards" game has cast over the industry for so many years. Instead, if a vendor purports to be able to deliver on the promise that complexity in the development environment is removed, it will become very apparent to an enterprise in short order. It is not surprising that the entrenched IDE developer camps give you strange looks when you call their beloved Eclipse or Visual Studio "obsolete".

Research firms have noticed this aligning of the planets as well, with Forrester Research coining the term *Low-code Platforms* [34], which they define as differing neighborhoods of technology form factors that address subtly different applications types. The common theme among Low-code Platforms is the enablement of rapid creation, quick setup and deployment of applications with minimal traditional "hand coding". Driven by the accelerating demand for responding system-of-engagement opportunities, applications need to be deployed in days, not months. From a pure development perspective, the fastest way to reduce uncertainty and accelerate value delivery is to build less stuff. For example, rather than hand rolling Hibernate mapping files [35], higher forms of leverage can reduce development time and mapping errors. Numerous other opportunities to reduce the degrees of freedom through bundling stacks of technologies together are also inherent in these platforms, with an MVC controller tightly integrated along with the associated languages. Examples emerging in industry include vendor offerings from OutSystems [36], Alpha Software [37] and even Microsoft Sharepoint [38] for development of workflow oriented applications. You can think of it as the resurgence of *PowerBuilder for the Web*. Simultaneously, Write-Once-Run-Anywhere (WORA) [39] is now a given with these platforms due to the simultaneous publishing of hybrid applications on both web and mobile, or facilities like Adobe PhoneGap [40] doing the translations automatically. While not perfect, the strategy definitely has a drastic acceleratory effect by doing much of the heavy lifting for developers. Taking "low-code" one step further is to reduce the inherent complexity in typical web and mobile application development so that subject matter experts can be in the driver seat. To illustrate that Hyper Agility is real and puts into serious question many of the productiivty practices that have become popular, consider the cloud-delivered IDE design window illustrated in Figure 11.14:

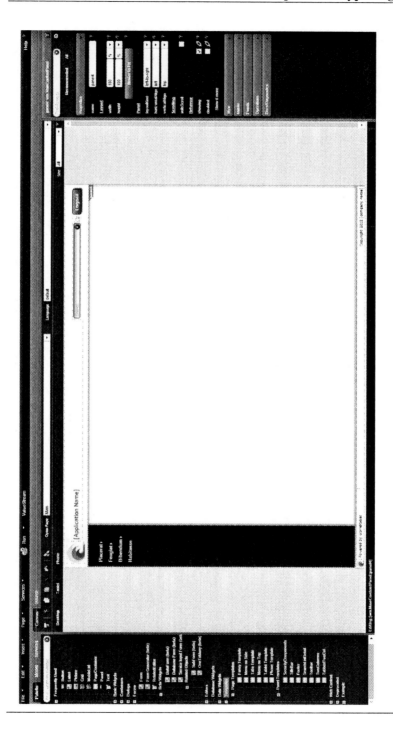

Figure 11.14 – Cloud–based Visual AJAX IDE

In the previous figure, we see that the IDE is a web application requiring no costly environment setup. It is an example of a visual IDE that simplifies the creation of the front-end of the application. In the left side DOJO [41] widget menu, you can see basic widgets for such things as labels, text and images, but also shown is a complex grid widget. Such a widget enables rapid presentation of result sets, linked to an accompanying form. Due to the fact that drag-and-drop Ajax (in this example) does not require coding knowledge or experience, the use of Wireframes is moot because the actual system user interface is created live by the person(s) that will care about the look and feel. Information Architecture and UX Design coaches can work closely with the SME developer in exchanging ideas from their extensive prior specialized experience. Also shown is the ability to reuse templates for rapid layout configuration. Such templates could be developed by Information Architects so that SME developers could be guided efficiently towards ease-of-use designs. Also of significance is the ability to simultaneiously design for both Web, Tablet and Phone, through the integration with Adobe Phonegap in this specific IDE example. CSS (Cascading Stylesheets) [42], which are templated, are always accessible in detail by developers to make small tweaks, as illustrated in Figure 11.15:

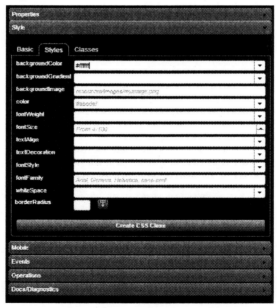

Figure 11.15 – Access to CSS Detail

The details of DOM (Domain Object Model) [43] are hidden, and with a framework like DOJO, events are bound (DOJO.Hitch) behind the visual objects such that access to developing dynamic behavior is easily accessible. Again, technology experts can pair with the SME developer to help them express the desired behavior in code in servant leadership fashion. Figure 11.16 illustrates access to the asynchronous events and binding to either client-side Javascript or server-side services:

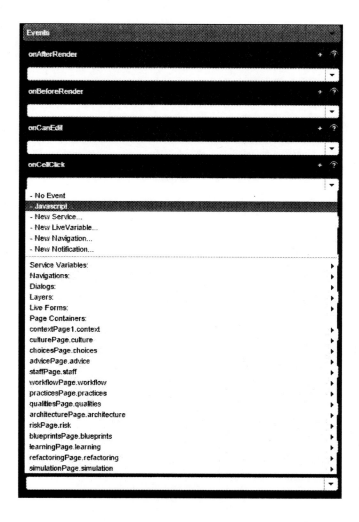

Figure 11.16 – JavaScript bound to DOJO Events

Once an event type is selected, access to the source code in context rather than in flat-file form eases the understanding by the SME of the system flow. Such an "event driven" paradigm was made popular by Visual Basic back in the early 1990's [44]. Figure 11.17 illustrates the simple editor and build environment:

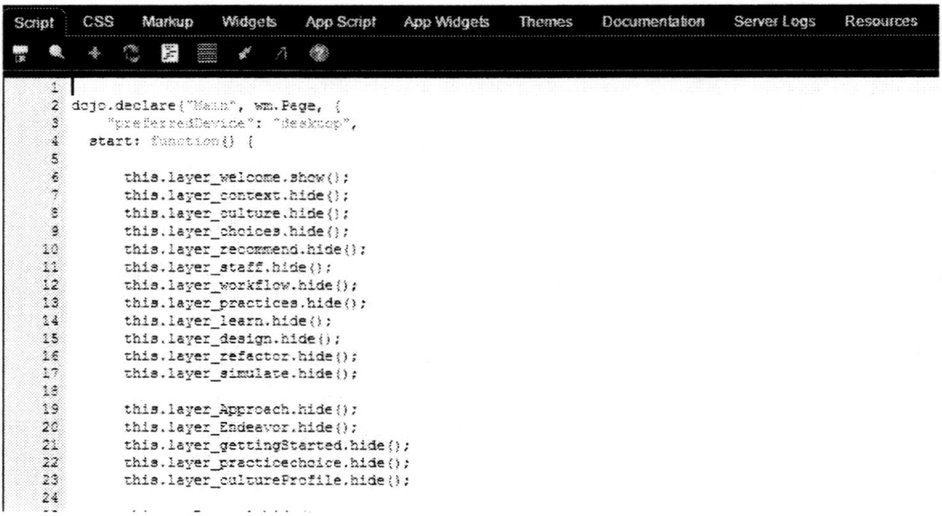

```
1
2  dojo.declare("Main", wm.Page, {
3      "preferredDevice": "desktop",
4      start: function() {
5
6          this.layer_welcome.show();
7          this.layer_context.hide();
8          this.layer_culture.hide();
9          this.layer_choices.hide();
10         this.layer_recommend.hide();
11         this.layer_staff.hide();
12         this.layer_workflow.hide();
13         this.layer_practices.hide();
14         this.layer_learn.hide();
15         this.layer_design.hide();
16         this.layer_refactor.hide();
17         this.layer_simulate.hide();
18
19         this.layer_Approach.hide();
20         this.layer_Endeavor.hide();
21         this.layer_gettingStarted.hide();
22         this.layer_practicechoice.hide();
23         this.layer_cultureProfile.hide();
24
```

Figure 11.17 – Javascript and Server-side Java IDE

Note that most of the complexity with coding AJAX (Asychronous Javascript and XML) [45] applications is the timing sensitivities of the programming paradigm. This is where specialist developer expertise can keep SMEs out of trouble. Similarly, much of Rich Internet Application (RIA) Online Transaction Processing (OLTP) is about domain abstractions and data, so having data specialists working closely with a SME is necessary. However, by simplifying the presentation of the schema and mappings into a non-threatening form, attention can be focused on the numerous Hibernate HQL queries that are necessary in typical applications. If NoSQL [46] databases are leveraged, data experts can hide the details of JSON (Javascript Object Notation) [47] strings from the SME and flatten the data-model for them. Figure 11.18 illustrates the Hibernate mapping environment as a common example of abstracting the persistence layer details into visual form:

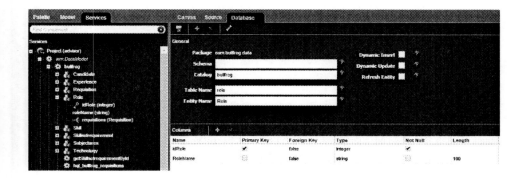

Figure 11.18 – Hibernate Mappings and Database Import

Most RIA web and tablet-based applications are transactional, and therefore many forms are required for all but trival applications. Modern PaaS delivery platforms provide a rapid Create-Read-Update-Delete facility for generation of forms. Obviously this saves time by automatically binding editors and button control widgets to the underlying relational data structure, again not requiring specialist developer expertise to implement. Figure 11.19 illustrates an example:

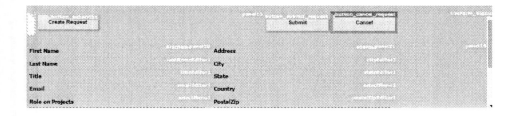

Figure 11.19 – Automatic CRUD Form Generation

Note that without such a Rapid Application Development (RAD) [48] environment for building modern web applications, the same application hand rolled with Spring [49] + Hibernate + Web flow + Spring Security [50] + JavaScript library takes about a week to setup. It would require a lot of XML for Spring config files and annotation in java code, hand mapping hibernate HBM files plus deciding on frameworks and JavaScript libraries, manually creating Cascading Stylesheets and reading documentation if not abstracted to this level.

If attempting such a Hyper Agility strategy in your enterprise, you will likely hear highly emotive rhetoric that such an environment is "not a real development platform". Rebuttal can be waged by explaining that tight integration with technologies such as Javascript, JSON, Spring MVC, Hibernate, SOAP, REST, RSS [51], jQuery [52], CSS, HTML5 Canvas [53] and Google Code and Cloud Foundry is implicit with these revolutionary PaaS platforms. It would be difficult to argue that such technologies are not "industrial strength". Similarly, while it is obvious that such a change may feel threatening to entrenched fiefdoms within IT, the opportunity with such an evolution is that a higher value-add contribution is possible and to be expected with onshore personnel. Career paths focused on understanding the business domain of an enterprise brings IT closer to their long standing stakeholders and blurs the line of division. People with a passion for technology can still deliver huge value in such a value stream configuration, but their positioning changes from reactive follower to one of servant leader. "Towering expertise" as it is referred to in the Toyota Product Development System [54] is still sought after for specializations, only that the application of this expertise is closer to the actual need rather than many steps removed. Modern practice has always suggested that closer, more collaborative relations exist between the business domain and IT; unfortunately the "how" to make this real so that hyper productivity emerges has been missing until now.

Undoing "Viruses of the Mind"

"In the future, the system must be first...and the first object of any good system must be that of developing first-class men"

The quote above comes from the first "management consultant", Frederick Winslow Taylor circa 1911. He represents probably the biggest Piñata for most labor activists within software development in relation to his Scientific Management [1]. The beef that many anti-management biased "humanists" have with Taylor comes in the form of his *Time and Motion Studies* [2]. While lost in the annals of history, he was one of the first "system thinkers" within the world of business. Some have attempted from time to time to correct the misconception (see The Lean Startup) that he advocated "human automatons" in mindless sweatshops. These attempts have yielded limited success, and the collateral damage is that Science has been stereotyped by many in the field of Information Technology to mean a lack of humanity and creativity. It is almost as if the ideology of Science and the Philosophies of Reason are threatening to some, and propagating an opposing world view serves some purpose or agenda. The rhetoric and populist meme's in this regard have come fast and furious and with a formidable support system to keep the anti-science ideas healthy and propagating. Most notable among these is the Agile Movement, with a constant beating of the drum for *changing the world of work* [3]. This movement has arguably devolved beyond its original intent to become a vehicle for blatant profiteering [4] and anti-capitalism/anti-management sentiment [5]. Where once the culture was firmly rooted in the customer focused and innovative Adhocracy cultural quadrant, it has now drifted into the Clan quadrant and is increasingly inward looking and self serving. What started out as advocacy based on 12 pragmatic principles has contorted to become a giant vortex of all of societies pushes and pulls. It has even evolved to suggest some form of spiritual or metaphysical enlightenment in the newest metaphysics to hit the marketplace - *Being Agile* [6]. Perhaps the attraction of this form of market differentiation is that the philosophical notion of "being" is the oldest question in the book [7]. In similar differentiating fashion, so too is the fascination with eastern culture as the end-all-be-all. Today's current state of rhetoric seems to continuously put-down western culture in favor of eastern ideals and traditions, suggesting that American ingenuity is no match for their Japanese counterparts [8]. All-in-all we see the continuation of the east-west polarization rather than integration of ideas from the philosophical lineages which pit Platonism against Heraclitanism, *Epistime* against *Techne*, Drucker versus Nonaka-san [9].

In his infamous 1991 paper (which was the basis for the naming of this Epilogue) Richard Dawkins pointed out that popular ideas spread through society by design like viruses [10]. Similar to the small-world phenomenon [11] of modern epidemics, ideas spread rapidly through today's infrastructure and social networks.   Dawkins, a renowned Atheist, also controversially explored meme propagation in the context of organized religion and identified some key "symptoms" of infection of "Viruses of the Mind". Interestingly, an industry veteran and researcher identified some dubious parallels within the domain of software development methodology [12,] which could be termed *The Agile Virus*. From Dawkins paper, we can ponder the following symptoms associated with the current state of Agile infection:

- *"The patient is impelled by some deep, inner conviction that something is true, or right, or virtuous: a conviction that doesn't seem to owe anything to evidence or reason, but which, nevertheless, the believer feels as totally compelling and convincing."* In the case of dogmatic methodology debates like the recent Test-Driven Development (TDD) debacle, even when counter-efficacy claims are given, various fallacies are thrown out to uphold these innate yet irrational feelings and passion.

- *"The believer typically makes a positive virtue of faith's being strong and unshakable, despite it not being based upon evidence."* This symptom is apparent when one hears "low-trust" culture rhetoric in the context of deflection when attempts to gain evidence of efficacy or confer the same rights to openness and transparency to investors are made.

- *"There is a conviction that 'mystery', per se, is a good thing; the belief that it is not a virtue to solve mysteries but to enjoy them and revel in their insolubility."* Unfortunately, this one is extremely convenient in the consulting business, as the old mantra from the hey-day on the 1990's suggests "maintain the mystery" at all costs to lengthen engagements.

- *"There may be intolerant behavior towards perceived rival faiths (in the case of business, methodologies). Believers may be similarly violent in disposition towards apostates or heretics, even if those espouse only a slightly different version of the faith."* Look no further on this one to the recent trashing of SAFe (Scaled Agile Framework) by one of the "fathers" of Scrum with the defamatory attack "The Boys of RUP are back in town" [13].

- *"The particular convictions that the believer holds, while having nothing to do with evidence, are likely to resemble those of the believer's parents"* Well, every time you hear 2nd Generation Agilist's talk of the "forefathers", you know that this symptom is being exhibited.

- *"If the believer is one of the rare exceptions who follows a different religion from his parents, the explanation may be cultural transmission from a charismatic individual."* Ever notice how charismatic software "thought leaders" are - ironically, they used to refer to themselves as evangelists.

Sound familiar? The *elephant in the room* is that many have felt that this ailment has been infecting our industry for too long. Even talking about such unorthodox feelings is taboo. Many have felt it either too socially or politically hot to call out. A few brave souls flirt with making a stand against such orthodoxy from time to time, but the inevitable result is that a gang of thugs, likely experienced in activism, pummel them. For my part, in the past I have been cautioned against references to religion or even my personal stance to methodology as that of agnosticism. Yet I feel that it is time for those with an ethical perspective to stand up for what is right and just. In effect, stand up for those who pay us to develop software. I guess the last straw that has led to me writing this Epilogue is my recent observations of how religious memes is creeping into the software development methodology conversations [14], almost as if those invoking it know full well the power that such a memeplex wields. Other senior veterans in the industry have picked up on this phenomenon as well [15]. Perhaps all the profitable differentiation ideas are tapped out. I would argue that most business executives would agree with the *separation of church and state*, and that going down that road represents a very slippery slope indeed. What bears special scrutiny is the bolstering yet polarizing effects that such a community reinforcement system would bring, and the potential for damage within businesses. In the case of software development, such a blatant play for power, and the resultant polarization that would result would at best represent the massive infusion of *Semmelweis Reflex* [16] and at worst would mimic the Crusades.

Whatever the incumbent method or body of knowledge, enterprise leadership must break out of "politics as usual" and the type of election cycle that happens every 18 months or so within large enterprises related to methodology. To achieve this, organizations must break down the division, dogma and rhetoric and foster unity of purpose. Effort, expenditure and passion must be refocused back towards software investments and their investors. This requires a powerful antidote for the viruses that have taken over in the world of software methodology. This antidote just so happens to be Scientific Management and the mindset of endless experimentation and exploration towards *Operational Excellence*. The industry must increase its degree of curiosity, step out of its comfort zone, and start experimenting with the kinds of innovative value stream configurations that have been described in Chapter 11 that seriously challenge the status quo.

All the other agendas must be left at the door because software development is first and foremost an economic activity, and the nature of the competitive economy is changing rapidly. Enterprise IT must jolt themselves out of the collective trance that somehow the status quo performance is acceptable.   The business deserves better outcomes, and the petty bickering that goes on within IT portfolios is harming these outcomes.   The business would just like folks to focus on an *honest day's pay for an honest day's work*.   The business would just like software development professionals to be in the same boat as themselves as they confront the daily competitive threats to the enterprises very existence.   The business is tired of all the IT methodology jargon, which from Wikipedia is very telling:

> *Much like slang, it can develop as a kind of shorthand to discuss ideas among a group, and can be chosen deliberately and create a barrier to communication, serving as a secret language or "argot" to provide an in-group with needed differentiation and an aura of superiority/correctness or "shibboleths".*

There has been a flu going around for some time now in our industry, and it can best be described as a mutated strain of the well-known "Irrational Exuberance" strain from the Dot.com bubble.   Everyone within Enterprise IT needs to get a shot to counter its effects or risk deeper symptoms and a more dire prognosis.   Such a shot should bring with it a return to ethical behavior, win-win conditions for both business stakeholders and IT professionals, elevation of status and the value proposition to innovators, a shift from containing enterprise-level concerns as "impediments" to *seeking first to understand* such issues - the list goes on.   The embracing of contextual and cultural diversity, and tolerance to alternative points of view should return in quick succession.   The "Age of the Customer" is demanding that IT start helping the business compete and stop being part of the problem, and a **good dose of business reality** might go a long way to reversing this disease.

Bibliography:

Chapter 1:

[1] Roger Sessions, *"The IT Complexity Crisis: Danger and Opportunity"*, ObjectWatch, 2009.

[2] Kim, Gene., *"The Phoenix Project"*, IT Revolution Press, Oct 2014.

[3] Stuart E. Dreyfus, Hubert L. Dreyfus, *"A Five-Stage Model of the Mental Activities Involved in Directed Skill Acquisition"*, Washington, DC: *February,* 1980.

[4] Gary L. Neilson, Bruce A. Pasternack, Karen E. Van Nuys *"The Passive Aggressive Organization"*, Harvard Business Review, December 2005.

[5] MacKinsey Global Survey, *"Organizing for Successful Change Management"*, June 2006.

[6] Gartner Inc., *"Gartner Worldwide IT Spending Report"*, 2013.

[7] Humphrey, W. S., *"Managing the Software Process"*, Reading, Reading, Massachusetts: Addison Wesley, 1989.

[8] Scott Ambler, *"Dr. Dobbs 2010 IT Project Success Rates"*, www.drdobbs.com, *February,* 2008.

[9] Standish Group, *"The Standish Group Report- Chaos"*, www.standishgroup.com 1994-2013.

[10] Bruce W. Tuckman, *"Development Sequence in Small Groups"*, Psychological Bulletin, 1965.

[11] SEMAT (Software Engineering Methods and Theory) Initiative, www.semat.org. *circa December* 2009.

[12] Schein, E. H. *"The corporate culture survival guide: Sense and nonsense about culture change"*; San Francisco: Jossey-Bass Publishers, 1999.

[13] Stenojovich, Maja, *"Rhetorical Analysis of Successful Brands in Social Media Discourse"*, Gonzaga University, 2012.

[14] Andrews, Richard, *"A Theory of Contemporary Rhetoric"*, Rutledge, 2013.

[15] DeMarco, Tom, *"Software Engineering: An Idea Whose Time Has Come and Gone?"*, IEEE Software, July/August 2009.

[16] Griss, M. L., *"Software reuse: From library to factory". IBM Systems Journal 32"*, IBM Systems Journal #32, 1993.

[17] McBeen, Pete., *"Software Craftsmanship: The New Imperative"*, Addison Wesley Professional; 2001.

[18] Scott, Ridley. *"Apple Computer 1984 Commercial"*, http://en.wikipedia.org/wiki/1984_(advertisement), 1983-1984.

[19] Orwell, George, Fromm, Erich; *"1984"*, Signet Classics, City, 1950.

[20] Apple Computer, *"Get a Mac Commercial"*, http://en.wikipedia.org/wiki/Get_a_Mac.; TBWA\Media Arts Lab 2006-2009.

[21] Christensen, Clay M., *"The Innovators Dilemma"*, Harvard Business Press, Boston, 1997.

[22] Hanks, Nancy, *"Making faces across the gulf"* Science Vol. 173 no. 3996 p. 479, 1971.

[23] Gerald F. Davis, Doug McAdam, W. Richard Scott, Mayer N. Zald *"Social Movements and Organization Theory (Cambridge Studies in Contentious Politics)"* Cambridge University Press, 2005.

[24] Project Management Institute, *"A Guide to the Project Management Body of Knowledge (PMBOK®)"* Fourth Edition, 2008.

[25] Kent Beck, et al. *"Manifesto for Agile Software Development"*, 2001.

[26] *"The Scrum Alliance, Transforming the World of Work"*, www.scrumalliance.org.

[27] Project Management Institute, *"PMI Agile Community of Practice"*, http://www.pmi.org/Certification/New-PMI-Agile-Certification.aspx.

[28] *"Agile is Totalitarinism"*, http://anti-agile.com.

[29] Mayer, Tobias, *"The Peoples Scrum"*, Dymaxicon May 2013.

[30] Bulajewski, Mike, *"The Agile Labor Union"*, West Space Journal, Issue 2, Summer 2013.

[31] Frances Hutchinson, Brian Burkitt, *"The Political Economy of Social Credit and Guild Socialism"*, Jon Carpenter Publishing, City, 2006.

[32] Martin, Robert et al., *"Manifesto for Software Craftsmanship"*, http://manifesto.softwarecraftsmanship.org.

[33] Wikipedia, *"Arts and Crafts Movement"*, http://en.wikipedia.org/wiki/Arts_and_Crafts_movement.

[34] Ruskin, John, *"The Stones of Venice"*, De Capo Paperback, 2003.

[35] Smith, Adam, *"An Inquiry into the Nature and Causes of the Wealth of Nations"*, 1776.

[36]Wikipedia,*"CraftUnionism"*, http://en.wikipedia.org/wiki/Craft_Unionism

[37] M Heusser, *"No Estimates in Action: 5 Ways to Rethink Software Projects"*, CIO Magazine, November 2013.

[38] Dweck, Carol., *"Mindset: The New Psychology of Success"*, Ballantine Books, Palo Alto, 2007.

[39] Russell, Bertrand, *"The History of Western Philosophy"*, Simon and Schuster/Touchstone, 1967.

[40] Wikipedia, *"Dogma"*, http://en.wikipedia.org/wiki/Dogma.

[41 Wikipedia, *"Age of Enlightenment"*, http://en.wikipedia.org/wiki/Age_of_Enlightenment.

[42] James, William, *"Pragmatism (Philosophical Classics)"*, Dover Publications, 1995.

[43] Kruchten, Philippe., *"Voyage in the Agile Memeplex"*, ACM Queue, Volume 5 Issue 5 City, 2007.

[44] Dawkins, Richard, *"The Selfish Gene"*, Oxford Paperbacks, 1976.

[45] Barney G. Glaser; Anselm L. Strauss, *"The Discovery of Grounded Theory: Strategies for Qualitative Research"*, Aldine Transactions, 1967.

[46] Illari, Phyllis, Russo, Fredrica, *"HCausality: Philosophical Theory meets Scientific Practice"*, Oxford Press, Oxford, 2014.

[47] *"Agile Anarchy"*, *"Business Craftsmanship"* http://agileanarchy.tumblr.com/post/16218188061/welcome-to-agile-anarchy; http://businesscraftsmanship.com.

[48] Baker, Sam, *"ObamaCare Website has cost $840 Million"*, National Journal, July 2014.

[49] Albanesius, Chloe, *"Toyota Recalls Prius Hybrids over Software Glitch"*, PC Magazine, February, 2014.

[50] *"Patriot Missile Defense: Software Problem Led to System Failure in Dhahran"*, US Government Accountability Office, February, 1992.

[51] Thomson, Rebecca, *"British Airways Reveals What Went Wrong at Terminal 5"*, Computer Weekly, May, 2008.

[52] Government Accountability Office, *"New Denver Airport: Impact of the Delayed Baggage System"* Briefing Report, 10/14/94, GAO/RCED-95-35BR.

[53] Douglas Isbell, Don Savage, *"Mars Climate Orbiter Failure Board Releases Report, Numerous Actions Underway in Response"*, NASA Jet Propulsion Laboratory, November, 1999.

[54] Professor J. L. Lions, *"Ariane 5 Flight 501 Failure"*, ESA Inquiry Board, July 1996.

[55] Tom Philpott., *"Military Update: Mullen pulls plug on problem-plagued DIMHRS pay program"*, Daily Press, February 2010.

[56] Glannon, Joseph, *"The Law of Torts"*, Aspen Publishers, 2010.

[57] Paul Sarbanes, Michael Oxley, *"Corporate and Auditing Accountability and Responsibility Act"*, United States House of Representatives, 2002.

[58] Sir Henry Sumner Maine, *"Ancient Law: Its Connection with the Early History of Society and its Relation to Modern Ideas"*, Henry Holt & Company, 1906.

[59] *"Institute for Electrical and Electronic Engineers"*, www.ieee.org.

[60] *"International Standards Organization"*, www.iso.org

[61] Information Systems Audit and Control Association (ISACA), *"Control Objectives for IT – COBIT"*. www.isaca.org.

[62] Wikipedia, *"Professional Association"*, http://en.wikipedia.org/wiki/Professional_association

Chapter 2:

[1] Thomas, Dave, *"Agile is Dead - Long Live Agility"*, http://pragdave.me/blog/2014/03/04/time-to-kill-agile.

[2] Cockburn, Alistair, *"Oath of Non-Allegiance"*, http://alistair.cockburn.us/oath+of+non-allegiance.

[3] *"The Anti-agile Manifesto"*, http://antiagilemanifesto.com.

[4] Gualtieri, Mike, *"Agile Software is a Cop-out"*, Forrester Research, http://blogs.forrester.com/mike_gualtieri/11-10-12-agile_software_is_a_cop_out_heres_whats_next.

[5] Wikipedia, *"Scotsman Fallacy"*, http://en.wikipedia.org/wiki/No_true_Scotsman

[6] K. Beck, *"Test Driven Development: By Example"*, Addison Wesley Professional, 2002.

[7] K. Beck, *"eXtreme Programming Explained: Embrace Change"*, Addison Wesley, 1999.

[8] James O. Coplein, *"Why Most Unit Testing is Waste"*, RBCS http://www.rbcs-us.com/documents/Why-Most-Unit-Testing-is-Waste.pdf.

[9] Heinemeier-Hansson, David , *"TDD is dead: Long live testing"*, http://david.heinemeierhansson.com/2014/tdd-is-dead-long-live-testing.html, April 2014.

[10] Kent Beck, Martin Fowler, David Heinemeier-Hansson, *"Is TDD Dead?"*, Google Hangout , https://plus.google.com/events/ci2g23mk0lh9too9bgbp3rbut0k, May 2014.

[11] Leemans, Sander, *"Validation of CERN's Finite State Machines"*, Eindhoven University of Technology, June, 2012.

[12] McQuivey, James, *"Digital Disruption: Unleashing the Next Wave of Innovation"*, Amazon Publishing, February 2013.

[13] Christensen, Clay M., "The Innovators Dilemma", Harvard Business Press, 1997.

[14] Bertrand Meyer, *"Object-oriented Software Construction"*, Prentice Hall PTR, 2000.

[15] D'Souza, Desmond; Wills, Alan Cameron, *"Objects, Components, and Frameworks with UML: The Catalysis(SM) Approach"*, Addison Wesley Professional, 1998.

[16] H. Rahmandad, N. Repenning, J. Sterman, *"Effects of Feedback Delay on Learning"*. "System Dynamics Review Vol. 25, No. 4; Oct.-Dec. 2009.

[17] W. Royce, *"Managing the Development of Large Software Systems"*, Proc. Westcon, IEEE CS Press.1970, pp. 328-339.

[18] Mark Kennaley, *"SDLC 3.0: Beyond a Tacit Understanding of Agile"*, Fourth Medium Press, 2010.

[19] Beck, Kent, *"jUnit Pocket Guide"*, O'Reilly Media, September, 2004.

[20] Duvall, Paul, Glover, Andrew *"Continuous Integration: Improving Software Quality and Reducing Risk"*, Addison Wesley Professional, 2007.

[21] Wikipedia, *"Wiki"*, http://en.wikipedia.org/wiki/Wiki.

[22] Dean Leffingwell, *"Scaling Software Agility: Best Practices for Large Enterprises"*, Addison Wesley, 2007.

[23] *"The Scaled Agile Framework"* , http://www.scaledagileframework.com.

[24] Schwaber, Ken, *"unSAFe at any Speed"*, https://kenschwaber.wordpress.com/2013/08/06/unsafe-at-any-speed.

[25] Atkins, Lyssa, *"The Coaches Coach Shares Her View on SAFe"*, InfoQ, October, 2014.

[26] The Open Group *"TOGAF v9"*. www.opengroup.org/togaf , 2009.

[27] Scott W. Ambler, Mark Lines *"Disciplined Agile Delivery: A Practitioner's Guide to Agile Software Delivery in the Enterprise"*, IBM Press 2012.

[28] Scott Ambler, *"Agile UP"*, www.ambysoft.com 2002-2005.

[29] Scott W. Ambler *"Agile Modeling: Effective Practices for eXtreme Programming and the Unified Process"*, Wiley Press 2002.

[30] Scott Ambler, First I., *"Disciplined Agile Delivery Lifecycles"*, http://disciplinedagiledelivery.wordpress.com/lifecycle, Nov. 2014.

[31] Scott Ambler *"The Agile Scaling Model (ASM): Adapting Agile Methods for Complex Environments"*, IBM whitepaper, 2009.

[32] Barry Boehm, Richard Turner, *"Balancing Agility & Discipline: A Guide for the Perplexed"*, Addison Wesley, 2003.

[33] Eric Ries, *"The Lean Startup"*, Crown Business, 2011.

[34] Henry Mintzberg, James A. Waters, *"Of Strategies, Deliberate and Emergent"*, Strategic Management Journal - July Wiley Blackwell 1985.

[35] Clough, Richard, *"How General Electric Wants to Act Like a Startup"*, Bloomberg BusinessWeek, August 2014.

[36]Rob Go, *"What Lean Startups are NOT"*, NextView Ventures, February 2010.

[37] David J. Anderson, *"Kanban: Successful Evolutionary Change for your Technology Business"*, Blue Hole Press, 2010.

[38] James P. Womack, Daniel T. Jones, Daniel Roos; *"The Machine that Changed the World : The Story of Lean Production"*, Harper Perennial, 1991.

[39] J. D. C. Little,*"A Proof of the Queuing Formula L= λ W"* Operations Research, 9, 383-387 (1961).

[40] E. Goldratt, *"The Goal: A Process of Ongoing Improvement"*, North River Press, 1992.

[41] Karl Scotland, *"Availagility Blog"*, http://availagility.co.uk/2008/10/28/kanban-flow-and-cadence/.

[42] Kim, Gene., *"The Phoenix Project"*, IT Revolution Press, Oct 2014.

[43] *"Velocity Conference"*, O'Reilly, San Jose June 2009.

[44] Jez Humble, David Farley *"Continuous Delivery"*, Addison Wesley Professional, August 2010.

[45] *"Lean Startup Conference"*, Neo, December 2012.

[46] *"Getting Started with Amazon Web Services: Deploying an Application"*, Amazon Digital Services, 2014.

[47] Wavemaker Inc., *"Wavemaker Studio"*, www.wavemaker.com.

[48] International Business Machines, *"IBM Bluemix"*, www.ibm.com/software/bluemix.

[49] R. Collin Johnson, *"IBM Unveils Cognitive Systems Institute"*, EE Times, October 2013.

[50] *"The Software Development Practice Advisor"*, Software Development Experts -www.software-development-experts.com/sdpa.aspx.

[51] Kennaley, Mark, *"US 20120311519 A1 - System and method for providing expert advice on software development practices"*, USPTO, June 2011.

[52] Godfrey-Smith, Peter, *"Theory and Reality: An introduction to the philosophy of science"*, University of Chicago Press 2003.

[53] T Bollerslev, JM Wooldridge, *"Quasi-maximum likelihood estimation and inference in dynamic models with time-varying covariances"*, Duke, 1992.

[54] Marc C. Kennedy, Anthony O'Hagan, *"Bayesian calibration of computer models"*, Journal of the Royal Statistical Society, January 2002.

[55] Richard Sutton, Andrew Barto, *"Reinforcement Learning: An Introduction (Adaptive Computation and Machine Learning)"*, Bradford Books, March, 1998.

[56] Theodore Sheskin, *"Markov Chains and Decision Processes for Engineers and Managers"*, CRC Press, November 2010.

[57] Christopher Bishop, *"Neural Networks for Pattern Recognition"*, Oxford University Press, January 1996.

[58] Nick Bassiliades, Guido Governatori, Adrian Paschke , *"Rule-Based Reasoning, Programming, and Applications: 5th International Symposium, RuleML 2011"*, Springer, December 2011.

[59] Timothy Ross, *"Fuzzy Logic with Engineering Applications, Third Edition"*, Wiley, March 2010.

[60] William Clancey., *"Artificial Intelligence Notes on "Epistemology of a rule-based expert systems"*, Elsevier Volume 59 Issues 1-2, February 1993.

Chapter 3:

[1] Henderson-Sellers, Brian, *"Situational Method Engineering - State of the Art Review"*, Journal of Universal Computer Science Volume 16 no 3, March 2009.

[2] Harmsen, A. F., *"Situational Method Engineering"*, Moret Ernst & Young Management Consultants, 1997.

[3] Philippe Kruchten, *"The Rational Unified Process: – An Introduction"*, Addison Wesley, 2000.

[4] IBM Rational, *"IBM Rational Method Composer 7.5"*, www.ibm.com/software/awdtools/rmc/

[5] Cockburn, Alistair, *"Crystal Clear: A Human-Powered Methodology for Small Teams: A Human-Powered Methodology for Small Teams"*, Addison Wesley Professional, October 2004.

[6] Barry Boehm, Richard Turner, *"Balancing Agility & Discipline: A Guide for the Perplexed"*, Addison Wesley, 2003.

[7] Scott Ambler *"The Agile Scaling Model (ASM): Adapting Agile Methods for Complex Environments"*, IBM whitepaper, 2009.

[8] Kruchten, Philippe, *"The Frog and the Octopus—Experience Teaching Software Project Management"*, Proceedings of the Canadian Engineering Education Association, Queens University, Kingston Ontario, 2011.

[9] Mike Gualtieri, Mark Kennaley *"Techno-politics Podcast: Agile Software is not the Cats Meow"*, Forrester Research, 2012.

[10] *"Scrumbutt"*, Scrum.org, https://www.scrum.org/ScrumBut.

[11] Ioannis Stamelos, *"Investigating the extreme programming system-An empirical study"*, Springer, 2006.

[12] Ambler, Scott, *"Big Modeling Up Front (BMUF) Antipattern"*, http://www.agilemodeling.com/essays/bmuf.htm, 2005.

[13] Defense Science Board, *"Acquiring Defense Software Commercially"*, Office of the Undersecretary of Defense For Acquisition and Technology, Washington D.C. , June 1994.

[14] Defense Systems Management College, *"Earned Value Management Textbook, Chapter 2"*; Defense Systems Management College, EVM Dept., 1997.

[15] Paul Solomon, *"Performance Based Earned Valuet"*. IEEE Computer Society Press, November , 2006.

[16] Morgan, Edmund M. *"Uniform Code of Military Justice - UCMJ"*, http://www.ucmj.us, Library of Congress, 1950.

[17] *"Joint Requirements Oversight Council - JROC"*, 10 US Title 10 › Subtitle A › Part I › Chapter 7 › § 181.

[18] Robert L. Mitchell, *"Meet Cobol's Hardcore Fans"*, ComputerWorld, August 2014.

[19] Michael Riley, Ben Elgin, Dune Lawrence, Carol Matlack, *"Missed Alarms 40 Million Stolen Credit Card Numbers: How Target Blew It"*, Publisher, City, March 2014.

[20] IBM *"VSAM Record Level Sharing (RLS) Overview"*, http://www-01.ibm.com/support/docview.wss?uid=swg27010925.

[21] Wikipedia, *"Job Command Language (JCL)"*, http://en.wikipedia.org/wiki/Job_Control_Language.

[22] Wikipedia, *"Time Sharing Option (TSO)"*, http://en.wikipedia.org/wiki/Time_Sharing_Option.

[23] Wikipedia, *"ISPF-Software Configuration Library Management (SCLM)"*, http://en.wikipedia.org/wiki/ISPF.

[24] Ivar Jacobson, Maria Ericsson, Agneta Jacobson, *"The Object Advantage: Business Process Reengineering with Object Technology"*, ACM Press, 1995.

[25] Dimitris Manolakis, John Proakis, *"Digital Signal Processing (4th Edition)"*, Prentice Hall, April 2006.

[26] Wikipedia, *"Quantization - Signal Processing"*, http://en.wikipedia.org/wiki/Quantization_(signal_processing).

[27] Larose, Daniel, T., *"Discovering Knowledge in Data: An Introduction to Data Mining"*, Wiley Series on Methods and Applications in Data Mining, June, 2014.

[28] Cyril Northcote Parkinson, *"Parkinson's Law"*, The Economist, 1955.

[29] Watts, Duncan J., *"Small Worlds"*, Princeton Studies in Complexity, August 1999.

[30] Caldarelli, Guido, *"Scale Free Networks"*, Oxford University Press, June 2007.

Chapter 4:

[1] Wharton Executive Education, , *"Culture as Culprit: Four Steps to Effective Change"*, The University of Pennsylvania.

[2] John Kotter, "Leading Change", *Harvard Business Press January*, 2010.

[3] Deal T. E., Kennedy, A. A., *"Corporate Cultures: The Rites and Rituals of Corporate Life"*, Penguin Books, Harmondsworth, 1982.

[4] Prosci Corporation, *"Best Practices in Change Management Report"*, 2003.

[5] Version One, "State of Agile Survey", http://www.versionone.com, 2005-2013.

[6] Schein, Edgar, *"Organizational Culture and Leadership: A Dynamic View"*, Jossey-Bass, San Franscisco, 1992.

[7] Dawkins, Richard First I., *"The Selfish Gene"*, Oxford University Press, Oxford UK, 1976.

[8] www.Wikipedia.com.

[9] Dawkins, Richard, *"Viruses of the Mind. In Dennett and His Critics: Demystifying Mind, ed. B. Dalhlbom, 13-17"*, Blackwell Publishers, Malden, Massachusetts, 1995.

[10] Speel, H. C., *"Memetics: On a conceptual framework for cultural evolution"*, Kluwer, Dordrecht, Holland, 1996.

[11] MacKinsey Global Survey, *"Organizing for Successful Change Management"*, June 2006.

[12] Kim Cameron, Robert Quinn, *"Diagnosing and Changing Organizational Culture"*, Jossey Bass, *2006*.

[13] Burke, Brian, *"Gamify: How Gamification Motivates People to do Extraordinary Things"* ; Gartner Press, 2014.

[14] Richard Thaler, Cass Sunstein, *"Nudge: Improving Decisions About Health, Wealth and Happiness"*, Yale University Press, 2008.

[15] Clay Christensen, "The Innovators Dilemma", Harvard Business Press, 1997.

[16] Peter Senge, *"The Fifth Discipline: The Art and Practice of the Learning Organizations"*. Doubleday Business, 1994.

Chapter 5:

[1] W. Royce, *"Managing the Development of Large Software Systems"*, Proc. Westcon, IEEE CS Press.1970, pp. 328-339.

[2] Tom Gilb, Dorothy Graham, *"Software Inspection"*, Addison Wesley, January, 1994.

[3] H. Rahmandad, N. Repenning, J. Sterman, *"Effects of Feedback Delay on Learning"*. "System Dynamics Review Vol. 25, No. 4; Oct.-Dec. 2009.

[4] David Wagg et al., *"Adaptive Structures: Engineering Applications"*, Wiley, July 2007.

[5] Barry Boehm, *"Software Engineering Economics"*, Englewood Cliffs, NJ: Prentice-Hall, 1981.

[6] B. Boehm, C. Abts, A.W. Brown, S. Chulani, B. K. Clark, E. Horowitz, R. Madachy, D. Reifer and B. Steece. *"Software Cost Estimation with COCOMO II"*. Prentice Hall PTR, July 2000.

[7] Jonathan Mun, *"Modeling Risk: Applying Monte Carlo Risk Simulation, Strategic Real Options, Stochastic Forecasting and Portfolio Optimization"*, Wiley, July, 2010.

[8] J. Rick Turner, Julian F. Thayer, *"Introduction to Analysis of Variance: Design, Analysis and Interpretation"*, Sage Publications Inc., April 2001.

[9] Bernt Oksendal, *"Stochastic Differential Equations – An Introduction with Applications"*, Springer, 2003.

[10] B. Boehm, *"Anchoring the Software Process"*, IEEE Software, 1996.

[11] Mathews, Scott H., Datar, Vinay T. and Johnson, Blake. *"A Practical Method for Valuing Real Options"*. Journal of Applied Corporate Finance, Spring 2007, (19), No. 2, pp. 95-104.

[12] Mikael Collan, Robert Fuller, Mezei Jozsef , *"A Fuzzy Payoff Method for Real Option Valuation"*, Institute for Advanced Management Systems Research, Abo Akademi University, October 2008.

[13] Hakan Ergdogmus, *"Valuation of Learning Options in Software Development Under Private and Market Risk"*, National Research Council of Canada, 2002.

[14] Khaneman, Daniel, *"Thinking, Fast and Slow"*, Farrar, Straus and Giroux, 2011.

[15] George Miller, "The magical number seven, plus or minus two: Some limits on our capacity for processing information" Psychological Review 63 (2): 81-97. 1956.

[16] Charles Spearman, Jenkins, James J. (Ed); Paterson, Donald G. "The Abilities of Man. Studies in individual differences: The search for intelligence". (Ed). (1961).

[17] Neal Ford et al, *"97 Things Every Software Architect Should Know: Collective Wisdom from the Experts"*. O'Reilly Media, 2009.

[18] Sven Johann, Eberhard Wolff, *"Managing Technical Debt"*. InfoQ, May 2013.

[19] S. Levine et al, *"The Control Handbook"*, IEEE Press, 1995.

[20] Peter Senge, *"The Fifth Discipline: The Art and Practice of the Learning Organizations"*. Doubleday Business, 1994.

[21] Martin Fowler, Rebecca Parsons, *"Domain Specific Languages -DSL"*, Addision Wesley, 2010.

[22] Snowden, D.J. Boone, M. *"A Leader's Framework for Decision Making"*. Harvard Business Review, November 2007.

[23] Snowden, D.J. Boone, M. *"Complex Adaptive Systems"*. Harvard Business Review, November 2007.

[24] Kennaley, Mark, *"US 20120311519 A1 - System and method for providing expert advice on software development practices"*, USPTO, June 2011.

[25] Abdel-Hamid, Tarek; Madnick, Stuart, *"Modeling the Dynamics of Software Project Management"*, MIT Alfred P. Sloan School of Management, February, 1988.

[26] Madachy, Ray, *"Software Process Dynamics"*, Wiley IEEE Press, January, 2008.

[27] Object Management Group, *"Software Process Engineering Meta-model Specification"*. www.omg.org 2005.

[28] Frederickson, J; Haumer, Peter, *"Unified Method Architecture US 8639726 B2"*, USPTO, January, 2014.

[29] Tarr, P.; Ossher, H.; Harrison, W.; Sutton, S., *"N Degrees of Separation: Multidimensional Separation of Concerns"*, Publisher, City, Date.

[30] Ivar Jacobson, Pan Wei Ng, *"Aspect-Oriented Software Development with Use Cases"*, Addison Wesley, 2005.

[31] Erich Gamma, Richard Helm, Ralph Johnson, John Vlissades, *"Design Patterns: Elements of Reusable Object-oriented Software"*, Addison Wesley Professional, November 1994.

Chapter 6:

[1] Michael Porter, *"Competitive Strategy: Techniques for Analyzing Industries and Competitors"*. Free Press, 1998.

[2] Mary Poppendieck, Tom Poppendieck *"Lean Software Development: An Agile Toolkit"*. Addison-Wesley, 2006.

[3] J. P. Womack, D. T. Jones, (1996). *"Lean Thinking: Banish waste and create wealth in your corporation"*. New York: Free Simon & Schuster.

[4] Jackson, Michael, *"System Development"*, Prentice Hall, 1983.

[5] Cox, James III; Schleier, John, *"Theory of Constraints Handbook"*, McGraw Hill Professional, 2010.

[6] Adzic, Gojko, *"Specification by Example: How Successful Teams Deliver the Right Software"*, Manning Publications, June 2011.

[7] David J. Anderson, "Kanban: Successful Evolutionary Change for your Technology Business", Blue Hole Press, 2010.

[8] J. D. C. Little, *"A Proof of the Queuing Formula L= λ W"* Operations Research, 9, 383-387 (1961).

[9] Shenhav, Yehouda, *"Manufacturing Rationality: The Engineering Foundations of the Managerial Revolution"*, Oxford University Press, March 2002.

[10] Douglas McGregor, *"The Human Side of Enterprise"*, New York: McGraw-Hill, 1960, p. 132.

[11] Michael L. George, *"Lean Six Sigma: Combining Six Sigma Quality with Lean Production Speed"*, MacGraw-Hill, 2002.

[12] Auditing Standards Board of the American Institute of Certified Public Accountants (AICPA), *"Statement of Auditing Standards-70: Service Organizations"* and *"Statemenn of Auditing Standards – 94: The Effect of Information Technology on the Auditor's Consideration of Internal Control in a Financial Statement Audit"* AICPA AU Section 324 para. 02, 1993-2006.

[13] Ross, Jeanne, Weill, Peter, Robertson, David *"Enterprise Architecture as Strategy: Creating a Foundation for Business Execution"*, Harvard Business Review Press; 2006.

[14] J. P. Womack, D. T. Jones, (1996). *"Lean Thinking: Banish waste and create wealth in your corporation"*. New York: Free Simon & Schuster.

[15] The Open Group *"TOGAF v9"*. www.opengroup.org/togaf , 2009.

[16] James O Coplein, Gertrud Bjørnvig, *"Lean Architecture: For Agile Development"*, Wiley, July, 2010.

[17] Cohn, Mike, *"User Stories Applied: For Agile Software Development"*, Addison Wesley, 2004.

[18] J. Zachman, *"A Framework for Information Systems Architecture"*, IBM Systems Journal Vol 26, No 3, 1987.

[19] Mark Kennaley, *"The 3+1 Views of Architecture – in 3D"*. Working IEEE Conference on Software Architecture -WICSA 2008.

[20] P. Kruchten, *"The 4+1 View Model of Architecture"*, IEEE Software, volume 12, issue 6, 1995.

[21] http://www.agilemodeling.com/essays/changeManagement.htm.

[22] Gantt, Henry L., *"Organizing for Work"*, Harcourt, Brace, and Howe, New York, 1919. Dupont *"Critical Path Method"*, 1957.

[23] Ivar Jacobson, Magnus Christerson, Patrik Jonsson, Gunnar Ovargaard, *"Object Oriented Software Engineering – a Use Case Driven Approach"*, Addison Wesley, 1992.

[24] Mario Barbacci et al, *"Quality Attributes"*, Technical Report CMU/SEI-95-TR-021 ESC-TR-95-021, Software Engineering Institute, Carnegie Mellon University, 1995.

[25] Martin Fowler, *"Continuous Integration"*, martinfowler.com/articles/continuousIntegration.html, 2006.

[26] James Morgan, Jeffrey Liker, *"The Toyota Product Development System: Integrating People, Process, and Technology"*. Productivity Press, 2006.

[27] Clinger-Cohen, *"Information Technology Management Reform Act"*, *"Federal Acquisition Reform Act"*, 104th Congress, Washington D.C. , February 1996.

[28] Cici Albert, Lisa Brownsword, *"Evolutionary Process for Integrating COTS-based Systems - An Overview"*, Technical Reports CMU/SEI-2002-TR-009, Software Engineering Institute, Carnegie Mellon University, 2002.

[29] Ivar Jacobson, Grady Booch, James Rumbaugh, *"The Unified Software Development Process"*, Addison Wesley Object Technology Series, 1999.

[30] Mark Kennaley, *"EPIC+ : An amplification of Package Acquisition Best Practices"*. www.software-development-experts.com.

[31] D. Winterfeld, W. von and Edwards, *"Decision Analysis and Behavioral Research"*, Cambridge University Press, Cambridge, England, 1986.

[32] Thomas Saaty, *"The Analytic Hierarchy Process"*, McGraw-Hill, New York, NY, 1980.

[33] C. Kepner, B. Tregoe, *"Kepner Tregoe Rational Process"*. www.kepner-tregoe.com. 1958.

[34] Rick Kazman, Jai Asundi, Mark Klein, *"Making Architecture Design Decisions: An Economic Approach"*, Technical Reports CMU/SEI-2002-TR-035 ESC-TR-2002-035, Carnegie Mellon University, 2002.

[35] Rick Kazman, Mark Klein, Paul Clements, *"ATAM: Method for Architecture Evaluation"*, Technical Reports CMU/SEI-2000-TR-004, Software Engineering Institute, Carnegie Mellon University, 2000.

[36] Office of Government Commerce (UK), Majid Iqbal, Michael Nieves, *"IT Infrastructure Library (ITIL) Service Strategy"*; and Vernon Lloyd ,Colin Rudd, *"ITIL Service Design"*; and Shirley Lacy, Ivor Macfarlane, *"ITIL Service Transition"*; and David Cannon, David Wheeldon , *ITIL Service Operation."*; and George Spalding, Gary Case, *"ITIL Continual Service Improvement"*. The Stationery Office, 2007.

[37] IEEE Computer Society, *"Guide to the Software Engineering Body of Knowledge – SWEBOK"*, IEEE Press, 2004

[38] T. Ohno, (1988). *"Toyota Production System: Beyond Large-Scale Production"*. New York: Productivity Press.

[39] Carey Schwaber, *"The Forrester Wave: Process Centric Configuration Management"*. Forrester Research Q4 2005.

[40] Lo Giudice, Diego, *"The Forrester Wave Service Virtualization And Testing Solutions"*, Forrester Research, Q1 2014.

[41] International Business Machines, *"IBM UrbanCode"*, http://www-03.ibm.com/software/products/en/ucdep/.

[42] Parasoft Inc. *"Parasoft Service Virtualization"*, http://www.parasoft.com/service-virtualization.

[43] Margo Visitacion and Liz Barnett, *"CA Process Continuum: Greater Depth, Lower Cost, but Still a Big Product"*. Forrester Research June 2001.

[44] Page-Jones, Meilir, *"7-Stages of Software Expertise"*, Wayland Systems, 1990.

[45] Lindstrom, Lamont, *"Cargo Cult: Strange Stories of Desire from Melanesia and Beyond"*, December 1993.

Chapter 7:

[1] *"Idea: Skunkworks"*, The Economist, August 25, 2008.

[2] Mark C. Layton, *"Agile Project Management for Dummies"*, Wiley, April, 2012.

[3] Joshua Eichorn, *"Understanding AJAX: Using JavaScript to create Rich Internet Applications"*, Prentice Hall, August 2006.

[4] Matthew David, *"HTML5: Rich Internet Applications (Visualizing the Web)"*, Focal Press, July 2010.

[5] Cecile Drew, Kathryn Hale, Adrian O'Connell, *"IT Spending Worldwide Q3 2014"*, Gartner, September 2014.

[6] Ingrid Lungren, *"Gartner: 102B App Store Downloads Globally In 2013, $26B In Sales, 17% From In-App Purchases"*, Tech Crunch, September, 2013.

[7] Christof Ebert, Capers Jones, *"Embedded Software: Facts, Figures and the Future"*, IEEE Computer, 2009.

[8] *"Over $25Billion: Size of Embedded Software Engineering Market"*, RTC Magazine, March 2009.

[9] Dan Vesset et al, *"IDC Market Analysis: Worldwide Big Data Technology and Services 2012-2015 Forecast"*, International Data Corp, March 2012.

[10] Louis Columbus, *"Gartner's ERP Market Share Update Shows The Future Of Cloud ERP Is Now"*, Forbes Magazine, May 2014.

[11] Robert L. Mitchell, *"Meet Cobols Hardcore Fans"*, ComputerWorld, August 2014.

[12] Eclipse Foundation, *"Risk-value Lifecycle"*, http://epf.eclipse.org/wikis/openup.

[13] Kahn, Kenneth *"The PDMA Handbook of New Product Development"*. Second Edition. Hoboken, NJ: John Wiley & Sons, 2005..

[14] Corey Ladas, *"Scrumban - Essays on Kanban Systems for Lean Software Development"*, Modus Cooperandi Press 2009.

[15] International Business Corporation, *"Rational Team Concert"*, http://www-03.ibm.com/software/products/en/rtc.

[16] Jeff Gothelf, Josh Seiden, *"Lean UX: Applying Lean Principles to Improve User Experience"*, O'Reilly Media, March 2013.

[17] Steve Mulder, Ziv Yaar, *"The User Is Always Right: A Practical Guide to Creating and Using Personas for the Web"*, New Riders, August 2006.

[18] Christina Wodtke, Austin Govella, *"Information Architecture: Blueprints for the Web (2nd Edition)"*, New Riders, February 2009.

[19] International Business Machines, *"Rational Requirements Composer"*, http://www-03.ibm.com/software/products/en/rrc.

[20] David Cavallo, *"Emergent Design and learning environments: Building on indigenous knowledge"*, IBM Systems Journal Volume 30, 2000.

[21] Graeme Simsion, Graham Witt, *"Data Modeling Essentials, Third Edition"*, Publisher, November 2004.

[22] Rob Moffat, *"Round-trip Engineering Remixed"*, DZone, February 2012.

[23] Scott W Ambler, Pramod J. Sadalage, *"Refactoring Databases: Evolutionary Database Design (paperback) (Addison-Wesley Signature Series (Fowler))"*, Addison Wesley, March 2006.

[24] Oracle Corporation, *"MySQL Workbench"*, http://www.mysql.com/products/workbench.

[25] Eric Ries, *"The Lean Startup"*, Crown Business, 2011.

[26] K. Beck, *"Test Driven Development: By Example"*, Addison Wesley Professional, 2002.

[27] Duvall, Paul, Glover, Andrew *"Continuous Integration: Improving Software Quality and Reducing Risk"*, Addison Wesley Professional, 2007.

[28] Nada daVeiga, *"Change Code Without Fear"*, Dr. Dobbs, February 2008.

[29] SourceForge, *"Cruise Control"*, http://cruisecontrol.sourceforge.net.

[30] GitHub, *"jUnit Team Wiki"*, https://github.com/junit-team/junit/wiki

[31] Matt Wynne, Aslak Hellesoy, *"The Cucumber Book: Behaviour-Driven Development for Testers and Developers (Pragmatic Programmers)"*, Pragmatic Bookshelf, February 2012.

[32] Jez Humble, David Farley *"Continuous Delivery: Reliable Software Releases through Build, Test, and Deployment Automation"*, Addison Wesley Professional, August 2010.

[33] International Business Machines, *"UrbanCode"*, https://developer.ibm.com/urbancode/products/urbancode-deploy.

[34] Geoffrey Moore, *"Systems of Engagement and the Future of Enterprise IT: A Sea Change in Enterprise IT"*, IIAM Whitepaper, 2011.

[35] Cristina Bianchi, Maureen Steele, *"Coaching for Innovation: Tools and Techniques for Encouraging New Ideas in the Workplace"*, Palgrave MacMillan, May 2014.

[36] Paul Clements, Linda Northrop, *"Software Product Lines: Practices and Patterns"*, Addison Wesley Professional, August 2001.

[37] Randy Heffner, Christopher Mines, Eric Wheeler, *"The Forrester Wave: API Management Solutions Q3 2014"*, Forrester Research, September 2014.

[38] Wikipedia, *"Representational State Transfer - REST"*, http://en.wikipedia.org/wiki/Representational_state_transfer.

[39] Mike Gualtieri, *"Predictive Apps Are The Next Big Thing In App Development "*, Forrester Research, August 2013.

[40] Kyle McNabb, Josh Bernoff, *"The CIO's And CMO's Blueprint For Strategy In The Age Of The Customer"*, Forrester Research, 2013.

[41] Wikipedia, *"Focus Groups"*, http://en.wikipedia.org/wiki/Focus_group.

[42] Docco, *"Docco Javascript Document Generation"*, http://jashkenas.github.io/docco.

[43] Techopia, *"Using mySQL to Create a Database Model"*, http://www.techotopia.com/index.php/Using_MySQL_Workbench_t o_Create_a_Database_Model

[44] Axure Software Solutions, *"Axure RP"*, http://www.axure.com.

[45] iRise, *"iRise Collaboration Visualization Framework"*, http://www.irise.com.

[46] Proto.io, *"Proto.io"*, https://proto.io.

[47] Roger Lee, *"Entrepreneurs must go Mobile First or Die"*, TechCrunch, July 2014.

[48] Joab Jackson, *"HTML5 finished - finally"*, PC World, October 2014.

[49] Jon Duckett, *"JavaScript and jQuery: Interactive Front-end Web Development"*, Wiley, June 2014.

[50] Adobe Corporation, *"Adobe PhoneGap"*, http://phonegap.com.

[51] Sencha Inc., *"Sencha Architect"*, http://www.sencha.com/products/architect.

[52] Appcelerator Inc., *"Titanium Studio"*, http://www.appcelerator.com/titanium/titanium-studio.

[53] Michele Pelino, *"Building The Business Case For A Bring-Your-Own-Device (BYOD) Program"*, Forrester Research, December 2014.

[54] Dan Siroker, Pete Koomen, *"A/B Testing: The Most Powerful Way to Turn Clicks Into Customers"*, Wiley, August 2013.

[55] Sarah Ervin, *"Agile Performance Testing – Proactively Managing Performance"*, DZone, April 2014.

[56] Wikipedia, *"Software-as-a-Service"*, http://en.wikipedia.org/wiki/Software_as_a_service.

[57] Cloudbees Inc., *"Cloudbees Continuous Delivery"*, https://www.cloudbees.com.

[58] Electric Cloud, *"Ship.io Continuous Integration for Mobile"*, https://ship.io.

[59] Jez Humble, David Farley *"Continuous Delivery: Reliable Software Releases through Build, Test, and Deployment Automation"*, Addison Wesley Professional, August 2010.

[60] Lex Friedman, *"Developers stymied by Mac App Store Delays"*, MacWorld, October 2012.

[61] Martin Fowler, *"Feature Toggle"*, http://martinfowler.com/bliki/FeatureToggle.html, October 2010.

[62] Brad Appleton, *"Streamed Lines"*, http://www.bradapp.com/acme/branching, 1998.

[63] Victor Farcic, *"Feature Toggles (Feature Switches or Feature Flags) vs Feature Branches "*, Java Code Geeks, , August 2014.

[64] Aslan Brooke, *"Use Canary Deployments to Test in Production"*, InfoQ, March 2013.

[65] Lauren Brousell, *"5 Reasons to Build an Enterprise Mobile App Store"*, CIO Magazine, April 2013.

[66] Names, *"Programs"*, Publisher, Date.

[67] Patrick Gray, *"Tapping into the real-world value of reference architectures"*, Tech Republic, January 2013.

[68] Lee Ackerman et al, *"IBM Redbook: Strategic Reuse with Asset Based Development"*, IBM Press, May 2008.

[69] Jeff Gothelf, *"Building in-house innovation teams: Small, collocated, dedicated, self-sufficient"*, Perception is the Experience Blog, June 2013.

[70] Faisal Hoque, *"The 3 Pillars of the Innovation Economy"*, Fast Company, February 2013.

[71] Steven Melendez, *"The Key To Successful Pair Programming? Patience And Humility"*, Fast Company, October 2014.

[72] Mario Barbacci et al, *"Quality Attributes"*, Technical Report CMU/SEI-95-TR-021 ESC-TR-95-021, Software Engineering Institute, Carnegie Mellon University, 1995.

[73] Karl Scotland; *"Minimum Marketable Features"*, Availagility Blog 2008.

[74] *"The Fault Tree Handbook"*, US Nuclear Regulatory Commission, January 1981.

[75] Wikipedia, *"Requirements Traceability"*, http://en.wikipedia.org/wiki/Requirements_traceability.

[76] Object Management Group, *"System Modeling Language -sysML"*, http://www.omgsysml.org.

[77] Object Management Group, *"Model Driven Architecture - MDA"*, http://www.omg.org/mda.

[78] Lee Ackerman, *"Patterns-Based Engineering: Successfully Delivering Solutions via Patterns"*, Addison Wesley, July 2010.

[79] Bertrand Meyer, *"Object-oriented Software Construction"*, Prentice Hall PTR, 2000.

[80] D'Souza, Desmond; Wills, Alan Cameron, *"Objects, Components, and Frameworks with UML: The Catalysis(SM) Approach"*, Addison Wesley Professional, 1998.

[81] International Business Machines, *"IBM Rhapsody"*, http://www-03.ibm.com/software/products/en/ratirhapfami.

[82] International Business Machines, *"IBM Rational Asset Analyzer"*, http://www-03.ibm.com/software/products/en/raa.

[83] The Mathworks Inc., *"MatLab"*, http://www.mathworks.com/products/matlab/?s_tid=hp_fp_ml. Jul-Sept 1986.

[85] Peter Flach, *"Machine Learning: The Art and Science of Algorithms that Make Sense of Data"*, Cambridge University Press, November 2012.

[86] Joshua M. Epstein, *"A Generative Social Science: Studies in Agent-Based Computational Modeling (Princeton Studies in Complexity)"*, Princeton University Press, 2006.

[87] John Sterman,. *"Business Dynamics: Systems Thinking and Modeling for a Complex World"*, McGraw-Hill, 2000.

[88] Google Inc., *"Google Analytics"*, http://www.google.com/analytics.

[89] Craig Borysowich, *"Developing a Conference Room Pilot"*, Toolbox.com, August 2009.

[90] Rally Software, *"Portfolio Kanban"*, https://help.rallydev.com/portfolio-kanban-board

[91] Rosalind Radcliffe, *"Using IBM Rational Team Concert for System z and the Jazz platform Parts 1-4"*, IBM Developerworks, May 2009.

[92] International Business Machines, *"Job Control Language"*, http://en.wikipedia.org/wiki/Job_Control_Language [93] Names, *"LPAR"*, Publisher, Date.

[94] International Business Machines, *"Rational Development and Test Environment for System Z"*, http://www-03.ibm.com/software/products/en/ratideveandtestenviforsystz

Chapter 8:

[1] Smith, Adam, *"An Inquiry into the Nature and Causes of the Wealth of Nations"*, 1776.

[2] Andy Friedman, *"Responsible Autonomy versus Direct Control in the Labour process"*, Capital & Class, 1977.

[3] Marx, Karl, *"Capital: A Critique of the Political Economy"*, Penguin Classics, 1993.

[4] Weber, Max., *"Economy and Society: An Outline of Interpretive Sociology"*, University of California Press, 1978.

[5] David H. Freedman, *"Corps Business: The 30 Management Principles of the US Marines"*, Collins 2000.

[6] Cyril Northcote Parkinson, *"Parkinson's Law"*, The Economist, 1955.

[7] Thomas W. Malone, Robert Laubacher, Tammy Johns, *"The Big Idea: The Age of Hyperspecialization"*, Harvard Business Review, June 2011.

[9] Massachusetts Institute of Technology, *"MIT Center for Collective Intelligence"*, http://cci.mit.edu.

[10] International Business Machines, *"IBM Smarter Application Development and Management (ADM)"*, http://www-

935.ibm.com/services/us/gbs/application-management/application-development-management.

[11] Thomas L. Jackson, *"Hoshin Kanri for the Lean Enterprise: Developing Competitive Capabilities and Managing Profit"*, Productivity Press, August 2006.

[12] Saul Kassin, Steven Fein, Hazel Rose Markus,*"Social Psychology"*, Cengage Learning, February 2013.

[13] Karl Scotland; *"Minimum Marketable Features"*, Availagility Blog 2008.

[14] Wikipedia, *"Post Fordism"*, http://en.wikipedia.org/wiki/Post-Fordism

[15] Thomaas Humphrey, *"Marshallian Cross Diagrams and Their Uses before Alfred Marshall: The Origins of Supply and Demand Geometry"*, Federal Reserve Bank Richmond Economic Review, Vol. 78, No. 2, March/April 1992.

[16] Guy Gilliland, Raj Varadarajan, Devesh Raj, *"Code Wars: The All-Industry Competition for Software Talent"*, Boston Consulting Group, May 2014.

[17] Gartner *"Gartner Says Sales of Tablets Will Represent Less Than 10 Percent of All Devices in 2014"*, Gartner Consulting, October 2014.

[18] Dan Vesset et al. *"Market Analysis: Worldwide Big Data and Technology and Services 2012-2015 Forecast"*, International Data Corporation, March 2012.

[19] G. Weinberg, *"Quality Software Management Vol. 4: Anticipating Change"*. 1997: Dorset House.

[20] Cockburn, Alistair, *"Shu-Ha-Ri"*, http://alistair.cockburn.us/Shu+Ha+Ri.

[21] Stuart E. Dreyfus, Hubert L. Dreyfus, *"A Five-Stage Model of the Mental Activities Involved in Directed Skill Acquisition"*, Washington, DC: *February*, 1980.

[22] Page-Jones, Meilir, *"7-Stages of Software Expertise"*, Wayland Systems, 1990.

[23] Red Hawk, *"Self Observation: The Awakening of Conscience: an Owner's Manual"*, Hohm Press, September 2009.

[24] Jack Zenger, Joseph Folkman, *"Getting 360-degree Reviews Right"*, Harvard Business Review, September 2012.

Chapter 9:

[1] Geoffrey Moore, *"Crossing the Chasm: Marketing and Selling High-Tech Products to Mainstream Customers"*, Harper Business, July 2006.

[2] Jesse Jacoby, *"Change Accelerator"* EmergentConsultants.com.

[3] Linda Ackermann Anderson, Dean Anderson, *"The Change Leader's Roadmap: How to Navigate the Complexities of Your Organization's Transformation"*, Being First Inc., 2009.

[4] *"Boston Consulting Group Change Delta"*, Boston Consulting Group, http://www.bcg.com/expertise_impact/capabilities/people_organizati on/change_management.

[5] Bridges, William, *"Transitions: Making Sense of Life's Changes, Revised 25th Anniversary Edition"*, Da Capo Press, August 2004.

[6] *"People Centered Implementation (PCI)"*, Change First Inc., http://www.changefirst.com/what-is-pci.

[7] Prokesch, Steven, *"How GE Teaches Teams to Lead Change"*, Harvard Business Review, January 2009

[8] *"Accelerated Implementation Methodology (AIM)"*, Implementation Managements Association http://www.imaworldwide.com.

[9] John Kotter, "Leading Change", *Harvard Business Press January*, 2010.

[10 Kübler-Ross, E. *"On Death and Dying"*, Routledge, 1969.

[11] LaMarsh Global *"Managed Change Approach"*, http://www.lamarsh.com.

[12] Lewin, Kurt, *"Frontiers in Group Dynamics - Channels of Group Life; Social Planning and Action Research stages of change"*, Human Relations 1947.

[13] Pritchett Consulting, *"Pritchett Change Management MethodologyModele"*, http://www.pritchettnet.com/change-management-methodology.

[14] Jeffrey Hiatt, *"ADKAR: A Model for Change in Business, Government and our Community"*, Prosci Learning Center Publications, August 2006.

[15] Tavistock *"Institute for Human Relations"*, http://www.tavinstitute.org.

[16] Eric Trist & Kenneth Bamforth, *"Some social and psychological consequences of the longwall method of coal getting"* – Human Relations, 1951

[17] Wikipedia *"Kurt Lewin"*, http://en.wikipedia.org/wiki/Kurt_Lewin.

[18] Massachusetts Institute of Technology"*Center for Socio-technical Systems*", http://ssrc.mit.edu.

[19] Herzberg, Frederick , *"The Motivation to Work"*, New York: John Wiley and Sons, 1959.

[20] Pink, Dan, *"Drive: The Surprising Truth About What Motivates Us"*, Riverhead Books, 2011.

[21] Steven Reiss. *Who Am I? The 16 Basic Desires That Motivate Our Actions and Define Our Personalities*. City: Berkley Trade, 2002.

[22] *"IBM to invest $1 billion to create new business unit for Watson"*, Reuters, January 2014.

[23] R. Colin Johnston, *"Cognitive Systems Initiative"*, EE Times, October 2013.

[24] Khaneman, Daniel, *"Thinking, Fast and Slow"*, Farrar, Straus and Giroux, 2011.

[25] Corey Ladas, *"Scrumban - Essays on Kanban Systems for Lean Software Development"*, Modus Cooperandi Press 2009.

[26] E. Goldratt, *"The Goal: A Process of Ongoing Improvement"*, North River Press, 1992.

[27] Wikipedia, *"5-whys"*, http://en.wikipedia.org/wiki/5_Whys.

[28] Wikipedia, *"Fishbone Diagram"*, http://en.wikipedia.org/wiki/Ishikawa_diagram.

[29] Chip Heath, Dan Heath, *"Made to Stick"*, Random House, 2007.

[30] Nick Rozanski, Eoin Woods, *"Software Systems Architecture with Stakeholders Using Viewpoints and Perspectives"*, Addison-Wesley, 2005.

[31] IEEE Architecture Working Group, *"IEEE Recommended Practice for Architectural Description of Software-Intensive Systems"*, IEEE Std 1471-2000, IEEE, 2000.

[32] Mario Barbacci et al, *"Quality Attributes"*, Technical Report CMU/SEI-95-TR-021 ESC-TR-95-021, Software Engineering Institute, Carnegie Mellon University, 1995.

[33]] Thomas Saaty, *"The Analytic Hierarchy Process"*, McGraw-Hill, New York, NY, 1980.

[34] D. Winterfeld, W. von and Edwards, *"Decision Analysis and Behavioral Research"*, Cambridge University Press, Cambridge, England, 1986.

[35] Ivar Jacobson, Pan Wei Ng, *"Aspect-Oriented Software Development with Use Cases"*, Addison Wesley, 2005.

[36] Len Bass, Paul Clements, Rick Kazman, *"Software Architecture in Practice"*, Addison-Wesley Professional, 1997.

[37] Santiago Comella-Dorda et al, *"A Process for COTS Software Product Evaluation"*, Software Engineering Institute at CMU/National Research Council of Canada/ TECHNICAL REPORT CMU/SEI-2003-TR-017 ESC-TR-2003-017, July 2004.

[38] Software Engineering Institute. *"CMMI for Development, Version 1.2"*. CMMI-DEV (Version 1.2, August 2006). Carnegie Mellon University Software Engineering Institute. 2006.

[39] *"CMMI Institute"*, http://whatis.cmmiinstitute.com

[40] *"Standard CMMI Appraisal Method for Process Improvement (SCAMPI), Version 1.1: Method Definition Document"*, Software Engineering Institute - Carnegie Mellon University, December 2001.

[41] Information Systems Audit and Control Association (ISACA), *"Control Objectives for IT – COBIT"*. www.isaca.org.

[42] Gary Hamel, Michele Zanini ,*"Build a change platform, not a change program"*, McKinsey, October 2014.

Chapter 10:

[1] Hutchins, Edwin, *"Cognition in the Wild"*, The MIT Press, Cambridge Massachusetts, 1995.

[2] Eric Bonabeau, Guy Theraulaz, Marco Dorigo, *"Swarm Intelligence: From Natural to Artificial Systems (Santa Fe Institute Studies in the Sciences of Complexity)"*, Oxford University Press, 1999.

[3] Wikipedia, *"Scotsman Fallacy"*,
http://en.wikipedia.org/wiki/No_true_Scotsman

[4] Wikipedia, *"Fideism"*, http://en.wikipedia.org/wiki/Fideism.

[5] Peter Senge, *"The Fifth Discipline: The Art and Practice of the Learning Organizations"*. Doubleday Business, 1994.

[6] Argyris, C; *"Teaching Smart People How to Learn"*, Harvard Business Review, Cambridge MA, 1991.

[7] Wikipedia "Chris Argyris",
http://en.wikipedia.org/wiki/Chris_Argyris .

[8]   Wikipedia,   *"Donald   Schön"*,
http://en.wikipedia.org/wiki/Donald_Sch%C3%B6n .

[9] Argyris, C; Schon, D; *"Organizational Learning: A Theory of Action Perspective"*, Addison-Wesley, Reading MA, 1978.

[10] Robert Flood, Norma Romm, *"Diversity Management: Triple-loop Learning"*, Wiley, September 1996.

[11] Basili, Victor R., Caldiera, Gianluigi, *"Improving Software Quality by Reusing Knowledge and Experience"*, MIT Sloan Management Review, Fall 1995.

[12] John Foreman, *"Data Smart: Using Data Science to Transform Information into Insight"*, Wiley, November 2013.

[13] Eric Siegel, Thomas Davenport, *"Predictive Analytics: The Power to Predict Who Will Click, Buy, Lie, or Die"*, Wiley, February, 2013.

[14] Anthony Ulwick, *"What Customers Want: Using Outcome-Driven Innovation to Create Breakthrough Products and Services"*, McGraw-Hill, August 2005.

[15] V. Basili, G. Caldiera, H. Dieter Rombach, *"The Goal Question Metric Approach"*. 1994

[16]   Highsmith,   Jim,   *"Velocity   is   killing   Agile"*,
http://jimhighsmith.com/velocity-is-killing-agility, November 2011.

[17]   Agile   Alliance,   *"Relative   Estimation"*,
http://guide.agilealliance.org/guide/relative.html.

[18] *"International Function Point User Group"*, http://www.ifpug.org.

[19] Giuliano Antoniol, Chris Lokan, Gianluigi Caldiera, Roberto Fiutem, *"A Function Point Like Metric for Object-oriented Software"*, Empirical Software Engineering, 1999.

[20] Software Technology Support Center, *"Guidelines for Successful Acquisition and Management of Software Intensive Systems"*, USAF, 1996.

[21] Roy Clemmons, *"Project Estimation Using Use Case Points"*, Crosstalk Journal of Defense Software Engineering, February 2006.

[22] *"What is the Difference Between Absolute and Relative Risk?"*, Stats Simplified, George Mason University.

[23] James Duggan, *"The Hall Pass has been Repealed: The Evolution of Application Lifecycle Management"*, Gartner ITxpo Symposium 2008.

[24] Carey Schwaber, *"The Forrester Wave: Process Centric Configuration Management"*. Forrester Research Q4 2005.

[25] Ivar Jacobson, Maria Ericsson, Agneta Jacobson, "The Object Advantage: Business Process Reengineering with Object Technology", ACM Press, 1995.

[26] ISO/IEC 20000-1:2011 IT Service Management System Standard.

[27] Office of Government Commerce, *"IT Infrastructure Library - Service Transition"*, The Stationery Office, 2000.

[28] *"Open Services Lifecycle Collaboration"*, http://open-services.net.

[29] Eclipse Foundation, *"Eclipse Mylin Project"*, http://eclipse.org/mylyn.

[30] Organization for the Advancement of Structured Information Standards (OASIS) *"Oasis Open Data Protocol v4 - OData"*, https://www.oasis-open.org/committees/tc_home.php?wg_abbrev=odata

[31] Tasktop Inc., *"Tasktop Sync"*, www.tasktop.com

[32] OpsHub Inc., *"OpsHub Integration Manager"*, www.opshub.com

[33] *"Carmageddon II: LA Drivers Told To Prepare For Another 10-Mile 405 Freeway Closure"*, Huffington Post, July 2014.

[34] International Business Machines, *"IBM Rational Insight"*, http://www-03.ibm.com/software/products/en/rtl-insight.

Chapter 11:

[1] Blasingame, Jim, *"The Age of the Customer: Prepare for the Moment of Relevance"*, SBN Books, Boston, January 2014.

[2] Blank, Steve, *"Why Lean Startup Changes Everything"*, Harvard Business Review, Boston, May 2013.

[3] David Cavallo, *"Emergent Design and learning environments: Building on indigenous knowledge"*, IBM Systems Journal Volume 39 #3&4, 2000.

[4] Frederick Brooks, *"The Mythical Man-Month, Essays on Software Engineering – Anniversary Edition"*, Addison Wesley, 1995.

[5] Gartner *"Gartner Says Sales of Tablets Will Represent Less Than 10 Percent of All Devices in 2014"*, Gartner Consulting, October 2014.

[6] Hawken, Paul. "*Disintermediation: an economics buzzword that neatly explains a lot of the good that is going on*" CoEvolution Quarterly, 1981.

[7] Carr, Nicholas, "*The Big Switch: Rewiring the World, from Edison to Google*", W.W. Norton & Company, June 2013.

[8] Leong, Lydia, "*Research Roundup for Cloud Infrastructure as a Service*", Gartner, July 2012.

[9] Press, Gill, "*Digital Marketing Battle Map: CMO vs CIO and Gartner vs. Forrester*", Forbes Magazine, July 2013

[10] Michael Polanyi, "*The Tacit Dimension*". University of Chicago Press, 1967.

[11] James Surowiecki , "*The Wisdom of Crowds*", Anchor, August 2005.

[12] M. Waldrop, "*Complexity: the emerging science at the edge of order and chaos*". London Viking, 1992.

[13] Nonaka, I., and Takeuchi, H., "*The Knowledge-Creating Company: How Japanese Companies Create the Dynamics of Innovation*", Oxford University Press, New York 1995.

[14] Clarke D, Whitney H, Sutton G, Robert D. "*Detection and Learning of Floral Electric Fields by Bumblebees*", Science Magazine Vol 340 no 6138 pp. 66-69, April 2013.

[15] Gabriel Szulanski, "*Exploring Internal Stickiness: Impediments to the Transfer of Best Practice Within the Firm*", Strategic Management Journal, Vol. 17 Special Issue - Knowledge and the Firm; Winter 1996.

[16] Wilbur Schramm, "*The Process and Effects of Mass Communication*", Urbana: University of Illinois Press, 1954.

[17] Goldratt, Eliyahu M., "*What Is This Thing Called Theory of Constraints*", North River Press, 1999.

[18] F. Paternò, "*End User Development: Survey of an Emerging Field for Empowering People*", ISRN Software Engineering, vol. 2013.

[19] International Business Machines, "*IBM Bluemix*", www-ibm.com/software/bluemix.

[20] Wavemaker Inc., "*Wavemaker Visual Ajax*", www.wavemaker.com.

[21] Wikipedia, "*Representational State Transfer - REST*", http://en.wikipedia.org/wiki/Representational_state_transfer.

[22] Wikipedia, "*Simple Object Access Protocol - SOAP*", http://en.wikipedia.org/wiki/SOAP.

[23] Google Corporation, *"Google Code"*, https://code.google.com.

[24] Cloud Foundry Foundation, *"Cloud Foundry"*, http://www.cloudfoundry.org/index.html.

[25] Alistair Cockburn, *"Walking Skeleton"*, http://alistair.cockburn.us/Walking+skeleton.

[26] Ken Power, *"Stage Performer Metaphor"*, XP 2010.

[27] *"Propceedings of Gesture-based Interaction Design: Communication and Cognition"*, CHI Toronto Workshop, 2014.

[28] Wikipedia, *"Post Fordism"*, http://en.wikipedia.org/wiki/Post-Fordism.

[29] Scaled Agile Inc., *"Scaled Agile Framework (SAFe)"*, http://scaledagileframework.com.

[30] Wikipedia, *"Moore's Law"*, http://en.wikipedia.org/wiki/Moore's_law.

[31] Wikipedia, *"Fourth Generational Programming Languages - 4GLs"*, http://en.wikipedia.org/wiki/Fourth-generation_programming_language

[32] Microsoft Corporation, *"Microsoft Access"*, http://office.microsoft.com/en-ca/access.

[33] Wikipedia, *"SAP Sybase Powerbuilder"*, http://en.wikipedia.org/wiki/PowerBuilder

[34] Clay Richardson, John R. Rymer, *"New Development Platforms Emerge For Customer-Facing Applications - Firms Choose Low-Code Alternatives For Fast, Continuous, And Test-And-Learn Delivery"*, Forrester Research, June-August, 2014.

[35] RedHat Inc., *"Hibernate"*, http://hibernate.org.

[36] Outsystems Inc. *"Outsystems Platform"*, http://www.outsystems.com.

[37] Alpha Software, *"Alpha Anywhere"*, http://www.alphasoftware.com

[38] Microsoft Corporation, *"Microsoft Sharepoint"*, http://office.microsoft.com/en-ca/sharepoint

[39] Mary Jo Foley, *"Microsoft closing in on Write-Once-Run-Anywhere says CFO"*, CNet, February 2013.

[40] Adobe Corporation, *"Adobe PhoneGap"*, http://phonegap.com.

[41] Matthew A. Russell, *"DOJO The Definitive Guide"*, O'Reilly Media, June 2008.

[42] Ben Frain, *"Responsive Web Design with HTML5 and CSS3"*, Packt Publishing, April 2012.

[43] Wikipedia, *"Document Object Model"*, http://en.wikipedia.org/wiki/Document_Object_Model.

[44] Wikipedia, *"Visual Basic"*, http://en.wikipedia.org/wiki/Visual_Basic

[45] Jon Duckett, *"JavaScript and jQuery: Interactive Front-end Web Development"*, Wiley, June 2014.

[46] MongoDB, *"NoSQL Databases Explained"*, http://www.mongodb.com/nosql-explained

[47] W3Schools, *"JavaScript Object Notation -JSON Tutorial"*, http://www.w3schools.com/json

[48] Martin, James *"Rapid Application Development"*, Macmillan, May 1991.

[49] Wikipedia *"Spring Framework"*, http://en.wikipedia.org/wiki/Spring_Framework

[50] Wikipedia, *"Spring Security"*, http://en.wikipedia.org/wiki/Spring_Security

[51] Wikipedia, *"Really Simple Syndication - RSS"*, http://en.wikipedia.org/wiki/RSS

[52] Bear Bibeault, Yehuda Katz, *"jQuery in Action Second Edition"*, Manning Publications, July 2010.

[53] W3Schools, *"HTML Canvas Tutorial"*, http://www.w3schools.com/html/html5_canvas.asp

[54] James Morgan, Jeffrey Liker, *"The Toyota Product Development System: Integrating People, Process, and Technology"*. Productivity Press, 2006.

Epilogue:

[1] Frederick W. Taylor *"The Principles of Scientific Management"*, New York: Harper Bros., 1911. & The System Company. 1911. *"How Scientific Management is Applied"*. London: A. W. Shaw Company, Ltd.

[2] Elton Mayo, *The Human Problems of an Industrialized Civilization* (1933).

[3] The Scrum Alliance - www.scrumalliance.org.

[4] Ambler, Scott, *"Certified ScamMaster"*, Ambysoft, http://www.ambysoft.com/certification/scam.html, 2012.

[5] *"Agile Anarchy Blog"* https://agileanarchy.wordpress.com/2011/04/25/scrum-is-not-project-management.

[6] Moreira, Mario, *"Being Agile: Your Roadmap to Successful Adoption of Agile"*, Apress, October 2013.

[7] Wikipedia, *"Ontology"*, http://en.wikipedia.org/wiki/Ontology.

[8] Peggy Kenna, Sondra Lacy, *"Business Japan: A Practical Guide to Understanding Japanese Business Culture (Paperback)"*, MacGraw-Hill, 1994.

[9] Sally Helgesen, *"The Practical Wisdom of Ikujiro Nonaka"*, Strategy and Business, November 2008.

[10] Dawkins, Richard, *"Viruses of the Mind. In Dennett and His Critics: Demystifying Mind, ed. B. Dalhlbom, 13-17"*, Blackwell Publishers, Malden, Massachusetts, 1995.

[11] David Easley, Jon Kleinberg, " *Networks, Crowds, & Markets: Reasoning about a Highly Connected World*" Cambridge University Press, 2010.

[12] Kruchten, Philippe., *"Voyage in the Agile Memeplex"*, ACM Queue, Volume 5 Issue 5 City, 2007.

[13] Schwaber, Ken, *"unSAFe at any Speed"*, https://kenschwaber.wordpress.com/2013/08/06/unsafe-at-any-speed.

[14] Richard Epstein, *"Software Development as Spiritual Metaphor"*, West Chester University of Pennsylvania, June 2004.

[15] Cottmeyer, Mike, *"Religion, Politics and Agile"*, LeadingAgile Blog, February 2014.

[16] Wikipedia, *"Semmelweis Reflex"*, http://en.wikipedia.org/wiki/Ignaz_Semmelweis.

Index

B

D

G

H

J

M

N

O

P

S

T

U

W